BRUTAL TRUTHS, FRAGILE MYTHS

BRUTAL TRUTHS, FRAGILE MYTHS

POWER POLITICS AND WESTERN ADVENTURISM IN THE ARAB WORLD

Mark Huband

A Member of the Perseus Books Group

Photographs courtesy of Mark Huband except where otherwise indicated.

Published in the United States of America by Westview Press, A Member of the Perseus Books Group, 5500 Central Avenue, Boulder, Colorado 80301-2877, and in the United Kingdom by Westview Press, 12 Hid's Copse Road, Cumnor Hill, Oxford OX2 9JJ.

Find us on the world wide web at www.westviewpress.com

Westview Press books are available at special discounts for bulk purchases in the United States by corporations, institutions, and other organizations. For more information, please contact the Special Markets Department at the Perseus Books Group, 11 Cambridge Center, Cambridge, MA 02142, or call (617) 252-5298 or (800) 255-1514, or email special.markets@perseusbooks.com.

Library of Congress Cataloging-in-Publication Data

Huband, Mark.
  Brutal truths, fragile myths: power politics and Western adventurism in the Arab world / Mark Huband.
    p. cm.
  Includes bibliographical references and index.
  ISBN 0-8133-3753-4 (alk.paper)
  1. Arab countries—Politics and government—1945–   2. Nationalism—Arab countries.   3. Islam and politics—Arab countries.   4. Qaida (Organization)   5. Iraq War, 2003.   I. Title.
DS39.H83   2004
909'.09749270829—dc22

                                                                    2004007957
                                                                    CIP

The paper used in this publication meets the requirements of the American National Standard for Permanence of Paper for Printed Library Materials Z39.48—1984.

Interior design by Reginald Thompson
Typeface used in this text: 12-point AGaramond

10   9   8   7   6   5   4   3   2   1

For Olivier and Zara, my dear children
"Intoum Oumry"

CONTENTS

ACKNOWLEDGMENTS

WHATEVER SUCCESS I MAY HAVE HAD IN LEARNING ABOUT THE Arab world has been entirely due to the readiness of friends, colleagues, and acquaintances, in the countries from Morocco to Iraq, to help me overcome my preconceptions, ignorance, and bewilderment. The political cauldron of the Arab world is subject to more propaganda than any other region, owing to the resonance of the challenges it throws up to global political, religious, and business interests. A region that is the birthplace of three religions, has the world's largest oil reserves, and can make or break the careers of politicians across the West is unlikely to be easily permitted its own voice. But through all the misrepresentation, propaganda, and lies, its own numerous, varied, and passionate voices remain strong, and I hope this book makes them a little clearer. For guiding me in the long process of learning, I would like to thank the following: in Rabat, Ali Bouzerda, Kamar Bencrimo, Ahmed Marzouki, and André Azoulay; in Algiers, Abdelaziz Belkhadem, Mostafa Bouchachi, and the late Abdelkader Hachani; in Tunis, Moncef Marzouki, Osama Romdani, and Mostafa Benjafa; and in Cairo, Mohamed Younes, Adel el-Labban, Yousef Boutros-Ghali, Hania Sholkamy, Ziad Bahaa Eddin, Mohamed Sid Ahmed, Karima Khalil, Max Rodenbeck, Mahmoud Moheildin, Jim

Muir, and Nabil Osman. For being an endless source of inspiration, insight, and knowledge about the Middle East, I would like to thank David Hirst. I am extremely grateful to my colleague Judy Dempsey for her great encouragement over the years and for her assistance when visiting Israel, and to Robin Allen for his generosity and hospitality and for so readily sharing his treasure trove of knowledge of the Gulf region. In the immediate aftermath of the September 11, 2001, terrorist attacks in the United States, I was able to devote a great deal of time to examining the rise of al-Qaeda, and I would like to thank Will Lewis and Hugh Carnegy at the *Financial Times* for having given me the great opportunities they did, as well as Charles Clover for his photographs of Iraq. Finally, I am extremely grateful to my parents, David and Ann Huband, for their invaluable comments on the first draft of this book.

PROLOGUE

On Thursday afternoons I often tried to leave Cairo early, long before sunset, to spend the weekend amid the mesmerizing lilt of the desert dunes as the vast sky was turning from its palest blue to violet and red, the stars appeared, and the magic of the pyramids watched us like faces without eyes from their plateau. The Pyramids Road—*Sharia al-Ahram*—was always an endless jam of creeping traffic, until a fine new bypass was flung up with the spectacular speed that the builders of Egypt have been perfecting since long before even Cheops died, cutting an hour off the journey to the southern road that plied through the desert to the oasis of Fayoum. On one such Thursday, only days before the eagerly awaited bypass was opened, the evening sun bore down on the crammed cacophony. Then, just before a junction that lies in the shadow of the soaring wonder of the pyramids, an unfamiliar flurry of police activity brought the traffic to an additional halt. We waited. A siren in the distance, approaching from the Alexandria Road, heralded the event. First a police motorcycle cavalcade, then a series of military trucks, then cars—some old, some shiny new—then, in their midst, a vast stretch limousine, which swung at speed to make the sharp left turn, its blackened windows reflecting the jam on our side of the road, a second clamor of police motorcycles bringing up the rear of what had been (I counted) a convoy of two hundred cars, all speeding the 600-mile journey from, I realized, the Libyan border.

Colonel Muammar Gadaffi was coming to town, hidden behind the blackened windows of the stretch limousine that UN sanctions forced him at that time to use when traveling. Ever since Libya had been accused of (and on August 13, 2003, effectively admitted to by agreeing to pay compensation to the families of the victims) being behind the 1988 bombing of Panam flight 103 over Lockerbie, Scotland, Gadaffi had been grounded by sanctions that imposed an air embargo on his country. Consequently, he swung through the deserts, cities, and oases of North Africa in his Cadillac; pitched a vast tent in the grounds of the Kubba palace when he came—as he occasionally did—to Cairo; and was given the freedom to roam the Egyptian countryside, speaking more freely, and often more controversially, to large, bemused crowds than any Egyptian politician ever dared do.

Just as the traffic on *Sharia al-Ahram* had been ordered to stop, it was equally brusquely ordered to go. We drove out into the desert, pondering the spectacle of power that had been Gadaffi's motorcade.

The spectacle is part of the substance of political life in the vast and varied Arab world. The idea of an Arab world is in itself a spectacle, a fragile myth draped in a mixture of European "Orientalist" fantasies and, much more important, the intense clamor for political substance that has dominated the seemingly endless battle between partial success and bitter failure in the region for much of the past century. The elements of unity in the Arab world in which the peoples of the region have retained a readiness to believe are themselves diminishing. On October 24, 2002, Gadaffi announced—in disgust at its inertia and ineffectiveness—that he would even leave the Arab League, the regional grouping that seeks to bind the Arab identity into a meaningful political entity with the power to assert

Colonel Muammar Gadaffi of Libya.

real influence on the world stage. He never actually carried out his threat.

Meanwhile, the cultural and historical riches, the magnificence of the Arabic language, the intensity of religious belief, the humor, the academic and emotional response to the crises and calamities with which the region is beset, have often remained in the hands of those least able to protect them for the future—a future when these qualities will undoubtedly be transformed into the tools of modern nation building. That process of nation building—the transformation of potential into reality—is dependent upon the practice of power being transformed. It is dependent upon the near-impossible being allowed to happen, as the Gordian knot of historical pressures, confused identities, and outrageous injustices is allowed to be unraveled, and the rigidity of power is allowed to give way to variety, liberty, and the confidence to believe that it is better to chance reform than stagnate, even if the risk involved is enormous.

As they emerged into the 1990s and a decade of new possibilities that at certain moments appeared to promise a major shift in fortunes, innovators within the Arab world exposed the full extent to which the levers of power were either ill-equipped to innovate or simply averse to change. "Arab culture is in a constant state of becoming," wrote the Arab nationalist academic Halim Barakat in 1993. "This state results from internal contradictions, new social formations and the utilization of resources such as oil, encounters with other cultures, and innovativeness. There would not have been any need to assert this fact were it not for the misrepresentation of reality by both Western Orientalists and traditional Arab scholars."[1] This need, he argued, stems from the tendency of both Western scholars and Arab traditionalists to emphasize the constancy and rigidity rather than the dynamism and pluralism of Arab society.

To non-Arabs, the Arab world is characterized almost solely by the Arab leaders. Lying beneath the leadership, however, is the social reality from which all the profound social and political currents determining the trends within the Arab world as a whole have emerged. Throughout the region there is a striking contradiction between the practice of autocratic rule and the vulnerability of the autocrats. Generally, through ill-use of the media, a strangely *inefficient* use of brutality and intimidation, and poor political judgment, autocracy has with a few notable exceptions remained remarkably vulnerable. The periods during which the leaders' consolidation of power has been apparent have in most instances been accompanied by real opposition to it. In modern times few Arab leaders, beyond those Gulf leaders cushioned by massive oil wealth, have really enjoyed anything resembling halcyon days. The real currents in society have produced a momentum of their own, which has rarely been successfully co-opted or eliminated by the elites. Meanwhile, for leaders pursuing political programs, "successive failures have been disheartening and frustrating at times . . . [But the] progressive nationalists are coming to realize that bridging the gap between reality and the dream is a long-term goal achievable only by a popular national movement that undertakes to change the fundamental social structures that order society."[2]

Unlike Eastern Europe, much of sub-Saharan Africa, and selected countries in Asia, the Arab world has entered the twenty-first century affected by relatively few of the positive changes brought about by the end of the Cold War and the collapse of the Soviet Union. Part deliberate and part due to political impotence, the relative absence of profound change, in concert with the parts of the world by which the Arab world is surrounded, has focused attention on the institutions of authority that have been responsible for both stability and stagnation. The flamboyance of the Libyan leader is really a curious, if telling and certainly symbolic, sideshow in the much bigger picture of the region. Leadership has been born into absolute power and seen it practiced with a mixture of huge arrogance and extraordinary paranoia, the one feeding the other. Deep ambiguity and intense distrust have wracked the relationship between the leaders and the led. On the one hand, the apparatus of states across the region has sought to suppress anarchy, while on the other, there is not a state in the region that has not used torture against the very same people whose protector it claims to be.

But while internal debates or conflicts rage with vicious and merciless candor—if only clandestinely—the nations still succeed in creating common, albeit loose, positions in the face of common threats, dominated by the affront to Arabs across all classes and regions presented by the behavior of Israel. Within countries, the populations of the region are torn between loyalty to the nation and loathing of the practices of states, but within the region the tension is between the demand for the self-respect the history and richness of their culture clearly deserves and the frustration at its failure to build wealth, create stability, and gain respect in the eyes of a Euro-American dominated world that has fully thrown in its lot with the Europeanized Israeli population.

Torn by such conflicting pressures, the holders of power have sought credibility through manipulation of history, diplomatic maneuvering, ultimately fruitless military campaigns, and a monopoly of brutality. While its leaders remain equipped with what is in reality a fragile grip on power, the future of the Arab world will be in large part determined by the ability of leadership to reform. But can it do so without unleashing the probably uncontrollable pressures that its undoubted shortcomings have been responsible for building up over so many decades? The Arab world is in desperate need of change, but it is unlikely that the systems of government in the region can be flexible without breaking down altogether, thus making a gradual process of change necessary to prevent chaos, even if this means autocratic governments remaining in power for a while longer.

In a climate dominated by religious extremism, antagonism towards the West and Isreal, and the invasion of Iraq, the West should be extremely careful not to destabilize the leaders of the Arab world, however unsavory many of them are. The only enduring change in the region will come from within, and any attempt to rush to reform will result in a surge in support for extremism. On the one hand, the clamor for reform is strong. But on the other, populations from Morocco to Kuwait are not necessarily *reformist*, and many are reactionary. People have not necessarily sought relief from dictatorship per se but rather an end to the dictators they know, whose longevity and lack of vision have turned stability into stagnation: "Once political ideas were appropriated by governments, they were in danger of losing their meaning," wrote Albert Hourani in 1991. "They became slogans which grew stale by repetition, and could no longer gather other ideas around them into a constellation, mobilize social forces for action, or turn power into legitimate authority. The idea of nationalism seemed to have suffered this fate."[3] Individual leaders have come and gone, but their replacements have sought to represent continuity rather than change. While incumbent leaders are associated with political stagnation, what are by nature rather conservative societies have sought a political language that will disavow them of the accusation of being revolutionary, while allowing them to express their wish for political change—but change that may in the end produce similar stagnation. Stifled dynamism stalks the region, while there is far less to show for the resulting stability than millions of people would like, and the question continues to be asked: What is actually holding the status quo together?

1

SOLDIER-KINGS AND POTENTATES

RULE AND MISRULE IN THE ARAB WORLD

THE ARAB WORLD IS RIPE FOR CHANGE. BUT AS WITH MOST phenomena in this region, change will probably not be noticed until some time after it has happened and may thus not be seen as having happened at all. Discretion and secrecy are central to the political creed, and the region's rulers will seek tight control over whatever takes place. More than a decade after the end of the Cold War, styles of government across the region have barely changed. But as the benefits and purpose of political rigidity become impossible to explain, the edifices will unravel, even as the inherent caution of Arab society dictates a slow pace of change. This is so because although the old ideas that political classes promoted and imposed to bind the complex region together have been discredited, whatever may replace them has yet to fully transpire—though political Islam remains the most likely candidate. There are many ways to hold on to power, and the soldier-kings and potentates of the Arab world have sought to

shift their appeal to stay in place. Some—though certainly not all—
no longer routinely assert their autocratic credentials with an eye on
the glory of their nations. Some have been busy seeking to modernize, as long as this does not mean they also have to democratize. Experiments at reordering the power structures of the Arab world with
an eye on retaining the political creed of Arab unity have been the
main casualty of this process and may actually have inspired it. The
economic and political *disunity* of the Arab world has been cemented
by the promotion of national rather than regional or "Arab" interests
and by individual countries pursuing incorporation into global capi-
talism, in Egypt's case in ways reminiscent of its nineteenth-century
economic history. Countries have sought to reach bilateral trade
agreements with the European Union or with other Arab states and
to accede to the World Trade Organization. In many ways these initiatives mark the definitive end of efforts to create the kind of leadership that Gamal Abdel Nasser, independent Egypt's founding leader
and Arab nationalism's champion, envisioned for Egypt when he
mused four decades ago: "I do not know why I always imagine that
in this region in which we live there is a role wandering aimlessly
about in search of an actor to play it. And I do not know why this
role, tired of roaming about in this vast region, should at last settle
down, exhausted and weary, on our frontiers, beckoning us to move
to dress up for it as nobody else can do."[1]

As the Arab world lurched toward war in the Gulf in 1991,
Egypt still saw itself as the heart of an Arab identity that sought to
draw strength from unity. But by the end of the 1990s, that "unity"
was based on concerns for regional security and stability, disillusionment with attempts at political unity, and the recognition that the
search for common Arab interests could not depend upon the identification of historical foes but required more solid foundations between allies. The divisive impact of Iraq's aggression, its invasion of
Kuwait, and its development of weapons of mass destruction

(WMD) at a time when other Arab states were arguing that the Middle East should be a WMD-free zone to force Israel into nuclear disarmament were the most destructive elements: "I told Saddam: 'you didn't listen to my advice in 1991. You criticized me. If you had listened to me then, we would have avoided what's happening now,'" Egypt's President Hosni Mubarak told me in 1998. "I don't trust Saddam. The Iraqis are all of one nature. Even if there was not Saddam there would be another one. This is their nature."[2]

The Iraqi regime's isolation from other Arab states was fatal. The region's second largest oil producer, led by a secular regime that was a potential bastion against Islamist Iran and Muslim fundamentalist groups elsewhere, chose to aggress against rather than cooperate with its Arab neighbors. While rejecting U.S. and U.K. strategies to precipitate the overthrow of President Saddam Hussein, Egypt's President Hosni Mubarak said: "It is high time the Iraqi regime took responsibility for the suffering it has brought Iraqis."[3] Egypt's major concern was with its own regional prestige. "Saddam misjudged Arab opinion when there were protests against the bombing of Baghdad in December [1998]," was how one senior Egyptian official dismissed Iraq's strategy. "He thought Arabs were supporting him. But in fact they were just supporting the Iraqi people."[4] In response to this growing isolation, Mohammed Saeed al-Sahaf, Iraq's then foreign minister (who later grabbed headlines in the war of 2003 when he insisted, even as Saddam's regime was on the run, that the U.S.-led coalition would crumble), condemned Arab criticism of Iraq, which he said "can only be described as the insistence of some states not to follow a sound Arab course in the framework of the Arab League, and to continue a policy of creating axes and blocs."[5] In response, an editorial issued by Saudi Arabia's official news agency described President Saddam Hussein as a "disease that should be removed, so peace and security can return to Iraq and its people. The holding of an Arab summit or a ministerial meeting in which Saddam Hussein and his gang take part will not be successful under the circumstances."[6] Arab League determination not to allow divisions to emerge within its ranks on the Iraqi issue ultimately succeeded, by preventing the fora at which such divisions could be created from being convened. On January 24, 1999, Iraqi delegates stormed out of a meeting of Arab League foreign ministers in Cairo, in protest at their refusal to condemn the air strikes then taking place and their call for an end to Iraqi threats against Kuwait.

But the League's move did not strengthen the Arab states' role either in the affairs of their region or on the wider world stage. And for a few more years Saddam Hussein's face continued to be the only one smiling on the streets of Baghdad: Saddam with a child on his knee, Saddam wearing a fishing hat, Saddam making policy at a table, Saddam greeting a crowd. Everywhere the image of the Iraqi leader beamed from walls, pillars, pedestals, and statues. The regime behind the smile, and the Iraqi assumption that the country would reassert its role in the Middle East and the wider Arab world, remained focused on ensuring that it retained power until conditions changed. "The regime is highly unpopular. But this is coupled with a sense of total helplessness about being able to do anything about it, which has meant that nobody will do anything about it," an Iraqi academic told me in Baghdad in 1998. "Anybody who thinks he can take an organized action against Saddam is a fool. Saddam is our safety valve. However awful he is, he keeps the country together, and if he goes it would be the end of Iraq. If he goes nobody would be able to assert any sort of control over the country."[7]

CROSSING RED LINES

The vitriol Arab leaders have poured upon each other as the region has sought to build its strength through often vicious "self-examination" has more often thrown up barriers than constructed any kind of regionwide political unity. Today, Egypt's body politic is torn between the weight of the Arab nationalist legacy bequeathed it by Nasser and domestic pressures that have ultimately undermined the idea of the most populous Arab country exercising meaningful regional leadership. The real ability—and therefore the real need—to provide *pan*-Arab leadership is open to question. Equally, the need for regional leadership has perhaps become anachronistic, while such efforts have been more akin to normal diplomacy than to hegemony. A sense of lost influence permeates Egypt's domestic political agenda, unsettling efforts led on the regional level by Nasser and on the national and bilateral levels by his successor, Anwar Sadat. In this climate of inward-lookingness, in the wake of the collapse of the Arab–Israeli peace process upon which it had pinned so much hope and national prestige, the practice of power in Egypt has shifted from being a tool with which to build a modern state with regional and global ambitions to being dominated by security concerns in the face of its ongoing vulnerability to domestic pressures. "There is a quiet, silent struggle going on between the old authoritarian Nasserite wing and those who want to reform the economy and the politics," the Egyptian-American sociologist Saad Eddin Ibrahim told me as we sat in the shaded tranquillity of his garden in the Cairo suburb of Maadi in April 2001. He was waiting to hear whether he would go to jail. He had been accused by the Egyptian authorities of embezzling funds donated by the European Union to the research center he ran. The EU had long said that there had been no embezzlement, but his case was not really about embezzlement but rather about power. "The security oriented wing of the establishment has the upper hand. The liberal wing is not prepared to take on the security wing, which is dominated by Safwat Sherif, Zakariya Azmi, and Kemal Shazli. State security has become regime security. The phrase that I hear is that I have 'crossed red lines.' What are the red lines? There are four: Hosni, Suzanne, Gamal, Ala," he said, referring to President Mubarak, his wife, and their two sons.[8]

Two weeks before his arrest, Saad Eddin had written a speech for Mrs. Mubarak, which she had delivered in Geneva. Then the regime turned on him. His case reveals as much about the state of human rights in Egypt (examined in Chapter 5) as about the practice of power. In 1995 he had established the Independent Commission for Election Monitoring, to monitor elections to the *Majlis al-Shura*, the representative assembly. In 2000 he was told it would be unconstitutional to have nongovernment officials inside the polling stations for that year's elections, and the government said they would be barred. So he sought and received the approval of all the opposition parties to post election observers outside the polling stations. In a second incident, Saad Eddin publicly blamed the police for an upsurge in violence between Muslims and Copts at a town in Upper Egypt, al-Khosheh. When he was arrested he was also accused of espionage, on the basis that he had given a lecture at a conference at a defense college in the United States and had apparently angered President Mubarak when he referred to a "remote possibility" of the president's son Gamal inheriting the presidency, during discussions on the issue of succession following the death of President Asad of Syria in 1999. In 2002 Saad Eddin was sentenced to seven years in prison, though an appeals court ordered a retrial. The case rumbled on in a manner that has revealed it to be wholly political rather than a question of law, until he was finally freed in 2003. The message within the establishment was clear: The "security wing" had won the psychological battle by showing that it could flex its muscles throughout the system, intimidate Saad Eddin, and make clear that there was nothing—not even admittedly muted criticism from abroad—that could limit its assertion of power.

But to what end had the security establishment decided to assert—or reassert—itself?

In the mid-1990s, after Egypt had embarked on a program of extensive economic reform, one senior official at the heart of the decisionmaking elite said more than once that the opening up of the economy to the private sector had been permitted simply because there were fears within the regime that the entire edifice of power was about to crumble. Egypt needed money, and the ruling clique had no way of replacing the barter arrangements it had had with the countries of the former Communist bloc, which had permitted a command economy to trundle along without its shortcomings becoming a mortal threat to the regime. The challenge for the regime was to ensure that whatever economic changes were permitted, they did not undermine the military elite, whose ultimate approval was needed if the government was to attract the foreign investment necessary to finance measures that could avert social unrest. "What we do need is to develop the institutions that generate economic decisions. The right decisions were made in the early 1990s. Decisions were taken correctly. But there was no process. The interest in any physical experiment is repeatability. You have to be able to repeat it and get the same result. I want new institutions that underlie the new orientation of the economy to be developed," said Youssef Boutros-Ghali, the leading economic reformer in the Egyptian government in the late 1990s. "I want to spend lavishly on the institutions of governance. Because to my mind what caused the southeast Asia crisis and made it graduate to a catastrophe is fundamental flaws of governance, not the wrong economic decisions."[9] Such ambitions would require ceding power away from the center and dispersing it widely. But this has not happened in Egypt to the extent Boutros-Ghali knows is necessary, as the determination of the security wing to retain its tight grip on the nation has perpetuated the influence of an aging generation of politicians who have little intention of seeing their power diminish or their legitimacy questioned.

Improvements in "governance" would necessarily entail a readiness to reveal the way government works, bring transparency to decisionmaking, and forge a bond between the leaders and the led that would ultimately create accountability and give the population a capacity to influence decisions. This has not happened either, not in the context of the economic liberalization, and certainly not in the political arena, leading one analyst of the economic reform process to comment that "as long as economic liberalization remains limited it enables the rulers to play an important role in the economy, either as regulators or as producers and employers. As long as it is biased in favor of the rulers and their associates, it involves only superficial or fictitious redistribution of the ownership and control of economic resources."[10]

The implications of these limitations have not gone unnoticed. "Many of the flashier names in Egypt I wouldn't touch with a 10-foot pole. They are companies that are heavily leveraged and have no business strategy and are just keeping one step ahead of their creditors,"[11] a leading Egyptian banker told me at the height of the country's relative economic boom in the late 1990s. How the business elite made their fortunes is at the heart of how power has been exercised in the country. In 2001, officials at one of Egypt's largest publicly owned banks, the *Banque du Caire*, reckoned that 15 percent of loans it had made were nonperforming, 70 percent of them—estimated to be valued at more than $1 billion—having been made to private companies. Money was there, if one had the right connections. Four large state-owned banks had for decades been the milk cow of the business elite, guaranteed from collapse by the state, free of meaningful oversight from the Central Bank, ready to finance business ventures whose success was largely dependent upon using political clout to preserve monopolies, keep foreign investors out, and provide a platform for politically well-connected individuals. "You look into each institution, from the public sector companies to the ministries to the big newspapers, and you get the feeling that from the chairman down they are all huge institutions with one strong man on top," a leading private sector businessman told me. "You look into the organizations and find there is no one to replace him. What if this man disappears tomorrow?"[12]

Among the strong men on top, one who is symbolic of the power structure is Ibrahim Kamel. Surrounded by works of modern art in a large open-plan office in Cairo's twin city of Giza, he is rarely seen without a large cigar, dressed usually in a black polo-neck sweater and a dour suit, peering through large black-rimmed glasses. Reputed to have been a Maoist in his student days in the United States, Kamel has overseen the creation of a business empire—Kato—whose rise is difficult to explain in business terms alone. A longtime acquaintance of Osama al-Baz, President Mubarak's political adviser, Kamel expanded his company with startling speed from producing aromatic oils, to financing a luxurious apartment and hotel block in Giza (wherein the penthouse suite was sold for $14 million in 1998), to launching Scirocco, an aircraft manufacturing joint venture with Russian partners in which it holds a 75 percent stake and which planned to design and build the TU204–120 Rolls Royce–powered passenger jet at a factory near Moscow. More important, however, in 1997 Kato became the first company from an Arab country to invest in an Israeli company, spending a reputed $60 million on a 5 percent stake in Koor Industries, Israel's leading industrial group. Such an investment would never have been made without the approval of Egypt's ruling elite, in whose meeting rooms at the presidential palace in Heliopolis Ibrahim Kamel is often to be seen. Much of the finance for such deals is the result of arrangements between the oil-rich states of the region and those on the front line of the Arab–Israeli conflict. The use of finance as a weapon in the fifty-five-year war is one aspect of the armory Egypt has sought to develop, with Libyan funds often playing a key role in strategic investments, and the inner circle of Cairo's business-political elite building up their empires in part with an eye on ensuring that Israel does not use its privileged access to Western capital as a means of becoming the dominant economic power in the Middle East.

Having used the economic weapons of privatization, strategic investment, and sufficient liberalization to encourage some foreign investment, the Egyptian government has at least temporarily staved off the threat of the serious economic turmoil it faced in the early 1990s. In doing so, it has succeeded in its longer-term aim of averting any dilution of its power. It has thus halted any meaningful shift toward recognizing the breadth of the gulf between its vision of the country's political future and that which has emerged from the vast and varied social and political currents now at work on street level. "You can't foster an economic reform without some kind of political reform," said Salama Ahmed Salama, the most forthright of Egypt's social commentators, whose continued presence on the state-owned daily newspaper *al-Ahram* is nevertheless a sign that criticism is unstoppable. "We don't have the strong institutions that can express the political forces in the right way. It's what makes the society in some ways constipated—an unrelieved pressure which should find some legal way of expressing its concerns. The political parties aren't strong enough. On the one hand you have the Islamic trend, which can express itself in a reasonable way. On the other hand you have the trend of Arab nationalism, and you have the leftist trend that is still there. They all have certain roots in the population. The fact that you are dealing with these trends in the same way . . . you are dealing with a society that is constipated—by using the same mechanism for each of them which was used when society was static and stagnating."[13]

Salama continued:

You have liberated the energies in the society and you are telling everybody that it's a new system and you encourage civil society, but you are using the same mechanism as in the past—the police, the legal system. It's very bad.

Egypt depends upon a central government. It needs a very strongly convinced leader to initiate such a debate and to believe in it and to believe that it can be fruitful. This will come, because there's no other way. If you want to make the economic reform work, you have to find outlets for different political trends to be part of the system. In the media, censorship is a way of appeasing the conservative elements. The government is facing a very serious problem that it is dealing with badly. They are using the same mechanisms as a closed society. This is the contradiction.

The military influence in our society has been weakened since Mubarak came to power. He has tried to make a middle way, between the military and the [ruling National Democratic Party, the] NDP. He has succeeded to a great extent in moving the army out of daily life. With many of the old guard there are few of them who can get into a democratic debate without seeing people as hostile to them.

Government pressure on the press and the syndicates: these are expressions of the impasse facing the system. The government would like to see things move forward in a smooth way, but they don't know how to do it.[14]

Salama has rightly earned a reputation for plain speaking, berating his countrymen for shortsightedness when nobody else would voice their opinions, while somehow being spared victimization by the extreme nationalists or cultural fascists who write in a select number of Egyptian newspapers with the aim of crushing frank exchanges of views. However, the opening up of the state to which he refers has been a damage limitation process rather than a political creed, with the elite permitting the creation of new alliances in the centers of power, that have come to substitute for the largely ineffective political parties. These alliances are the government and the business sector, the business sector and some media, and the business sector and some political parties. This alliance building has created uncertainty about where the centers of power outside the presidential inner circle actually lie. Government has become a grouping of individuals who have personal ties to these different groups rather than a homogenous gathering of "yes men." However, by continuing to resist shifts toward building a powerful parliamentary democracy, the same individuals who put Saad Eddin Ibrahim in jail on spurious charges can use their influence with impunity.

"Which way does Egypt want to go?" asked Gamil Mattar, an analyst of Egypt's social and political trends. He answered the question with another question: "Which Egypt? You have a political elite that has been there for 40 years. They don't really have a political ideology. They are bureaucrats. Then you have other elites: westernized liberal democrats, the religious elite, and the [Islamic] fundamentalists. The official elite will try not to accelerate the westernization process because they are afraid of their power being taken by the anti-western elites: that is, the Islamists and the nationalists." The isolation of the elites from the mass of society has forged the new challenge, according to Gamil. "You have the Islamists: there is an Islamic revival. An Islamist mood. It wasn't there in the 1940s, when the masses were more modern. Now you [still] have them going along the path of modernization, but they are more anti-western now. There is tension: people want money, but when they return from Saudi Arabia with money and gadgets they are lost. The westernization process is responsible for this. There's westernization in terms of technology, but as a government they can't dare face the Islamic elite."[15]

Egypt has confronted the evolving challenge from Islamists with military pressure. It, like Algeria, has also sought to structure the situation since the end of the phase in the 1990s that saw both countries seriously threatened by Islamist political and military campaigns. In the process of doing so, they have largely failed to produce a political creed that harnesses the bedrock support for Islamism to a pluralist system of government. "The political parties don't represent social aspects. They represent cultural interests and differences," said Dia Rachwan, an analyst of Egypt's religious life and senior researcher at Cairo's al-Ahram Centre for Strategic Studies. He emphasized the failure to transpose the social reality onto the level of political life. "The 1952 revolution [which overthrew the monarchy and created the republic] was more profound than [the revolutions] in Eastern Europe. The values of the revolution were already in the minds of Egyptians before the revolution. The government is obliged with all the other political parties to safeguard the system institutionalized by the revolution. There are many obstacles to the reform, and I don't believe the government has the courage to push the reforms very far."[16]

Rachwan's view is probably far too idealistic, failing to recognize the gulf between the leaders with a vested interest in power and those they are leading, whose feelings about the virtues of political revolution would most likely be overwhelmingly negative, if they were ever consulted. Meanwhile, isolated and partially insulated, the Egyptian regime reserves its wrath for those within it who turn against it or reveal its secrets. It is rare that such things happen, but one morning in April 1999, Mohamed el-Ghannam appeared at my door. A highly educated colonel in the police force and the former legal adviser to the interior minister, Hassan al-Alfi, el-Ghannam had been instrumental in creating the government's response to the rising tide of Islamist violence in the early 1990s and was also privy to the security policy that the government applied to Egypt's six million Coptic Christians. Part of his role—vital at a time when the Islamist threat was great, and when treatment of the Copts was being widely criticized among Christian fundamentalists in the United States—was to explain the policy against the Islamists in a series of articles in the government newspapers. But then his father, an army general, died. The death turned Mohamed el-Ghannam bitter. He told me that his father was taken to a military hospital, where inadequate health care hastened his death. He was furious. After years of paying health insurance to the army, corruption within the service meant that the care was inadequate and the necessary medication unavailable. In a row beside his father's deathbed, he fought with a doctor, and in the melee his police pistol was fired. Even though the doctor was barely scratched by the bullet, the state exploited the incident as el-Ghannam mounted a campaign against official corruption. The case of the injured doctor hung over him for four years and was the ostensible reason for his being refused permission to leave Egypt. In the meantime he wrote in the Islamist newspaper *al-Shaab*, attacking corruption within the police force, the army, and the interior ministry. When the editor of *al-Shaab*, Magdi Hussein, was sued for libel by Hassan al-Alfi—el-Ghannam's former boss, whom the newspaper had accused of corruption—el-Ghannam offered himself as a witness for *al-Shaab*, but the pressure against him was too great and he remained silent while Magdi Hussein went to jail. For four years el-Ghannam received threatening telephone calls, had his car damaged, and lived in a state of nervous panic. In barely a whisper, he told me his story, his fear leaving him in a cold sweat on each of the numerous times he appeared, always impromptu, at my door. He wanted to get out of the country, and had arranged visas for Italy, where he had studied. But later, when he arrived at the Cairo airport, his exit stamps were scribbled out, and the police trapped him just before he stepped aboard the plane.

PRISONERS OF THE *MAKHZEN*

Mohamed el-Ghannam was eventually allowed to leave Egypt in 2001, the impression being that he was more of a thorn in the flesh if he stayed in Egypt than he would be if he were diluted in the plethora of dissident voices already, largely ineffectively, criticizing the regime from exile. Institutional rigidity could not accommodate the challenge he presented, even though the issues he had raised were ones that the regime—which has taken action against corrupt officials, and sacked Hassan al-Alfi for his failures as security minister when fifty-six foreign tourists and six Egyptians were slaughtered by Islamists in 1997—regards as a danger to itself if left unresolved. The regime wants to be seen to be leading and will silence commentators or critics, even if they are voicing views it does or could share. Egypt's government does not seek to be popular but to be strong; it cannot bear to appear to be catching up with the social trends that are leaping ahead of it, and yet it lacks the capacity to lead on all fronts. It is the major weakness of republican autocracy in much of the developing world, that it does not allow itself to shift its focus, due mainly to the clumsiness of decisionmaking and the weakness of institutions. This vulnerability is even more pronounced among the region's royal dynasties. The absence of an inbuilt capability to change without losing the aura of total power is a major weakness of Arab regimes.

In the gathering twilight of a cold autumn evening André Azoulay, King Hassan's economic adviser, delineated the boundaries that, if crossed, would make for a difficult time in Morocco: "Everything which touches the king is taboo."[17] It is now nearly a decade since I first stepped from a long corridor in the royal palace in Rabat into Azoulay's warm office, carpeted with deep red rugs, and listened to the calm, subtle listing of the rules of the game set by the *makhzen* into whose world I had stepped and of whose existence I had been unaware. Defining the *makhzen* was the first challenge, as the grip of those who were literally "to whom taxes are paid" extended into all areas of life, with the king at the center of what amounted to a semifeudal power structure.

"Morocco is a great waiting room," the daughter of Islamist leader Abdessalam Yassine told me. It was night outside. Her sitting room was bare but for a pastel painting of flowers on the wall. She stayed at home, read widely, and painted her paintings. She was waiting. Her father was waiting. I had seen her father once, when the *makhzen* appeared to have made the mistake of letting the façade of total power slip. The *makhzen* allowed me to see him when they should not have. Under a blood-red evening sky riot police had blocked the wet streets near the Ahmed Ben Said mosque across the Bouregreg River from my home in Rabat. Abdessalam Yassine had been under house arrest since December 1989, in a house not far from his daughter's. "From the government's point of view they want to see the reaction to a couple of hours' liberty," said an engineering student standing beside me in the mosque. "The lay political parties have no religious content to their programs. They don't face the issue of the Day of Judgment."[18] The next day, December 16, 1995, the riot squad barred the streets again. It rained a lot that winter. Yassine was no longer free. The student was right. Nothing had really happened. The event was an illusion, a test. Yassine's daughter went back to painting, and the riot squad eventually retreated.

"It's the human rights culture." The minister for human rights, Mohammed Ziane, was explaining to me why the restrictions on Sheikh Yassine's movements had initially been lifted. "You can't prevent someone from living just because he doesn't believe the same things as me. But if the democratic rules established by the king aren't respected by the [Islamists] then they won't be able to play a political role. . . . If there is one small word about Islam in their political program, their party will be forbidden."[19]

The king. The king. The king. Always the king. King Hassan of Morocco, as well as being hereditary head of state, was also Commander of the Faithful, *emir al-mumineen*, a direct descendant of the

Prophet Mohammed. Officially the guardian of Moroccan Islam, when Hassan died in 1999 this role was taken on by his son Mohammed. The Islamists view the king's religious leadership as one of Morocco's "contradictions." The king had been abroad when Yassine had his hours of liberty. Ziane was soon fired, and the human rights ministry was incorporated into the Ministry of Justice. Ziane was fired because he fell out with the *makhzen*, the power. But even though they wielded power, who were the *makhzen*?

In Egypt, the men of power could be listed. But in Morocco my friends were not able to tell me. Perhaps one could say the *makhzen* were whoever your enemy was. It was the power that opposed you. It was whatever stood in your way. It was a closed door, a telephone that would not be answered, an official who would not give you your papers. It was a lugubrious shadow. It had the power to frighten. *Makhzen* could mean anybody, and it was meant to be so. The king ruled the country. Should he alone be called *makhzen*? It was simpler, easier to pretend one did not know what went on, and to say simply that it is the *makhzen* who are to blame.

For some, the *makhzen* drove a Renault car. They would wait all day in the hot sun at a traffic light in Rabat near the famous patisserie on the Route Des Zaërs. Luck was with them when the traffic lights were red. The car would stop. They would rush to the window, which would be opened an inch or two, and press a damp note into the hand of the *makhzen*. In this case he wore a scarlet, brushed wool jacket. He had a mobile telephone, a Motorola radio, and a set of golf clubs in the trunk. He and I were on our way to the golf course. He had invited me to go along after keeping me waiting for three hours. He was Driss Basri, the minister of the interior, the fist of the *makhzen*. He had hinted that he would accord me an interview, because at that time Morocco was pretending to open its doors. We got into his car. He would not tell me what was written on the note pressed into his hand at the traffic light. I assumed it was an appeal for favor or mercy. We drove to his villa. Basri wanted to know the questions I intended to ask, and I related them in some detail. The car swung into his driveway, which was draped with bougainvillea, the scarlet of the king's man on earth. He said his press attaché would let me know about the interview, then left me to find a taxi home and continued on to the golf course. Eight months later I had had no news. Nothing happened; I had never really seen Basri; the *makhzen* could not allow itself to be seen. Morocco would keep its doors closed a little longer. I was not even certain Basri was the *makhzen*. Driss Basri was the shadow under which Morocco cowered.

Hundreds of miles away, in the Algerian desert to the southeast, the prisoners of the *makhzen* languished in the twilight world reserved for victims of the *makhzen's* betrayal. The martyr Mohamed Lasyad had died in the desert; now his name is on a prison. Mustapha Sirji swayed from one foot to the other. The *makhzen* had sacrificed him to their enemy. The prison lies inside southern Algeria, Morocco's rival. There were twenty-five hundred Moroccans like Mustapha Sirji in this and four other prisons. They had been captured in the mid-1970s when the Polisario Front launched a war of independence for the Western Sahara, the desert to the south of Morocco whose occupation King Hassan ordered in a bid to save his deeply unstable rule when Spain left the territory in 1975. The Polisario have their own territory inside Algeria, which arms and feeds them. That is where the Moroccan prisoners are kept, in prisons named after Polisario fighters like Mohamed Lasyad. Until 2000, Algeria and Morocco did not discuss the prisoners. They didn't exist. They were in the shadows, too difficult for the *makhzen* to contemplate, too easy to sacrifice. In Morocco the prisoners' families said nothing. To complain would be to doubt Moroccan sovereignty of the Western Sahara, which is treasonous. Basri's career depended upon maintaining this uncertainty. The United Nations

Driss Basri, Morocco's interior minister and architect of King Hassan's autocratic rule.

played along, financing circular moves portrayed as a solution to the non-war.

"I ask the others if I am a human being here, or if I am an animal," said Mustapha Sirji. The answer was clear. He had been there for almost twenty years. It was a red, scorching evening. The world was ablaze, the desert on fire. That month a comet had been edging its way across the sky. "We are Muslim. We believe in God. We pray. We are not the rocks. We are living in this inferno. We are the forgotten victims of this drama. We have our lives to live. I have lost my youth. We have lost our families. Every time we receive letters somebody has died. How long is this going to go on? Please will somebody notice us?"[20] The prison had an open courtyard of sand between the high walls, which the prisoners themselves had built. Outside was desert, then somewhere a border, farther away his family. He gave me a letter for them. Some other prisoners did the same. "We have offered to free them, but the Moroccans have refused, because to take them would mean they would have to give us

Polisario prisoners of war they are holding," said Polisario's Brahim Salem Bousseif. The jail echoed with the sound of prayers, and the burning sun sank beneath the Sahara outside. "But they won't, because they don't want to recognise Polisario or admit that this is a war," he said, as the men bowed, their prayers drawing to a close, the sun leaving the sky deep blue speckled with stars as the desert was plunged into darkness. I left the prisoners behind. "It's a fight to the death, even though we have a kind of peace now," said Brahim, his small, bespectacled, bearded face knotted by anxiety as he screwed up his eyes to watch the passing comet.[21] It is peace. It is war. Nothing happens.

The prisoners had been forgotten by the king who had sent them to fight a war over a territory whose retention was the foundation of his monarchy, the foundation of the power of the *makhzen*. Back in Rabat I put the prisoners' letters in a bright yellow mailbox near my house, their silence sealed in envelopes, the futility of their wasted lives never a subject uttered in the land of the *makhzen*. To have done so would have been taboo, and "everything which touches the king is taboo," André Azoulay had told me. In fact, everything was taboo, because everything touched the king.

A public road passed through the palace grounds. The gates were only closed at night. Perhaps the king wanted to be closer to the people. At his hunting lodge in Bouznika he was close to them. There, his retainers kissed both sides of his hand. Bowing and scraping, humbling themselves before their king, they kissed the hand that fed them. There were hundreds like them. In palaces throughout the country, scores of staff prepared meals every day as if the king were about to arrive. Usually he did not. The fate of the food was unknown. In his stretch dove-gray Cadillac, or his magnificent jet-black vintage Mercedes, the king may have been speeding in a convoy that included spare cars—a pale yellow Rolls Royce, a line of black Cadillacs, a fleet of *Gendarmerie Royale* on Harley Davidson motorbikes—to some other part of his large, varied, and beautiful kingdom. But despite the show, or perhaps because of it, he found his credit was bad. Outstanding bills meant that air ambulance companies began refusing to take royal patients to Paris unless they paid cash in advance. Housing agents in Rabat stopped dealing with some of the courtiers of the royal household because they didn't pay their rent on time. The keeper of the royal checkbooks used to move funds from one Western capital to another, to ensure that adequate funds were available whenever the king chose to visit. Then the story began to be told that this practice had come to an end.

But the courtiers still waited for the day when the king would arrive in the empty palaces they kept immaculate. The king had fed and housed their families for generations, and their loyalty was expected in return.

But something happened once, when it was not returned.

King Hassan had a court jester, whose job was to make the royal family laugh. In 1971 several hundred young army cadets, deceived into believing that the kingdom was under threat from foreign insurgents, attacked the king in another of the palaces, on the beach side at Skhirat. Binebine, the son of the court jester, was among them. The attack failed. When the king learned of Binebine's disloyalty, he summoned the royal clown and asked him why his son, who had grown up in the palace alongside all the other courtiers' children and royal offspring, had engaged in such treachery. The jester was swift in his reply: "He is not my son." Binebine was caught after the coup failed. He now lives in a small apartment in Marrakech. He, along with many of the others, had been tricked into staging the coup by Basri's predecessor as interior minister, General Mohamed Oufkir. Oufkir's 1971 coup failed, but he hid his involvement. In 1972 he tried to shoot down the king's plane. Afterwards he officially committed suicide by shooting himself in the back.

Then Basri took over from Oufkir as the shadow of the *makhzen*.
Oufkir was lucky. His wife Fatima was imprisoned with her five
children. That was the king's revenge for the general's treachery. The
children had cells of their own. One of them was three years old
when the family was locked up. In their prison, Fatima talked to her
children through the water pipes that linked their cells. In 1987 sym-
pathetic prison guards let them escape, but they were recaptured.

The young cadets, who had turned the Skhirat coup into a
bloodbath that resulted in pitched battles on the streets of Rabat
until forces loyal to the king reasserted control, were sent to Tazmamart. But Tazmamart does not exist: a prison high in the mountains, which until 2000 nobody but its inmates and their guards had
seen or spoken of. Its existence was illegal by Moroccan law, which
forbids incommunicado detention; another of Morocco's contradictions. The *makhzen* broke nobody's laws but its own. Tazmamart
did not exist on any map.

"We felt that we had been rejected by all Moroccans. Even people close to us couldn't say the word 'Tazmamart.'" In 1971 Ahmed
Marzouki was a junior army officer involved in the attack at Skhirat.
In 1973 he was sentenced to five years in prison. Eighteen years
later he was released from Tazmamart. "For mentioning the word
'Tazmamart,' children would be beaten by their parents. The guards
would say to us: 'nobody is thinking about you.' And nobody could
have been thinking about us, because there was no pressure within
the country saying: stop the arrests, stop the torture. It's that which
is terrible. In Tazmamart our only refuge was to dream. In my
dreams I was outside with my family. And when I woke up it would
be a shock. Now it's just the opposite: now I dream very often. I
dream about the time I was arrested and taken to Tazmamart. So it's
the torture and the journey that I dream about. It's always there.
When I was freed it took me three months to see anything, after
spending eighteen years in darkness. For eighteen years I saw noth-

ing. Blindfold, in a cell without windows. Eighteen years. I have rheumatism and stomach ulcers because we had no medication in Tazmamart. The only right we had was the right to die in silence."[22]

Abdellah Aaguaou, Mohammed Errahoui, and Ahmed Marzouki sat, eager-faced like the three young men they had once been, living the king's revenge long after the death of the ringleader, General Oufkir. Freedom's ghost drifted like the dim light among the termites of the run-down housing estate where we talked on the edge of the Moroccan capital, on the edge of Morocco, the country whose borders were for long their prison until they were finally allowed to travel abroad in 2000. Abdellah Aaguaou was innocent. He knew he was innocent because those found guilty of the attack on the king's plane had been executed. Under orders, he had loaded the fuel into the fighter plane that attacked the royal aircraft over Khenitra in 1972. He was sentenced to three years in prison for his unwitting role. He was released from Tazmamart nineteen years later. Of the sixty-one imprisoned there, twenty-nine came out. The rest perished in their cells, from disease, cold, possibly even the ultimate taboo in Islam: suicide.

"They are the lost years. In the Calvary of Tazmamart I saw strong men crying. I learned that at their heart the main characteristic of human beings is weakness. Whatever their sadism, people always find themselves exposing their weakness," said Aaguaou. "When we were released we realized that our families had been suffering even more than us. My mother was suffering more than me. Even after I was released she was always frightened that I wouldn't return if I went out. She died two years ago. She died in my arms. She suffered for what happened. And now we are free we have no way of fitting in."[23]

Then on July 23, 1999, King Hassan died. People cried, and even the prisoners of the *makhzen*—some of them at least—behaved like master practitioners of the Moroccan art of contradiction. "The best

thing that can happen is that a country identifies itself with somebody who identifies with them. The Moroccan identity is its monarchy. If it has survived it's because of its ability to change. The
monarchy has achieved a national unity,"[24] Raouf Oufkir, son of the
general whose attempted coups in the early 1970s had set the political tone for the following two decades, told me over mint tea and
pastries. Raouf had been incarcerated in his own cell for fourteen
years, his youth spent alone, the victim of the *makhzen* class of which
he had been a part until it turned on him and decided that it would
make him, his brother, his sisters, and his mother suffer.[25] The
makhzen would retain their power, but under a new king. Everything
would be different, but everything would stay just the same, because
in the minds of the people the power still lay in the hands of the distant and untouchable figures whose control remained dependent
upon the capacity to instill fear and mystery into daily life.

BACK TO THE FUTURE

This state of unchanging permanence, which the region's leaders
and many of its people have sought to make their political creed,
has created both a sense of identity, which was perhaps a necessary
part of the decolonization process, and a sense of isolation from a
range of global currents, which can broadly be defined as *modernization*. The nationalism that sought to build strong foundations for
the independent states of the Arab world also sought to rediscover
an Arab identity after centuries of Ottoman and European influence. An often-quoted maxim summing up the sentiment behind
this process is from a French visitor to Ibrahim Pasha, son of Egypt's
Ottoman ruler Muhammad Ali Pasha, who saw in the ruling family's strategy the aim of giving "back to the Arab race its nationality
and political existence."[26] But the process of doing so must necessar-

ily reconcile the two key features of the Arab identity: the political unity that had its foundation in the linguistic bond stretching from the Arab east, the *mashreq*, to the Arab west, the *maghrib*, and the unifying role of Islam. "Arab nationalist ideology was a development from Islamic modernism,"[27] wrote the American historian C. Ernest Dawn in 1991. "Throughout the nineteenth century, the contenders for office [in Arab countries] had to deal with the perceived inferiority of Islam or the East to the West. Various attempts to meet this problem had no satisfactory result. Arab nationalism arose out of the failure of its immediate predecessor and its ideological parent, Islamic modernist Ottomanism."[28]

It is almost a century since the birth of the ideological and cultural movement that eventually saw Arabs split decisively away from Turkish Ottoman influence. Arabs not only reasserted their Arab roots but also incorporated their Islamic identity within the political debate in a manner that, at least until the election of an Islamist-influenced party in the 1990s and later in November 2002, had contrasted sharply with the rigidly secularist political creed of modern Turkey. Today, the cultural-religious struggle remains at the heart of the friction dominating the Arab world. The linguistic aspect of the cultural struggle has, generally speaking, been a more effective tool with which to bind the Arab world than the religious aspects of identity, though this is now changing. As Albert Hourani wrote in *Arabic Thought in the Liberal Age:* "As far back in history as we can see them, the Arabs have been exceptionally conscious of their language and proud of it, and in pre-Islamic Arabia they possessed a kind of 'racial' feeling, a sense that, beyond the conflicts of tribes and families, there was a unity which joined together all who spoke Arabic . . . [With and since the birth of Islam, moreover,] Arabic became and has remained the language of devotion, theology and law."[29]

The institutional foundation of Arab nationalism—limited today to the existence of the politically ineffective but culturally significant

Arab League—has strengthened the use of Arabic in the regional diplomatic, political, and academic arenas in a manner that has complemented its importance as the language of the Holy Koran. But despite being equipped with this unique linguistic means to debate regional and national issues in a language understood across a vast range of diverse tribes, cultures, and religions, the challenge facing the region's rulers is to reconcile the religious and political lives of the Arab nations.

The challenge of Islamic fundamentalism and the issues it has spawned beyond the Arab world are examined in detail in the following chapters. But use of the religious-cultural identity as a political tool by hereditary leaders, in response to the groundswell of Islamist fervor that has intensified across the region throughout the past fifteen years, has become a key marker of the relations between the leaders and the led. The Moroccan monarch, in his guise as *emir al-mumineen*, the Commander of the Faithful, and the Saudi king as the Guardian of the Two Holy Places, have sought credibility in a religious-political identity. But where the rights of the ruler are semifeudal rather than derived from religious credentials, monarchs have sought to portray themselves as the modernizers, often in defiance of popular conservatism; the consequent fracturing of the relationship between the leaders and the led has shown credibility to be fragile, as occasional forays into reformism have demonstrated.

Gleaming under the harsh rays of the desert sun, the Cadillacs and sport utility vehicles of the Kuwaiti electorate jammed the narrow roads of the popular quarters, around schools turned over to a symbolic display of democracy. Taking advantage of a suspension of parliament prior to the election in July 1999, Emir Jabah al-Ahmed al-Sabah issued a decree that gave women the right to vote. In doing so, he transformed what would otherwise have been an unremarkable exercise in semidemocracy in the otherwise wholly undemocratic Gulf states into a poll whose outcome would have an influence over a real issue, because the parliament that would result from the election would be required to approve the decree. Demography meant that extending the franchise would make the female electorate nine thousand votes larger than the male electorate. When a delegation of women from across the political spectrum went to thank the emir for his decision, their representation from business, finance, and academia was itself symbolic of the discrepancy between the role women play in Kuwaiti society and the political influence they had until then been denied. "The decree caught everybody by surprise, and it threw all the parties into confusion," said Sulaiman Mutawa, an economic consultant and former minister of planning, who said the voting reform was a step toward addressing a range of political issues the ruling elite had failed to tackle. "What we have suffered from so far is the absence of leadership. There has tq be a firmness of authority, and that only happened once the parliament was dissolved."[30]

Reform through autocratic means has been an enduring feature of rule across the region. By ignoring the democratic process in their pursuit of reform, rulers such as the al-Sabah, or in a more complex case Crown Prince Abdullah of Saudi Arabia, have deferred the day upon which the process by which reform is achieved is recognized as integral to the actual reform. "It's an issue of both religion and culture," said Ali Ahmed al-Baghli, a former oil minister and a losing candidate for the Liberal group in the Kuwait election, speaking of the extension of the franchise, the point being that it was not an issue of politics. "The people who are most against it are the tribal people, while the rest have remained noncommittal. It's a shame that there's no clear opinion."[31] As a sign of how the mechanics of Kuwaiti democracy worked in favor of the ruling al-Sabah family, two-thirds of legislators would have had to vote against the decree to overturn it, while a simple majority was needed to approve it. "From the social point of view, the people of Kuwait are quite split on this issue. But you will find that the majority of people, both men and women, are against it. The decree was intended to split people, and to embarrass the Islamists,"[32] said Nasser al-Sane, an Islamist candidate.

However, the decree also symbolized recognition by the emir that the malaise in Kuwait's political life was creating huge dangers. "There seems to be the realization that the higher-ups have come to the conclusion that their main weakness is the prime minister and crown prince. They have given him all the chances to lead, but he has failed. He is not a decisionmaker. The status quo is the motto. Once the emir realized this, he gave his cousin [the prime minister] enough opportunities to prove himself and saw that we were hitting rock bottom, and he realized he had to closely watch things,"[33] one senior Kuwaiti official said. The shock of Iraq's invasion in 1990, the war that followed in 1991, thirteen years of sanctions against Iraq, and the regional instability now facing the Gulf had exposed Kuwait to its institutional shortcomings and weakness. Of the election that was supposed to have injected a new vibrancy into the stagnant political life, Suleiman Mutawa, the former minister, said: "None of the candidates really look beyond the walls of Kuwait. Most of them—instead of having issues—hark back to the government's inability: embezzlement, what the previous finance minister did. Twenty years ago the issues would have been pan-Arabism and the Palestinian issue. Meanwhile, we have two sources of wealth: oil, and human resources. We haven't paid attention to the future generations. I have told them: stop talking about housing problems and start looking at education. None of them really had a sense of the continuity in the Arab world. You care for your children, but you don't care about your grandchildren. What we have suffered from so far is the absence of leadership."[34]

However, the opening of the political system is far from certain to create a more vibrant social environment in the coming years, even with 122,000 women voters, as many of the new female voters were expected in the 2003 election to support Islamist parties opposed to a broader social role for women. "I think we were better off in terms of social opinions in the 1960s than in the 1990s," said Dr. Moudi al-Houmoud, the female assistant director of Kuwait University. "That part of the population that has tribal connections has had more influence in the 1970s–1990s. We have twenty-five districts, and 50 percent are rural. It's become a sizable part of our society. Those people have their own norms. With the Islamists, this has created a formidable bloc."[35] The *salafist* trend, which advocates a return to fundamental Islamic practices based on the Islam of the earliest caliphs, was the most vociferous in opposing women's political rights, while the *Ikhwan al-Muslimeen*—the Muslim Brotherhood—which had long controlled student politics at the university thanks to substantial female support, is also expected to attract a large bloc of women's votes in future elections.

Kuwait's parliament approved the emir's decree, but whether the emir's aim was visionary or opportunistic was—and remains—unclear. The ultimate control of power by the emir-appointed government rather than parliament is obvious. Meanwhile, the expansion of the franchise as a means of delivering a political blow to the ineffective parliamentarians served to stir up a debate about women's rights within the religious arena without bringing any wider political reform. In other words, it was tentative change, seen against the looming background of the threat from Iraq across the border, but nevertheless designed to serve a ruling family widely seen as out of touch with popular sentiments dominated more by religious conservatism than by political ideology. The discussion of women's rights also was more a reflection of the longer-term political stagnation than it was a sign of real vision. The same debate had been aired—admittedly not in the Gulf region—by opinion formers within the Ottoman empire as far back as the 1860s. Bernard Lewis, the Harvard historian of the Middle East, quoted the nineteenth-century Ottoman writer Namik Kemal, one of the leaders of the Young Ottomans, writing in the newspaper *Tasvir-I Efkar* in 1867, as saying: "'Our women are now seen as serving no useful purpose to mankind other than having children. . . . The reason why women among us are thus deprived is the perception that they are totally ignorant and know nothing of right and duty, benefit and harm. Many evil consequences result from this position of women, the first being that it leads to a bad upbringing for their children.'"[36] In a sweeping generalization that nevertheless seems to encapsulate prevailing attitudes within certain social classes and within major political and religious movements 135 years later, Lewis himself went on to say:

> The emancipation of women, more than any other single issue, is the touchstone of difference between modernization and Westernization. Even the most extreme and most anti-Western fundamentalists nowadays accept the need to modernize. . . . The emancipation of women is Westernization; both for traditional conservatives and radical fundamentalists it is neither necessary nor useful but noxious, a betrayal of true Islamic values. It must be kept from entering the body of Islam, and where it has already entered, it must be ruthlessly excised.[37]

For the soldier-kings and potentates the challenge from political Islam (hereinafter referred to as *Islamism*) has been treated as a modernist issue of security, as befits dictatorship, rather than as an intellectual and existential debate, of a kind that few of the incumbent regimes in the region would have the capacity to engage in effectively. The "modern" republican state has sought to uproot and destroy the Islamist threat, denying its relevance to society. This approach to the Islamist challenge has meant that issues such as women's rights have been treated by the modernizers with startling ambiguity. The innate conservatism of the Arab world has dictated even to the dictators that women cannot be seen in positions of real power. Some of the most outspoken women in the region are in fact Islamists, while the secular dictatorships have struggled to incorporate a formal recognition of women's political and social rights, just as they have struggled—and failed—to establish a legal footing for everybody else's political and social rights. For women as for the rest of society, the tools of dictatorship have been used to build modernist secular republicanism as a creed without principles, though obliged for the sake of pleasing Western governments to occasionally engage in wholly symbolic gestures toward pluralism, whether they be the creation of a consultative council in Saudi Arabia or a laughable presidential election in Tunisia, in which rivals to incumbent President Zine Abdine Ben Ali resigned themselves to electoral failure almost as a duty to the regime.

"These days dictators have a need to legitimize themselves with a parody of democracy. They used to be able to be frank. Now they need a façade. The aim is to trick the countries abroad. They take some ideas, then they falsify them. So, we are prisoners in our country, and the people are terrorized."[38] Secretly, the most forceful non-Islamist critics of Tunisia's police state had gathered in a home on a dark back street of Tunis. I had been given an address and told to avoid being followed by taking several taxis, a bus, and a tram, and then walking. I arrived late and the group was agitated, thinking that I may have had a repeat of a previous experience when the secret police had trailed me and two other journalists through the streets in a ludicrous game of cat and mouse. But I arrived with the dark, wet, lamp-lit street behind me apparently deserted.

"The politics is an instrument of the police," said Moncef Marzouki, the former head of Tunisia's human rights organization and the most consistent critic of the Ben Ali regime before he was forced to leave Tunisia in December 2001. Prior to the 1987 palace coup that brought the former interior minister to power and placed

Tunisia's founding father, Habib Bourguiba, under close observation at his home until his death on April 6, 2000, a political character had been forged in the country that had given the Islamist movement a public role alongside other political and social currents. Then the door to diversity was slammed shut. "Ben Ali needs for everything around him to be in unison. He has given the impression of changing things. But the direction is towards assuring allegiance to the state. He started with the Islamists. Then the mission was transferred to attacking all the rest. He didn't attack the Islamists because they were Islamists, but because they could threaten him,"[39] said Mustafa Ben Jaafar, founder, along with Marzouki, of the Tunisian human rights movement.

Ben Jaafar's conclusion resonated way beyond Tunisia's well-policed borders. The first decade of the twenty-first century opened with a naïve hope that mortality might be the key to facilitating reform. Within months of each other, three political dinosaurs—King Hassan of Morocco, King Hussein of Jordan, and President Hafez al-Asad of Syria—were dead. Their place was taken by young inheritors, which showed that even republicanism had monarchical traits when Bashar al-Asad followed in his father's footsteps. In Egypt, the suggestion that a similar inheritance might take place, with Hosni Mubarak being replaced by his son Gamal, was an issue that contributed to Saad Eddin Ibrahim ending up in jail. In Libya, Colonel Gaddafi is grooming his son, while Saddam Hussein, before his sons' deaths in a shoot-out with U.S. forces, had long hoped that his psychopathic offspring Uday would follow him until his other son Qusay found favor. To all these leaders, the fundamental struggle has been against the societies they are leading, which have presented constant challenges to the legitimacy and relevance of their rule. There are no genuinely popular leaders in the Arab world, not necessarily due to dislike of the often personable individuals who have risen to supremacy, but more due to the social and economic failures that political stagnation and ill-used power have brought.

These failures have brought with them a new challenge. In the early 1990s, if political reform had brought greater openness, it is possible that the conflicts within countries would have remained centered on social and economic issues. But official resistance to political change has intensified pressure on both regimes and their critics to such an extent that the issues are now philosophical and religious. While only a few years ago the challenge presented by Islamist groups appeared to have been reduced to one of security, a new combination of circumstances is creating conditions in which a much more profound upheaval across the region has become all the more certain. Economic reform has not improved living standards, social life is generally as desperate as it ever was, and political life is as stagnant and frustrating as if the Cold War had never ended.

More important, however, is the failure to build a credible and satisfactory sense of identity, founded on the values that give the Arab world its character. The need for such a process has been brought into sharper focus by three events: the decision by the Israeli government of Ariel Sharon to destroy Palestinian resistance to Israel's colonial ambitions in Palestine, and the ensuing slaughter of Palestinians; the collapse of American credibility in the eyes of Arabs who once saw the United States as a useful voice in Middle Eastern affairs but now regard it as anti-Arab; and, most dramatically, the emergence of Osama bin Laden. It is against the background of these issues that the appropriateness of the political regimes to the process of creating and strengthening Arab identity can now be examined.

2

SEA BREEZE, DESERT WIND

CULTURE, IDENTITY, AND ARABISM

A RANDOM ARRAY OF LETTERS AND SYMBOLS FROM ALL THE world's known languages has been carved into the rough-hewn wall that encircles the *Bibliotheca Alexandrina*, the new library of Alexandria, the city that has cradled its own unique civilizational mixing for the past five thousand years. Beyond the coast road on which the library lies, the Mediterranean sparkles, while on the landward side the desert road forges south to Cairo and Upper Egypt. Alexandria's place between land and sea has played a vital role in forging its— and Egypt's—place in the Arab world.

The new library is an attempt to reassert the primacy of that role. "It's as if there are two different [cultural] winds. One is from the Mediterranean, and the other is from the desert. From the sea, it's nice. From the desert, it's hot," said Kamal el-Zoheiry, director of the Great Cairo Library, Egypt's largest until the opening of the Alexandria library in 2002.[1] He has a poignant sense of the currents of learning that have blown through Egypt. The cultural life sustained in ancient Alexandria over many centuries drew its lifeblood from both constant exposure to other centers of learning in the ancient world—Athens, Cos, Cyrene, Rome, Ephesus, Pergamon— and the relative openness and eclecticism of Ptolemaic rule, under which the city emerged as a center of learning. Today, with a $167 million budget provided by the Egyptian government, the UN Educational, Scientific and Cultural Organization (UNESCO), and other donors, ambitions for the Alexandria library are founded on the Ancient Library of Alexandria, created by Ptolemy Soter, King of Egypt, during the late fourth century B.C. Until it was burned down in an unexplained fire, probably in A.D. 391, the ancient library was said to have contained more than 500,000 texts from throughout the known world. The *Bibliotheca Alexandrina's* $1.5 million annual book budget is intended to lead to the creation of a collection numbering eight million books by 2020, along with up to four thousand newspapers and periodicals, fifty thousand manuscripts and rare books, and fifty thousand maps. Alongside these collections, the library intends to amass up to 250,000 audio and audiovisual aids, as well as establishing links to overseas computer databases and permanent Internet access.

The *Bibliotecha Alexandrina* is one of the most ambitious efforts undertaken in the Arab world to reconcile the historical variety that lies at the heart of Arab culture with the current climate of political rigidity, anti-intellectualism, and religious friction. Such efforts at relative openness have emerged from an almost indecipherable root. Governments such as that in Egypt, which have associated themselves with these experiments in enlightenment, are as guilty of perpetuating these negative facts of daily life as are many of the extremist and fundamentalist opponents they spent the 1990s trying to crush. "The US and Europe have many centers of learning. They are like candles for scholars to lead the way. Why do you deny for Egypt to have a candle lit in a dark tunnel? You need to light the way to change peoples' attitudes," Mohsen Zahran, the new library's director until 2001, told me in defense of the project.[2] By the time the library started to take shape, Egypt believed it had beaten off the domestic challenge posed by Islamic fundamentalism, but it was then to see many of those it had sought to crush reappear in the ranks of Osama bin Laden's al-Qaeda. Zahran's "dark tunnel" seemed to have bored its way onto the global stage, and the path toward the kind of enlightenment envisaged by Egypt's modernizers has since seemed even less certain.

Establishing the principles that lie behind the creation of the library is a highly complex task, as few Arab governments in recent years have felt obliged to explain cultural issues in anything more than oblique terms. Most are simply addressing daily crises, many of which derive from the fact that this is an era of dashed hopes, disappointed dreams, and political failure. Writing in 1982 about the intellectual climate that prevailed in the postindependence era of the 1950s and early 1960s, Albert Hourani observed, with great excitement if some apprehension, that:

> The most important of all the changes which came to the surface in these twenty years (1939–59) was this: the past was abolished, whether it were the past of "westernization" or the more distant past of the traditional societies. A new society was coming rapidly into existence. . . . The problems posed by the emergence of this new society were so new, complex and strange that the past no longer had lessons. The minds and imaginations of men might still look to the past for inspiration, and draw from it the lesson (whether justified or not) that the Arabs had been great before and could be great again; and they might regard the culture inherited from the past as the basis of national solidarity. But they no longer believed, for the most part, that they had received from the past an

unchanging norm of wisdom, a system of principles which had reg-
ulated and should always regulate the organization of society and
the activities of the State, whether that norm were derived from the
customs of the ancestors or the Sacred Law. The *Shari'a* indeed had
been abandoned with astonishing speed and completeness.[3]

Twenty years later, in a highly pessimistic collection of lectures published as part of the academic works rushed out in the
wake of al-Qaeda's attacks on the United States on September 11,
2001, the historian Bernard Lewis wrote: "If the peoples of the
Middle East continue on their present path, the suicide bomber
may become a metaphor for the whole region and there will be
no escape from a downward spiral of hate and spite, rage and self-
pity, poverty and oppression, culminating sooner or later in yet
another alien domination."[4]

One means by which the cultural and religious uncertainties
racking the Arab world can be addressed, and Lewis's predictions be
averted, is the gradual *re*introduction of variety in political, social,
and cultural life. This variety existed in the decades before the
emergence of the now discredited Arab nationalist creed. But its
reemergence is today challenged by Islamic fundamentalism—the
"dark tunnel" to which Zahran was referring. Most of the measures
taken by Egypt—and Tunisia, Jordan, Morocco, Algeria, and other
countries—to loosen social control within the preexisting tenets of
politico-militarist authoritarianism have been direct or indirect responses to the challenge of political Islam—*Islamism*. The challenge
has been met either by trying to lure people away from Islamism by
expanding freedoms or by imprisoning Islamists on such a large
scale that such expressions of faith are cowed by threats. Meanwhile, the complexities intrinsic in the process of opening society
are enormous, due largely to the absence of a pluralist model that is
not a copy of the Western model, rejection of which is an essential

part of the spirit of independence at the heart of the broader and longer term search for an Arab identity. Moreover, the close ties between Western states and the autocracies of the Arab world have meant that activists within much of Arab civil society, who could in theory draw upon Western models, instead find themselves distanced from the West by Western support for regimes whose reform or removal is necessary if social reform is to be introduced. The West—whatever its ideals—seems to be as much the enemy as the regimes themselves.

So, it is up to the Arab regimes and Arab civil society to fashion their own kind of pluralism, in the face of an Islamist challenge that is highly likely to prove victorious in more than one Arab country in the coming years. But a fundamental weakness of many of the region's regimes is the lack of clarity about what—beyond their own survival—they are trying to achieve. The message on the wall of the *Bibliotecha Alexandrina* says a great deal. Despite the world's languages being represented as a sign of the building's supposed global reach, the assembled letters intentionally make no sense at all. Although this is by design of the architects, the library's role as a focus for study and intellectual endeavor has been crippled by the confused environment into which it has emerged. As work progressed on the building, the Egyptian government revealed its lack of commitment to the principles that were purported to underpin its creation. The first, most startling example was a decision in 1998 to ban use by students at the American University in Cairo of a biography of the Prophet Mohammed by the widely respected French author Maxime Rodinson. The book had been available to students at the AUC since soon after its publication in English in 1971. But in May 1998, Salah Montasser, a rabid commentator on the government daily newspaper *al-Ahram*, took exception to the book. In an article entitled "A Book That Must Be Stopped," he claimed that it insulted Islam on fifty counts. Moufid Shihab, the minister of higher education, immediately demanded the book be withdrawn, without debate of the kind supposedly enshrined in the institutions his ministry oversees, including the *Bibliotheca Alexandrina*. Condemnation of the ban was swift but ineffective. "This is a contradiction in the minds of those in positions of responsibility," said Salama Ahmed Salama, the outspoken commentator writing in the same newspaper as Salah Montasser. "It shows that our educational philosophy is on the wrong track, and will produce a generation of intellectual cripples. This [ban] has reinforced extremism."[5] But Salama's view drew little public support. "I wouldn't like to have Rodinson's book. His book is a red flag," said Abdel Raouf al-Reedy, director of the Mubarak Public Library in Cairo and a former Egyptian ambassador to the United Nations, who now also serves on Egypt's Council for Foreign Relations. "Since it's become a problem and a symbol of anti-religion, I'm not going to be a hero and say I should have it. The principle for me is to spread the role of the [Mubarak] library and spread enlightenment, and not to be a vanguard for ideas that aren't accepted by society."[6]

As he leafed through the expanding collection of fabulous volumes that he hoped would one day attract scholars to Alexandria, Mohsen Zahran refused to say whether Rodinson's book would appear on the shelves. The library has now opened, with great fanfare. But the issues that dominated the cultural life of Egypt during its construction—and that are today even more acutely pressing, due to the absence of effective mechanisms allowing them to be debated meaningfully—remain at the heart of the enormous religious, existential, and cultural challenges facing the Arab world. The creation of a cultural institution dependent for its success upon intellectual freedom, at a time when the leading figures within such institutions are cowed rather than confident, is a stark reflection of how intense the conflict now being fought out is. "Our eyes are illiterate, so we should help the young by being acquainted with colors. How to look. How to challenge. The Egyptian child suffers because he is not acquainted with art. The child should be acquainted with the computer, should be able to read books and see paintings," Kamal al-Zoheiry told me. He continued:

The only hope for us is for us to learn the art of looking—to yourself and to the other. How to lessen our obeyance, not to be accustomed to obey others. It's ironic. It's very pharaonic, the art of writing. Our society is probably like a pyramid. But sometimes it's not a pyramid, it's an obelisk, because he (pharaoh) is so far from us. We are accustomed to have respect for old books, books on religion. So we neglected what was good in geography and architecture, which were always good in Islamic culture. You can't approach these things through orders. It's done by giving the chance for the eyes to develop. There's no danger. With a powerful government and powerful citizens things will go much better. It's in the interests of the government to have a good opposition. We need it.

On the battle over the Rodinson book, it's silly. There's a battle between those who want us to listen and those who want to help standards. The battle is continuing. There's a big cultural conflict. The problem is not only that we don't use dialogue in religion, but that we don't use it in other disciplines. Without this there will be no tolerance, not just in religion but in science. You can't have books which are against religion without there being freedom of research in other spheres. If you create that dialogue, then the problem of Rodinson would be just one of many issues.

Islam in Egypt is a little bit different, because you have a certain inheritance of mosques and art and libraries. We don't have any mountains in Egypt. We are obliged to be interwoven with the Copts. The villages are a mixture of religions, and religion is very deep. We have two different Islams: one from the Mediterranean Sea, and one from the desert.[7]

ILLUSIONS OF PARADISE

The search for images and symbols that will truly reflect how Arabs see their world, is ubiquitous. Images of paradise are painted in bright colors on the sun-drenched walls of the Sheikh Bashir el-Ibrahimi school off a side street in the Algerian capital, Algiers. Tranquil scenes of rural life depict children running through lush green fields and cattle being led to pasture on the hillsides. Sheikh Bashir was a heroic *mujahid*, a fighter in the war that cost one million lives and won Algeria its independence from France in 1962. His portrait was among the wall paintings of the "land fit for heroes" that the independence struggle was supposed to have created. On September 16, 1999, Algeria's president, Abdelaziz Bouteflika, strode past the paintings as he crossed the school playground to a polling booth. He was to cast his ballot in a referendum in which 98 percent of those who voted approved his plan to promote a *concorde civile*, a pact giving Islamic militants a limited amnesty in return for surrendering their arms and ending their military struggle by January 2000.

Algeria thought it had established its identity as a "popular republic," had clarified the identity of its heroes, and had painted their images on school walls against a background of peaceful rural scenery that contrasted sharply with the real horrors of rural life over the previous eight years. It was trying to bring itself to a turning point. The moment was supposed to be one at which those in power—the *pouvoir*, as they are popularly known—would finally recognize that the war they had fought as a means of eradicating the Islamist challenge was going nowhere. But Algeria's popular republicanism would be seen for the self-delusory anachronism that it was, although the populace allowed itself to hope that the rotten regime that was supposed to embody that republicanism might accept that it no longer represented the aspirations of anybody but its own corrupt and brutal military elite.

"I need a big vote in favor. It's important for me. I need a massive turnout to show the desire of the majority to impose its will on the minority,"[8] Bouteflika told me, before casting his ballot in the school hall, where posters promoting the referendum called it the "fin de l'eclipse"—the "end of the eclipse"—and depicted Bouteflika himself floating among clouds. According to the government, 85 percent of the electorate voted, and 98 percent voted in favor of the amnesty, which would allow Islamists not guilty of murder or rape during the years of violence in which thousands had died to return to their homes. They had until January 13, 2000 to give up their weapons and agree to the terms of the amnesty, though they would remain deprived of civic liberties like the right to vote, even if they did surrender.

After the deaths—mostly of civilians, thousands of whom had had their throats cut in appalling massacres carried out by extremists—of up to 100,000 people, the offer of such a pact was unlikely to have been rejected. The question was, and remains, what could it ultimately achieve?

"We didn't need to go to the referendum in order to know the extent of popular support in Algeria for peace and reconciliation. Those Algerians who abstained from voting are no less concerned for peace than those who voted,"[9] Abdelkader Hachani explained candidly. The third-ranking leader of the Islamic Salvation Front— the FIS, whose expected victory in the 1991 election had led the army to cancel the poll, thereby unleashing the civil war—had been released from prison after months of negotiation. In his tiny house at 22 Rue Gheddis Amar in Algiers's Islamist stronghold of Bab el-Oued, the youngest of the FIS's three senior leaders refrained from sounding completely dismissive of Bouteflika's efforts, but he was under no illusion about what this attempt to engineer a break with

Algeria's bloody past really amounted to: "The *pouvoir* can choose to respond to the result and the hope for peace, and can take the measures necessary for real reconciliation, or it can continue with the politics that it has taken the country into war until now. The referendum wasn't done in order to bring *concorde civile*, as the people who have always opted for confrontation will find an alibi to re-launch the conflict after 15 January (the end of the amnesty), as the discourse of the *pouvoir* remains exclusive."[10] The biggest threat to the *pouvoir* was that Hachani—alone among Islamists who had the opportunity to speak publicly—had the capacity to crisply analyze the evolving political landscape with a candor that recognized the horrors Algeria's Islamists had themselves meted out to the people:

> The reason for the violence was the exclusion. Regrettably I feel that even if we reach the point where the violence is gone, the reasons for its possible resurgence will always be there. The FIS was dissolved at the beginning of 1992, and there would not have been violence if the FIS had remained legal in 1992. But after the FIS was dissolved, the *pouvoir* arrested the leaders. The *pouvoir* pushed people to violence. All our positions are against violence. The option of violence: it was difficult to turn the other cheek. When we (the FIS leaders) were released, we opted for peace.
>
> We are legalistic. We won't impose anything on the Algerian people that they don't want. If the Algerian people don't want our program, then we expect the right to remain in opposition. People know that people remain firmly attached to the program the FIS offered originally. There's no better course than to let the FIS take its political role. If the movement is no longer popular, why has the *pouvoir* taken the position it has?[11]

To Hachani, the referendum was a strategic option chosen by those in power rather than a means by which the existential, religious, and social issues facing the brutalized survivors of the conflict, and which lay behind the horrific explosion of violence, could be reappraised. Today there is no greater trust or mutual confidence between the population of Algeria and the *pouvoir* than there ever was in the past. The same people remain in power, though with a slight ebbing of their total influence. By rigidly opposing a major change in the political landscape, the *pouvoir* has limited the capacity of both Bouteflika—a semidetached member of the ruling class who has criticized the military—and the various opposition groups, as well as civil society, to change the way Algeria is run and thereby definitively end the ongoing, if today far less widespread, violence. As Hachani told me:

> There are two forms of violence in Algeria: there's a violence which is fundamentally political and religious. That violence the Algerian people generally see as soluble. The other violence is criminal. The violence that is not a religious affair is criminal. We think that the priority is to rid the country of violence, but in a global and definitive way. All the parties that use violence must stop. To be definitive it must be a just peace.[12]

On November 22, 1999, six weeks after we met, Hachani was shot dead while leaving a dental clinic near his home in Bab el-Oued, ridding the *pouvoir* of an articulate critic and depriving moderates of an interlocutor. His murder, still unsolved today, served only the interests of the *eradicateurs*, the hard-liners within the military and political elite who saw their power as threatened by any form of political pluralism, whether it was the Islamists or secular opposition parties.

The Algerian army had by then resorted to any method in its effort to win a war that had cost at least 100,000 lives by the end of the 1990s.[13] The war had been fought by cruelly exposing the collapse of

Algeria and what it had once represented as a developing country with political depth. In their efforts to terrorize the population, which is far and away the main victim of the conflict, "The terrorists would pass as members of the security forces and, on our side, the military would disguise themselves as Islamists in order to carry out terrorist operations for which the Islamists could then be blamed,"[14] wrote Habib Souaidia, a former member of the Algerian army's special forces, in a devastating exposé—the only one of its kind published so far—of the excesses committed by the Algerian army. His account confirmed long-denied accusations that the army had been responsible for the slaughter of civilians on a vast scale. "Don't play with the fire: if there's terrorism you shouldn't be equivocal,"[15] Redha Malek told me in September 1999, in defense of the atrocities. The most outspoken critic of the FIS and the Islamist movement at the outbreak of the war, when he briefly occupied the position of prime minister, he had become infamous for declaring that "Fear must change sides." His battle cry had been taken up by the soldiers, whose exploits are described in Souaidia's harrowing account: The army should be allowed to terrorize the Islamists—and, by implication, the population that supported them—to achieve a victory for secular republicanism. For Malek, the brutality had clarified what secular republicanism meant:

> The vote in 1995 and the failure of the boycott call was the beginning of the changes. It showed a rejection of *intégrisme*. In 1995 it was Islamic terrorism that was rejected. Now it's political Islam that has been rejected. There were acts of genocide, collective massacres. It led to a shift of the population towards the state. Between 1995 and now there have been so many excesses that the population has come over to the state.
>
> The experience of the past seven years has been for many people the failure of the idea. What is happening now in Algeria is the

failure of political Islam. Because they chose Algeria in which to win the battle and take power, across the Maghreb and as far as Egypt. They chose Algeria because if you have Algeria you reach into the south, as far as Senegal.[16]

In the end, however, the determination of the *pouvoir* to reassert the virtues of secular republicanism, and in doing so to reassure itself of its own primacy, did not bring with it anything quite so clear-cut. The war has not been one out of which one set of ideas has emerged clearly victorious over another. Terror and fatigue lay behind the rejection of a boycott call made by the Islamists when Algerians were offered the chance to vote in 1995. The same feelings lay behind the support for the amnesty offered by President Bouteflika in 1999, though opposition parties put the turnout at 50 percent in Algiers and 35 percent elsewhere. People wanted an end to the war, but they still had little faith in the *pouvoir*. In short, the popular aspirations that existed in 1988, when the growing discontent that would soon be articulated by the FIS first emerged, remained both strong and unresolved more than ten years later. Shortly before his assassination, the FIS leader Abdelkader Hachani told me:

> One of the positive aspects of paying this heavy price is that there's been a political maturity achieved. It's very important. What is the responsibility of the FIS? We hope that we will be permitted to have the movement reunited. After ten years there's a political maturity. But it's only a potential. The only way to prove it has value is to allow it to reassemble.
>
> For Algeria and for our movement the most credible and acceptable way is through political means. It is for this reason that a return to peace is a strategic route. Peace must be the basis. The world has changed, there is globalization, and the world is moving rapidly.[17]

Part of the political maturity Hachani was referring to is to be seen in the ongoing reference to the cultural and social roots that have informed political life, and which no amount of brutality can fully extinguish. Emerging out of this process has been the Wafa party, which has sought to draw upon the body of support that lay behind the rise of the FIS, though without subscribing to the *inté-grisme*—Islamic rule—that lay at the heart of FIS's doctrine. Wafa's rise is a response to Algerians' huge disappointment with the *pouvoir,* and it received the strong support of the FIS leadership. "The regime is opposed to the handing over of political power through peaceful means. The support of the FIS for Wafa showed us that the FIS had retained the power of mobilization of the population,"[18] Mohamed Said, the party's spokesman, told me. He continued:

> People didn't vote for the FIS for religious reasons, but because the FIS had a language of change. People voted for change. People are very politicized. There's never been a religious problem in Algeria. There are social and economic problems. The other parties talk of economic and social problems, but they are not creative, because they are part of the official opposition. There are no real parties in opposition to the regime.[19]

More than six months later, the party's stance was even more pessimistic: "There's no national reconciliation. Who have they reconciled themselves with? Is the politics of 2000 different from in 1989? We are in the same situation. It's the same politics of eradication as in 1989,"[20] Ahmed Taleb Ibrahimi, the party leader and a former foreign minister, told me. Such was its likely popularity, Wafa had not been allowed to register as a party.

Despite the crushing of the FIS, the refusal of the military power in Algeria to accept that it is not representative of popular aspirations means that it can only be a matter of time before Western countries opt to discreetly support "moderate" Islamist government—that is, not overtly anti-Western—in countries that can reabsorb the current growing security threat to the West emanating from Islamist militant groups that have not given up the fight. The terrorist threat unleashed by al-Qaeda has encouraged its main ally in Algeria—*Group Salafiste pour la Predication et le Combat* or Salafist (Group for Preaching and Combat), known by its French acronym GSPC—to refocus much of its effort on Europe. Since late 2002, Algerian terrorist cells in Spain, Italy, France, and the United Kingdom have been exposed and their links with the GSPC established as a result of intelligence sharing between Algerian and European security services. A wave of arrests in Catalonia, Paris, London, and Manchester in January and February 2003 established how well-developed these cells' plans were for launching attacks using chemical weapons such as ricin poison and cyanide gas. To date it is unclear if their focus on Western Europe is a result of their failure to force the capitulation of the *pouvoir* in Algeria and the crumbling of their own popular support there in response to the atrocious violence suffered by civilians.

Meanwhile, the unraveling of the credibility of the *pouvoir* in Algeria, and the absence of a popular power base on which it can reliably draw, have been accompanied by recognition that a solution to the crisis can only come if there is a strong cultural and social affinity between the leaders and the led: "The Islamist current hasn't lost its basis of voices,"[21] said Abdelaziz Belkhadem, a former president of the National Assembly, who leads Algeria's Committee for Peace and Reconciliation and is now the country's foreign minister. "They have gained a lot in political maturity. They are more pragmatic. They are more exposed to the need to open up to the modern society. There are few who remain keen to use violence. There are those who go to the maquis (underground) because they misunderstood violence. They thought that it exalts God. There are some who can't come back from the maquis, who have committed atrocious crimes," he said in 1999, telling me when we met again in 2000, "The political Islamist current remains strong. The conflict in Islamism between the non-secular project and the secular project continues to exist. The cultural situation in Algeria is anti-secular."[22]

WHERE RIVERS MEET

"If most of society becomes like me, that will be my success."[23] His eye still on the future, by the time he began to identify himself with all that Sudan's Islamic government had become, Hassan el-Tourabi had already begun to see the twilight of his experiment with personal power.

No other country has proved so significant in creating the atmosphere out of which the radical Islamist trend has emerged in the twenty-first century. From the enormous office he occupied as speaker of the country's National Assembly, the architect of Sunni Islam's only effort to create an Islamic state in the modern Arab world eyed the rapidly flowing currents of the two Niles as they joined beneath the old metal bridge linking Khartoum with Omdurman. Power was flowing out of his hands, just like the water that Sudan's poverty and crisis situation allows to flow off into the desert unexploited. It was June 1997, and el-Tourabi's efforts to harness Sudan's future to the Islamic revival then burgeoning across the region were weakening, as the cost of using it as a weapon to confront secular government and cultural diversity beyond Sudan's borders in pursuit of an Islamic identity became too great.

It seemed barely months since the project el-Tourabi had launched was in its infancy, with secularists weakened and Western countries focused on globalization to an extent that had prevented a coherent response to the challenge from Islamism. "Our most serious problem in Sudan since independence has been the search for stable government. We have had a formal democracy ruled by tribal families. Then a military dictator. Because there's now a religious spirit, the military can't rule the government," he had told me back in 1993. "You can't have democracy without basing it on the spirit of the people. Throughout Africa there are parties, but they are tribal actually. And Islam is based on democracy. In the new Sudan there is no following of the [religious] sects and their relevant political parties. Revolutions run against the old order, and people don't join those sects anymore. People worked for them for the hereafter. But now people know that in the hereafter they don't get anything for working for these people."[24]

El-Tourabi's rejection of the old order, the alliance between his National Islamic Front (NIF) with a section of the army in which political Islam has a strong root, as well as his readiness to confront and reject a religious and cultural heritage while paying little heed to its residual importance for Sudanese, set him on an extremely isolated path. The Muslim Brotherhood, from which he extricated himself, as well as the religious conservatives of the Ansar and Khatmiyya sects, loathed his approach. "All this government has to claim that it is Muslim, is that it prays,"[25] one conservative religious leader told me in 1993, when we met after taking a circuitous drive to his modest house in Khartoum North to avoid detection by whichever branch of the security forces my accomplice expected was trailing us. Other religious critics of the government during its first years in power found its religious credentials overshadowed by the personality of el-Tourabi, which they saw as casting a pall over whatever claims the regime had to pursuing an Islamist path. Having rejected the models of the past—in particular the *Mahdist* state, whose descendants had reemerged during the democratic period but failed to rule the country with any success—the regime could only look to the future. Sudan's political heritage was rejected as a failure. The Western models that influenced it intermittently between 1956 and 1989 had collapsed. The traditional ruling elite had failed to lead. Military rule had not brought stability in the past. What was left? "Democracy is a relativism. We believe in absolutism in some areas, because we are religious people. Sudan is not exactly paradise, but it's getting better," Baha al-Din Hanafi, the director of President Bashir's political department, had told me. "I think Sudan is an Islamic model. The West will never find a better Islamic model with which to conduct a dialogue. We don't believe in violence and terrorism, and the West will never find a more rational political Islam than in Sudan."[26]

El-Tourabi did represent a break with the past practice of political power lying in the hands of Sudan's two main religious-political sects. He also defended his behind-the-scenes role; prior to becoming National Assembly speaker he had no official title despite being the most powerful man in the country: "I'm not interested in political office for myself," he told me, disingenuously as it turned out, his wish for power having made such a position unnecessary, until his ill-defined role became unacceptable to the government and he sought office. "Sudan has lost most of its intellectual leadership, who have gone abroad. People don't have to join the government to play a role."[27] But three years later he was elected to the National Assembly and appointed speaker. His influence had radically altered by 1997, but in the early years of the regime the fundamental question was whether the failure of their efforts to run the country was due to the political nature of the traditional movements or the religious position their leaders—or their leaders' forefathers—had occupied. Was religion a dead weight on the practice of politics, which had denied the chance of leadership to those seeking alternatives?

"The main political parties were committed to Islamization, but the Islamic program had to be nonpartisan. Before it was implemented there had to be a bill of rights clearly defining the rights of non-Muslims,"[28] Sadiq al-Mahdi, great-grandson of the Mahdi and the prime minister ousted by the military coup that brought the Islamists to power in 1989, had told me. The military guard, which had been posted in a green tent and armed with a heavy caliber machine gun mounted on an armored personnel carrier at the end of the street where his house lies in Omdurman, had been dozing as we drove quietly past on the sand road stretching the length of the grounds surrounding his house. A long, neat lawn spread out from beyond the terrace. A gravel path encircled the lawn, which was wilting in the soaring heat, leading to a summer house draped in the fantastic blossom of bougainvillea. It was cool inside, the scent of the blossom, the hum of bumblebees, and the occasional whiff of sand dust turned up by a rare breeze dousing the place with the timeless air of the desert. "The NIF, with its military allies, has really put aside all those principles," he went on. "According to the Koran, there's no way of establishing Islamic authority by a coup d'état, because anything that is based on compulsion is null and void."[29]

The fine line the government had been treading since the army–NIF alliance was formed in 1991 had led to the creation of parallel organizations, not only within the military forces but in all areas of the power structure. The early 1990s witnessed the eclipse of President el-Bashir as a real decisionmaker and his transformation into a front man behind whom lay the internal power structure of the NIF. El-Bashir's role was merely to sign decrees—occasionally *after* events, such as the execution of army officers allegedly involved in a 1992 coup attempt, had taken place. El-Tourabi dominated the daily decisionmaking process, in coordination with the foreign minister, Ali Osman Taha, the minister of state for foreign affairs, Ghazi Salah Eddin Atabani, and other key figures from the National Islamic Front. The NIF had itself been officially disbanded and renamed the Islamic Movement, though its key personnel remained the same. The inner circle of decisionmakers—the Higher Committee—was chaired by el-Tourabi. Its decisions affected all areas of government and determined future policies. The long-term strategy was to install NIF supporters in all areas of government and the armed forces. By 1995, up to one thousand senior non-NIF army officers had been dismissed from the army as part of the NIF's attempt to control its political identity.[30] Ultimately the intention was to replace the army with a Popular Defense Force loyal to the NIF. In the police force an estimated five hundred officers had been dismissed by 1995, the intention being to replace the state police with the Popular Police by 1999. In the civil service the aim was the same: to install a service totally loyal to the NIF by 2000.

To protect its transition to totalitarianism, the government had by 1993 created a security service intended to destroy the power of the political opposition. Naf'i Ali Naf'i headed an NIF-run department within the security apparatus—the Security Group—which was in effective control of all the state security departments. The same group controlled a series of "ghost houses" in Khartoum; these were residential villas in which opponents of the regime were held incommunicado for long periods without the government even being required to announce that an arrest had been made.

"Where society can manage, government has no business interfering. . . . Where society on its own manages to realize social justice, for example, then the government does not need to interfere," Hassan el-Tourabi had written in 1983.[31] The role of government in the creation of the Islamic state—as opposed to the maintenance of that state once it has been established—varies, el-Tourabi wrote, according to historical circumstances and the ability of the government to physically communicate with all those living within its domain. It has at its heart the assumption that

> the freedom of the individual ultimately emanates from the doctrine of *tawhid*[32] which requires a self-liberation of man from any worldly authority in order to serve God exclusively. Society, and

particularly those in power, is inspired by the same principle and the collective endeavor is not one of hampering the liberty of an individual but of cooperation toward the maximum achievement of this ideal. To promote this cooperation, the freedom of one individual is related to that of the general group. The ultimate common aim of religious life unites the private and public spheres; the *sharia* provides an arbiter between social order and individual freedom.[33]

A new constitution introduced in 1997 entrenched the military–religious alliance that had seized power in the 1989 coup d'état, while allowing a degree of political pluralism. El-Tourabi had focused his aspirations for leadership both within Sudan—in the "holy war" he fought against the non-Muslim south—and abroad, in the form of the Pan-Arab and Islamic Conference (PAIC), which in the early 1990s was a forum for Islamist groups from around the world and—crucially—had become the matrix through which Osama bin Laden expanded his contacts among Islamic extremists during his 1991–1996 sojourn in Sudan.[34] Intense international isolation and the implacable hostility of, among others, the United States, at international financial donor meetings, had by 1997 evolved into overt support by Sudan's neighbors for a military opposition to the government. In response, regime in Khartoum realized it had no choice but to reform itself. The pragmatism that Abdelaziz Belkhadem had discerned within some strands of the Islamist trend in Algeria began to emerge within the Sudanese regime at about the same time. But whereas the task of refocusing Islamist efforts in Algeria involved a painful and appallingly brutal phase within the Islamist movement—during which extremists such as those who joined the ranks of the GSPC and relative moderates like those who were once part of the FIS or its armed wing fought wars within wars—the task in Sudan had remained essentially one of winning

arguments. The ability to retain a degree of unity—through a mixture of coercion, common interest, repression, and intellectual
power—within the northern Sudanese Islamist movement had sustained el-Tourabi and the National Islamic Front (NIF) in power.
Power had itself strengthened that power. "If the NIF were not in
power, its support would be halved," al-Tayib Zain al-Abdin, a
moderate supporter of the NIF and onetime political associate of el-
Tourabi, told me in May 1997. "There are people within the NIF
who are not happy with what is going on."[35]

By the end of that year el-Tourabi symbolized the gulf between
the brutal truth and the fragile myth of power in the Arab world.

Despite seeming to have the power—both intellectual and administrative—to create in the political arena a society that reflected
the cultural and historical image and legacy of Muslim Arabism, el-
Tourabi found himself in the wilderness. In the end it was Omar
Hassan el-Bashir, the military president with whom el-Tourabi had
formed the ruling alliance, who drew support away from the NIF
leader and eventually placed him under house arrest, where he remained until late 2003. "But it wasn't just Bashir but people like us
who didn't like Tourabi having that much power, because of the
change that had taken place in Tourabi," said Sayyed Khattab, who
had been el-Tourabi's right-hand man in the PAIC and is now director of the Centre for Strategic Studies in Khartoum. "I think he became more and more obsessed with the idea of power itself, and
with his role in the history of Sudan. I think this has been there all
along, but we were just too innocent to see it."[36] Khattab related
how el-Tourabi would summon ministers to a "consultative committee," where they would be admonished for failing to carry out
his own directives rather than those agreed to by the cabinet. President el-Bashir would himself receive instructions from this committee, which grew to infuriate the head of state, Khattab revealed. On
one occasion Sudan's ambassador to Cairo—probably the most im-

portant diplomatic post for Sudan—was withdrawn by el-Tourabi without el-Bashir's knowledge, just as the president was about to visit Cairo. Such power play within the regime was the result of the policy failures—both domestic and foreign—that precipitated the crumbling of el-Tourabi's credibility on all fronts. "At the beginning the government hoped for influence in regional politics. After that they became arrogant, and then they realized after a very short time that this influence was beyond their capacity," said al-Tayib Zain al-Abdin. "In fact they weren't helping foreign [Islamic] groups. In fact, do they have an influence over other Islamic movements? I think not. It's nonsense."[37]

But in reforming itself in response to the animosity that had developed within the regime toward Hassan el-Tourabi, the key question facing the Sudanese government in 2003 was whether it could survive a transformation while retaining its Islamic credentials. Does Hassan el-Tourabi's personal failure in fact amount to the failure of the entire Islamic project that the military–religious alliance had launched, and that had given the regime its political identity? "Our current ideology: There's a lot more being said about empowering the society than used to be said," Sayed Khattab told me in Khartoum in 2001. "We are looking for a society in which good citizens are the norm and should have rights. This was a cradle of civilization even before Islam. Islam didn't come to Sudan through conquest. We feel that we have to try to do something in the area of religious dialogue. Not because it's fashionable, but because we are beset with the problem of having a country that is multireligious. So, we should start with this dialogue at home. The impression in the West is that this is a theocracy, because they are not going beyond the labels."[38]

The question remains as to whether a regime that has experimented disastrously with Sudanese society for more than a decade, but is now becoming relatively enriched by the exploitation of oil reserves in the south, is changing fundamentally or is simply more likely to fester as some of the pressures upon it ease. "For us the focus is now domestic. If you want to get into a position where you want to do all the things you want to do, then you had better have a strong country," said Khattab.[39] Indeed, despite its massive short-comings and failures, the regime may yet find that the weakness of its opponents, a peace agreement ending the war in the south, and the eclipse of the unpopular Hassan el-Tourabi will give it still more time to rule. On May 6, 2000, President Bashir fired el-Tourabi from his post as secretary-general of the ruling National Congress Party and then closed party offices, saying he was angered by his former ally's "habit of defying me,"[40] and accused him of encourag-ing the armed forces to turn against him. The previous January, el-Bashir had suspended parliament and declared a state of emergency, with the intention of depriving el-Tourabi of a political platform. By May he was accusing the Islamist leader of attempting to incite civilian militiamen to "rise up against the regime," to which el-Tourabi responded: "Bashir wants to please the west and the Arabs by undermining the religion of God. The Islamist movement is today ousted at the hand of the agents of the west."[41]

That el-Tourabi's assertions fell on deaf ears within the country, and no significant groundswell of support emerged to defy the mili-tary president, reflects deeply on the relationship between the indi-vidual and the idea within the sphere of political Islam. Just as it is widely accepted that the al-Qaeda leader Osama bin Laden is not necessarily indispensable to the ongoing terror campaign al-Qaeda has launched in the name of Islam, it is not the case that the archi-tect of Sudan's process of Islamization must remain at the heart of the power structure to see that process continue. "We still believe in an Islamic model which is capable of addressing the challenges of modernity, which are democracy, human rights, and minority rights," Ghazi Salah Eddin, a former stalwart supporter of el-

Tourabi who deserted him for President el-Bashir, told me. "We are becoming more conscious of our Islamic background and orientation. That is what keeps us moving and tied to our power base. Our power base is basically an Islamic one. The division that has taken place in our base has had a weakening effect on us. There's no doubt about this. Tourabi wasn't generally interested in debate. He wasn't put under house arrest because of his ideas. He was given a full chance to attack us and establish his own party. The turning point was his agreement with the SPLA," he said, referring to an individual initiative by el-Tourabi to strike a deal with southern rebels.[42] This deal was condemned by the government and led to the formerly all-powerful Islamist being placed under house arrest.

The government's refocusing on domestic issues was not only the result of the Western and African regional opprobrium it attracted by its ambitions to radicalize the entire Islamic world but was also due to the radical movements with which it had ties coming to regard the regime in Khartoum as too moderate. The movements with which el-Tourabi had links—al-Qaeda, the GIA in Algeria, Palestinian Hamas, and others—did not have the pressures on them that a government like that in Khartoum had to endure from other governments. Al-Qaeda and the GIA (prior to its demise in the late 1990s) became disillusioned with Khartoum, accusing it of succumbing to Western and Saudi Arabian pressure to moderate. By the late 1990s, el-Tourabi had few friends among Islamists and few friends—if any at all—among governments. "He was oblivious to the fact that the generations behind him had grown up, but he insisted on the old role of the sheikh," Ghazi Salah Eddin told me. He continued:

We look on it as a new phase. I am no longer interested in a movement that is inspired by one man. We are a country. We are a phase in history. We need to see how we can inspire a whole people, from an Islamic base. It's no longer the old phase of slo-ganism. It's much more practical and issue-oriented.

Despite our mistakes and shortcomings, people still believe that this is still the most serious group in terms of its commitment. People are cognizant of the fact that we are Islamists. We have to think of how we hand over to the next generation. We are not picking up momentum. We have been slowing down a bit.[43]

LOST GENERATIONS

Shivering in their cocktail chiffon, the grande dames of Cairo shuf-fled through the sand to the VIP seats, jewels sparkling in the flood-lights. The cold wind blowing in from the Sahara was not going to deter Egypt's elite as they gathered for yet another outdoor staging of *Aida*, Guiseppe Verdi's Nile-side melodrama, at the Giza pyra-mids on the edge of Cairo. It was an evening—in October 1998—to see and be seen, to sit only as the house lights dimmed, to ensure that everybody knew you were there at the occasion of the year.

Underlying it all, however, was a valiant attempt by the govern-ment to remind Egypt's extremists of just who runs the country, to prove that the war with the violent Islamist groups was over, and that there was no longer any question about who was in control. It was a highly significant gesture, hosting three thousand people for each performance—among them lesser European royals, cabinet ministers, fading rock stars, and the "permatan" *glitterati*—and hav-ing them spend an evening in the desert of a country where a year before Islamic militants had shot fifty-eight foreign tourists in cold blood.

"Not again," some Egyptians had been saying. "Can't they think of another opera to stage?" Certainly not. *Aida* has been claimed by Egypt as part of its cultural tapestry, so Wagner or Mozart would simply not do. Even though his most famous opera was really a colonial trick Verdi played on Egypt, the visual spectacle, the occasionally oriental feel to the music, and the typically silly operatic yarn leapt over the realities of modern Egypt and allowed the then imperial elite and its Egyptian satraps to dwell gloriously on the imagined pharaonic past.

"The reason everybody loves *Aida* is perhaps because it is just a fantasy. We don't know if that was what life was really like under the pharaohs," said Mustafa Nagui, chairman of the Cairo Opera House, and the driving force behind several previous open-air productions that had been staged in the southern city of Luxor. "The story of *Aida* doesn't interest me at all. What matters is that it is a spectacular show that has a relationship with Egypt," he said candidly, of a spectacle that was commissioned by Khedive Ismail, Egypt's former ruler, to commemorate the opening of the Suez Canal in 1869. But he did not claim that it reflects Egyptian sensibilities: "From a European perspective, the opera is about emotions. Love is victorious. From our point of view, the hero should not have loved Aida. He should have made his work and duty conquer his love," he said, adding: "The evidence of modern Egypt in this production lies in the simple fact that we were able to stage it. It's a production that nobody else can do, because we have the civilization. *Aida* belongs to us because we have the pyramids at which to stage it."[44]

Amid the chiffon and pearls, the desert crawled with police, security officers, soldiers, and surveillance squads. Every member of the audience, apart from the politicians, was frisked and scanned; handbags were searched and mobile telephones banned. But the real message to the Islamists was to be seen on stage. Braving the cold desert night, scores of near-nude men swooped and soared in a glaring display of immodesty. The opera aside, the leading ideologues of the modern Islamist movement were all either Egyptian or lived in

Giza pyramids, Egypt.

Egypt, and to this day they regard the pre-Islamic period, upon which *Aida* supposedly draws, as a heathen age. "The message in the opera is that there's no conflict between civilizations and religions," Mustafa Nagui told me. "When you see *Aida*, and you see people worshipping the sun and *Ra*, the message is that you can worship whoever you want. I am a very religious Muslim. But I understand how to be cultured. You must open your mind to everything before you choose what to believe."[45]

The confidence with which the Egyptian government approached the challenge from the religious extremists it had sought to annihilate in the mid-1990s now seems less obvious. The military threat to Egypt has shifted, as the extremist current has coalesced into the al-Qaeda network and refocused with immense ambition on Europe, the United States, and Saudi Arabia. But the political and existential questions that have spawned the extremism remain unresolved within the cradle of the Muslim world itself, and their dispersal globally has made the regimes the extremists initially sought to overthrow less rather than more powerful. Thus, regimes such as that of Egypt, which thought it had achieved victory and celebrated with opera in the desert, can draw little comfort from the fact that their allies in the West are so clearly threatened. Western insecurity can only create greater global insecurity, whose impact at a time of such immense political uncertainty in the Middle East provides little comfort to the secular regimes of the region. Moreover, the short-lived sense of victory over some of the Islamist groups that the region's regimes may have enjoyed has done profoundly little to create an environment conducive to peaceable coexistence between the multitude of cultural and religious trends the Arab world comprises.

Such a sense of uncertainty has produced wildly differing views about what the future holds.[46] On the one hand is the view that moderation has taken over, that the extremists are defeated, and that the Islamist movement is "facing a moral crisis."[47] This view holds that in the future, the success of Islamists will depend on their adherence to democratic principles. "There is no longer any real alternative."[48] In the wake of the September 11, 2001, terrorist attacks in the United States, this assessment would seem to be at odds with the global perception of the cultural-political currents now dominating the Middle East and parts of the broader Muslim world. The complexity of what is taking place within Islam, the new dimensions of radical Islamist relations with the West or "Christendom," and the credibility of the Western response to the terrorist threat since September 2001 have been obscured by the drama of the so-called Global War On Terror and by the absence of any clear signs that the U.S. administration of George W. Bush has developed a credible, long-term political response to the challenge.

Gilles Kepel is one of a growing number of writers seeking a way of broadening the debate over what Osama bin Laden and the al-Qaeda terrorist network really represent. In the immediate aftermath of the September 11 terrorist attacks, detailed accounts of al-Qaeda's activities, many of which had long been researched, were swiftly brought forward, printed, and distributed. Since then, a second wave has emerged, intended to be more considered, more informative, and drawing upon what happened in both the immediate and the more distant past, to project what might happen next.

As has been the case for intelligence agencies, academics have discovered that the "truth" about al-Qaeda has the potential for slipping from their grasp every time they think they have reached a sound conclusion. With the West now firmly in the gunsights of the extremists, one question remains vital: How should Western countries and their cultural, religious, and political institutions regard themselves in the relationship with their new enemy? The West is inextricably linked to the process that has created al-Qaeda. The birth of political Islam as long ago as the 1890s,[49] and its evolution into its most recent, and most violent, manifestation, in the form of al-Qaeda, can be traced directly to the role of outsiders in the Muslim world. But how far down the road to understanding the real implications of this role have those engaged in this process now gone?

Starting at the beginning of the century that spawned modern political Islam, it would seem that the answer to this question is: not far. In his series of lectures, Bernard Lewis portrayed the moral crisis described by Kepel instead as a crisis of *morale*, which he extended to the Islamic world in its totality. *What Went Wrong? The Clash between Islam and Modernity in the Middle East* traces the declining fortunes of the Caliphate led by the Ottoman empire until its defeat in 1918 and its abolition in 1924 by Kemal Ataturk. Lewis's assertions make vivid the extent of social decay, and he seeks to depict from what great heights the Islamic world has fallen since 1699, and the Treaty of Carlowitz, which marked the end of Ottoman expansion in Europe. He shows an acute awareness of how deeply significant is the Arab and Muslim sense of loss at the decline in the power and influence of the Islamic world. He writes of the Arab world today: "Modernizers—by reform or revolution—concentrated their efforts in three main areas: military, economic, and political. The results achieved were, to say the least, disappointing. . . . Worst of all is the political result: The long quest for freedom has left a string of shabby tyrannies, ranging from traditional autocracies to new-style dictatorships, modern only in their apparatus of repression and indoctrination."[50] The ability of the Ottoman empire to learn from European strengths, develop skills in European languages to facilitate diplomacy, and adopt European military methods and the like is made clear. But this ability to learn did not create modernity within the empire and merely made it more autocratic at a time when Europe had passed through or was becoming ripe for political and economic change. "The Ottomans, faced with the major crisis in their history, asked: 'What did we do wrong?' . . . The basic fault, according to these memoranda [by Ottoman scholars in 1699] was falling away from the good old ways, Islamic and Ottoman; the basic remedy was a return to them. This diagnosis and prescription still command wide acceptance in the Middle East,"[51] Lewis writes.

Vital to improving Western understanding of how the Middle East has reached the political crisis of today is the sense of failure created by both the fall of the Ottomans' Islamic state and the failure to replace it with dynamic, modern alternatives. Gilles Kepel adds a further failure to the catalogue detailed by Lewis. In *Jihad: The Trail of Political Islam*, he argues that the most recent wave of political Islam, which from the late 1980s until the mid-1990s appeared on the verge of toppling regimes and seizing political power, is now on the wane. Kepel identifies a new movement within political Islam that he calls *jihadist-salafism*, which he distinguishes from previous movements. It was born out of the Afghan *jihad* that drove the Soviet Union out of Afghanistan in 1989. "The international brigade of [Afghan] jihad veterans, being outside the control of any state, was suddenly available to serve Islamist causes anywhere in the world. . . . This milieu was cut off from social reality; its inhabitants perceived the world in the light of religious doctrine and armed violence. It bred a new, hybrid Islamist ideology whose first doctrinal principle was to rationalize the existence and behavior of militants. This was jihadist-salafism . . . Salafism advocated a return to the traditions of the devout ancestors,"[52] Kepel writes. Proof of how potent this return remains was found by U.S. investigators as they trawled through the possessions of the September 11 hijackers. Among what they left behind was a letter, found in the discarded bag of Mohamed Atta, the lead hijacker. It detailed instructions to the hijackers to carry out their allotted task "in the same way our good predecessors have done before you," and for them to be courageous "as our predecessors did when they came to the battle."

Despite the availability of this *jihadist* force, militants who were fired with the zeal created by the defeat of the Soviet Union and returned to their native countries in the early 1990s, as well as with the subsequent ferocity of the Islamist violence of the 1990s, could not ignore "[the] deeper reality . . . that the two opposing camps within the Islamist movement (the middle class rich and the disinherited young) were no longer able to provoke social upheaval on a scale that could lead to a lasting success like that of the [1979] Iranian revolution. The recurrent violence of the decade was above all a reflection of the movement's structural weakness, not its growing strength. No ideologist worthy of the name . . . [was] able to offer an overall vision that transcended social antagonisms,"[53] Kepel argues. It is a credible argument, though one he puts forward in a manner that leaves the reader needing more proof from the ground level of Islamist activism than he is able to provide. He follows through by saying that today's *jihadist-salafist* movement is the backbone of al-Qaeda, which (in a reference to the bombing of the U.S. embassies in Kenya and Tanzania in August 1998) he says is "cut off from its roots within society . . . [and thus] resorted to a brand of terrorism that was more or less covered by religious justification, and most of whose victims had nothing whatever to do with the designated enemy of the jihadists."[54] Though Kepel's argument is weakened by inadequate explanation of whether the failure of the Islamist movements to seize power was due to the overpowering might of the states they were fighting or to their isolation from their popular support, his conclusion is firm: "What is certain is that by losing the war on the ground, in an orgy of unspeakable atrocities [which led to popular support for the Islamists collapsing], the GIA (in Algeria) drastically weakened Islamism as a whole, not only in Algeria but in the rest of the Muslim world, where it was now obliged to expend much time and energy distancing itself from its more extremist elements."[55] The suggestion is that this defeat for Islamism is definitive.

So where then does Osama bin Laden fit into the new equation? By targeting the West itself, al-Qaeda is in a much stronger position to garner support from people who were horrified by Islamist violence while they were personally suffering from it in their own countries but who can support Islamist aims when the victims are non-Muslims in other parts of the world. In *The Shade of Swords: Jihad and the Conflict between Islam and Christianity,*[56] a leading Indian writer, M. J. Akbar, deftly shifts the center of gravity of the current crisis from the Middle East to south Asia and makes clear from the start that an understanding of Islam today requires a sound understanding of its roots, particularly with reference to his chosen subject, *jihad.* Akbar is at his most daunting when he characterizes the conflict in which the West is now engaged: "Time will tell how much America understands about the forces at play in its second Afghan war, but this too is an episode from a larger world conflict: only the roles are reversed. America is the Soviet Union this time. The nature of battle is different. One army is in the field, and the second is in the shadows."[57] He explains Osama bin Laden's rise to prominence as the result of Pakistan's radicalization rather than as the product of the Middle East situation, or even the product of a larger Islamic movement having emerged. Even so, he does not regard bin Laden as a definitive figure within Islam but more the result of political crisis: "All Muslims live in two dimensions: one is the circle of nationalism, the other a circle of brotherhood. . . . In an age of despair the need for a hero who can inspire pan-Islamic victories becomes acute. . . . There is no such hero on the horizon now. Despair can become a breeding ground for mavericks who believe in themselves and their version of the faith."[58]

But now it seems that the maverick has become the hero.

3

GOD AND THE MAVERICK

OSAMA BIN LADEN AND THE ISLAMIST CHALLENGE

When the darkness comes upon us
And we are hit by a sharp tooth, I say:
"Our homes are flooded with blood
And the tyrant is freely wandering in our homes."
And from the battlefield vanished
The brightness of swords and the horses.
And over weeping sounds now
We hear the beat of drums and rhythm.
They are storming his forts
And shouting: "We will not stop our raids
Until you free our lands."

IT WAS DURING A CONVERSATION FILMED IN NOVEMBER 2001, which appeared to definitively confirm al-Qaeda's role in the September

11 attacks in New York and Washington, that Osama bin Laden quoted the words cited above to a visiting Saudi sheikh: "We will not stop our raids until you free our lands." His goal was and is clear. It has been clear to him for the decade or more since U.S. troops occupied the Arabian peninsula and ousted Saddam Hussein from Kuwait in 1991. To the Western countries who failed to heed the threat contained in his *Declaration of War against the Americans Occupying the Land of the Two Holy Places* of August 23, 1996, bin Laden's message today has a double significance: First, it was a threat that was not taken sufficiently seriously except by a handful of U.S. officials, and which therefore exposed a large degree of ignorance and—possibly—arrogance on the part of those whose job it is to understand and confront such threats; second, it is a threat that has actually been carried out. The most significant act of Osama bin Laden is that he has carried out what he long threatened—publicly—to carry out. The global shock of the September 11 attacks was in part caused by the visual impact of the destruction but was in part the result of the attacks being so devastatingly successful. They forced the Western world to accept that "reality" could be created by forces completely beyond its control.

"This is a war being fought in the mind as much as anywhere else," wrote the Indian journalist M. J. Akbar in his powerful account of the likely future of Muslim–Christian relations. Akbar reflects on the need for the emergence of a Muslim hero in a time of disillusionment, but argues: "There is no such hero on the horizon now. Despair can become a breeding ground for mavericks who believe in themselves and their version of the faith."[1] But he is probably wrong, because in many ways there *is* a new "hero." It is bin Laden who is both the "maverick" and the "hero who can inspire pan-Islamic victories" and thereby win the war, by securing victory in the minds of those he seeks to have follow him, inspiring them to commit acts that will further debilitate the traumatized United

States and see it quit Islam's spiritual heartland. The steady with-drawal of U.S. forces from Saudi Arabia since the September 11 at-tacks suggests that bin Laden's demands are now being met. But in a war that is indeed also being fought in the mind, the strengths and weaknesses of the protagonists and an idea of who is winning can best be assessed by establishing how well each has undermined the credibility of the other in the eyes of their own and each other's con-stituencies. Akbar asserts that the loss of Afghanistan is as irrelevant to al-Qaeda as it is to the Taliban regime that allowed the terrorists to operate from there. "The Taliban, and Al Qaida, and many or-ganizations with a similar dream, can survive without a government, or even a country, because the recruitment is done in the mind. You cannot fight a battle in the mind only with Special Forces and cruise missiles. . . . Defeat is only a setback in the holy war. The jihad goes on," he writes.[2] He argues that the success of U.S., British, and Northern Alliance troops on the battlefield is significant but barely important in the global context. As remnants of the ousted Islamist regime mount sporadic attacks in the country, the victory over them seems less than definitive. But the context within which al-Qaeda has emerged explains much about its character and suggests that while its recruiting ground is vast and amorphous, its effectiveness as a network remains dependent upon organization and structure, even though the spirit it has inspired has taken root globally.

Khartoum's rattling yellow taxis ground their gears and juddered past the acacia trees, which cast squat shadows onto the two-story office on McNimr Street. The office door was locked, and the only evidence that this was once the engine room of what has now be-come a sprawling terrorist empire was a faded, orange sign on the wall that read "Taba." In an office on the upper floor of Khartoum's presidential palace, overlooking what was that day the dangerously high water of the Nile, Gutbi al-Mahdi, the head of Sudan's external intelligence service during bin Laden's stay in Sudan and now political adviser to Sudan's President Omar el-Bashir, peered through his thick spectacles and tried—in vain—to theorize convincingly: "We have to know how a terrorist is born. What happened to make him such a person?" said Gutbi.[3] He continued:

> The turning point in Bin Laden's life is very important. He left Sudan and he was very bitter. He felt he was doing good work in Sudan. He didn't commit any crime. Then he was thrown into Afghanistan. He left all his wealth here. He is broke. The [Sudan] government owes him a lot of money. He lost all his money in Sudan, because we confiscated all his property.
>
> There is nothing he can do in Afghanistan except fight. When he was expelled we expelled all his 200 people with him. These are people who feel they have absolutely no future. All doors are closed. And they are under nobody's control.
>
> We think these are the kinds of mistakes which we feel have contributed a lot to this situation.[4]

According to Gutbi, when bin Laden arrived in Sudan in 1991 he brought with him construction equipment worth $12 million and went on to invest $80 million by the time Saudi Arabian and U.S. pressure forced the Sudanese to expel him and his followers in 1996. The main flaw in Gutbi's analysis is that it suggests that bin Laden and the followers he was assembling into what would become al-Qaeda were somehow disconnected from the radicalization and orientation toward terrorism that was at the time taking root in Sudan and elsewhere. For Gutbi, as for other senior Sudanese officials, attitudes toward the al-Qaeda leader are influenced by the ways in which the Saudi extremist's experience of their country reflected upon their own credibility. Sudan's failure to resist U.S. and Saudi pressure for his removal was a major blow to the regime's standing among the radicals it had once sought to influence across the Islamic world. Pragmatism forced a change of political direction in Sudan, one of the results of which was the decision to ask bin Laden to leave.

But in hindsight, it is necessary to ask whether the al-Qaeda movement that emerged in Sudan in 1991–1996 perhaps intended to use Sudan in the way that it eventually used Afghanistan. While in Sudan, bin Laden liaised most closely with Ibrahim Sanoussi, Hassan el-Tourabi's assistant in the Pan-Arab and Islamic Conference (PAIC). This transnational body, while not overly influenced by the ultraconservative Saudi *wahhabism* or *salafism* practiced by bin Laden, was nevertheless a useful vehicle whereby the al-Qaeda leader could retain contacts with the then fledgling "global" Islamist movement. There has never been a suggestion that bin Laden sought to hijack the PAIC from el-Tourabi, but the global perspective it held was much closer to the vision bin Laden had of his own role than the modest, business-oriented functions Gutbi attributes to him. It is naïve to assert that had bin Laden remained in Sudan, he would have limited himself to using the businesses he housed at the offices of his Taba Investments company on McNimr Street to building roads. It is much more likely that he would have sought to lead Sudan along the same path that he led the Taliban after their seizure of power in Afghanistan in 1996. As Ali Osman Taha, currently Sudan's vice president, told me:

> I don't think bin Laden had a clear design of what he intended to do. It wasn't clear to me. It wasn't clear how deep and how far were his connections with the other groups: the Egyptians, Somalis, and others who were in Sudan. It wasn't clear that he had a design for all these groups, all of which had come on their own initiative.[5]

Taha's conclusion can be taken in several ways: either as doubting that bin Laden knew what he was doing, or recognizing that he wasn't confiding his plans to his Sudanese hosts. Given the extent to which bin Laden *was* planning while he was in Sudan, the latter view—about which even people like Taha would perhaps have been little informed—seems the more credible. In the early 1990s Sudan had opened its doors to a wide range of Islamists, some of them linked to terrorism. Taha himself was implicated in the attempted assassination of President Hosni Mubarak in the Ethiopian capital Addis Ababa in 1995, as two of those alleged to have been involved fled through Sudan. Taha denies the accusation. But it is unclear how informed the Sudanese authorities were, despite the would-be assassins' open identification with extremist and violent causes. The two passed through Khartoum's airport unhindered—just as many Arabs were doing at that time—leaving the country open to the accusation that it assisted them, when it was probably more likely that Sudan's lax security was being exploited. The administrative—if not political—sea change in Sudan, which has now ended with Hassan el-Tourabi in the political wilderness, stems from the Mubarak assassination attempt, when Sudanese officials began to worry that at least some of the foreign radicals in the country were dangerously out of control.

To date, few senior members of the Sudanese regime will acknowledge that the course and cause of bin Laden's radicalization was probably more strategic than it was simply the result of events. "Pressuring Sudan to kick out Osama bin Laden left him with no option but to fight. If they had been left in Sudan, they would have been content," Yahya Babicar, the deputy head of Sudan's intelligence service, told me.[6] The impression from such statements is that the regime in Khartoum had only a superficial idea of what bin Laden was planning. Had they looked into the network he was building up from the McNimr Street office and on the farms at which he was organizing military training, and had followed the tentacles the network was establishing among Sudan's neighbors, as well as its ties way beyond Africa and the Middle East, their conclusions would have been vastly different. Even though Sudan, since the September 11 attacks, has opened up at least some of its intelligence files on al-Qaeda operatives and obviously had information that has been useful to the CIA and other intelligence services now tracking al-Qaeda,[7] the extent to which bin Laden explained his operations inside Sudan and his future plans with the Sudanese government is far from clear. "We are helping [the United States] understand the bin Laden organization. Not by indicting people, but they have used our records and have met with some people who have helped give them an insight into the way that Osama bin Laden and his people are thinking," said Babicar.[8]

The tendency among Sudanese officials is to stress that banishing bin Laden to Afghanistan was a major cause of his radicalization. Whether this is indeed true is fundamental to understanding the depth, source, and ideology of al-Qaeda's and bin Laden's extremism. Either bin Laden's radicalism is the result of a succession of essentially political disappointments—the chaos that erupted in Afghanistan after the "victory of Islam" and the defeat of the Soviet Union, the Saudi refusal of bin Laden's offer to use his *mujahid* troops from Afghanistan to oust Saddam Hussein from Kuwait in 1991, and al-Qaeda's expulsion from Sudan—or it is indeed derived from a master plan with *jihad* as its main focus.

My sense is that, just as he did with the Taliban—to whom he was much closer ideologically than he ever was to the Sudanese regime—bin Laden *always* intended to infiltrate the body politic of Sudan and use the country as a launching pad for *jihad*. The disappointment Sudanese officials say bin Laden expressed turned to anger because he was denied the chance to do so and had to start all over again in Afghanistan. Potentially, he was just as dangerous while in Sudan as in Afghanistan, and sensing this—though perhaps without really knowing why—the Sudanese were willing to acquiesce to demands that he be expelled. This pattern is vital to understanding al-Qaeda today and assessing the character of the network post-Afghanistan. Bin Laden believes in structures and organization, and the hierarchy he created is both al-Qaeda's main organizational strength as well as the source of its credibility among Muslims. Al-Qaeda is not haphazard; there is a chain of command, orders are given, and plans are developed over time and distance. For this reason, al-Qaeda probably is now looking for a new base—which is what its name means. It will wait patiently for Afghanistan to once again fall into lawlessness, also retaining its support in Pakistan, expanding it within Kashmir, Bangladesh, Indonesia, and the Caucasus, while seeking to build support in sub-Saharan Africa. Then it will step in, just as it has done before, with money, people, and ambitious plans.

What will become clear when the discernible signs of this phase start to emerge is the extent to which the structures put in place during the 1990s have endured, even in the face of the U.S.-led war on terror. For this reason it will be necessary to retrace the course of al-Qaeda's development back to that padlocked office on McNimr Street. Only then will it become clear what the al-Qaeda phenomenon truly represents, by establishing its history as a part of a much larger, civilizational phenomenon that is likely in the long run to unravel the political makeup of the Middle East. Faith alone is not enough for al-Qaeda to succeed in this venture. Al-Qaeda and its affiliates require structures. The assertion by al-Qaeda's foes that they have dismantled these structures and thereby hindered its capacity to fulfill its mission are dangerously off the mark. Damage has been done to the al-Qaeda network, but it can replicate, adapt, and modify, because it is *the* new movement in the Islamic world, its predecessors—both religious and secular—having failed. As the Harvard scholar Bernard Lewis writes: "The two dominant movements of the twentieth century were socialism and nationalism. Both have been discredited, the first by its failure, the second by its success and consequent exposure as ineffective."[9] But as he has also said: "If the peoples of the Middle East continue on their present path . . . there will be no escape from a downward spiral of hate and spite, rage and self-pity, poverty and oppression, culminating sooner or later in yet another alien domination."[10] That alien domination—as the experience of Sudan and Afghanistan perhaps suggests—could far more easily be by foreign Islamists moving from one country to another within the Islamic world than by non-Muslims, against whom much of the Islamic world can and will continue to retain an effective resistance on many fronts. But to sustain its efforts and retain its credibility, al-Qaeda and its affiliates must secure and sustain a degree of organizational capacity into which new recruits can feed.

"THE BASE"

To understand what al-Qaeda envisages for the future, it is useful to know how it got to where it is today. In early 1991, Jamal Ahmed al-Fadl arrived in Khartoum.[11] With him he carried $57,000 and 17,000 Saudi rials, as he told a New York court in 2001 during the first major trial of al-Qaeda suspects. As Osama bin Laden's finance chief, he organized the rental of apartments for al-Qaeda members and bought farmland to be used for both growing crops and providing what he called "refresh [military] training . . . because al-Qaeda think when we were Sudan, we focus on the people that got training already [in Afghanistan]. If they need any operation or anything for the military purpose, the people got trained already, they just give them refresh in these farms."[12] The first farm was bought by al-Fadl in his own name, with $250,000 made available to him by Dr. Abdel Moez, an Islamic lawyer who ran al-Qaeda's *fatwa* committee, which issued religious rulings, and who was a member of its *shura* or legislative council. Al-Fadl was then instructed to buy a 40 feddan salt farm in Port Sudan for $180,000, the money being provided to him by al-Qaeda's Business Companies Committee. He then bought a 50 feddan farm at Damazine, one-third of which was used for military training and the rest for growing white corn, peanuts, sesame, and sunflowers, as well as for producing sesame and peanut oil. Tractors were imported from Czechoslovakia and Maz trucks from Russia for use on the farms, while al-Qaeda officials were dispatched to find export markets for produce.

Located at the Damazine farm was a group of Jordanian militants, the Abu Ali group. The group came under the al-Qaeda umbrella, and it was intended that they would carry out military activities in Jordan and Palestine. At his New York trial, al-Fadl said he was given $100,000 in cash to carry to Amman, the Jordanian capital, to hand to a member of the Abu Ali group. Al-Fadl was given the money by another al-Qaeda member, Abu-Fadhl, who had withdrawn it from al-Shamal Islamic Bank in Khartoum, where al-Qaeda had its account. He traveled to Jordan using a Sudanese passport with a false name, carrying the cash—which was all in $100 bills—in a bag full of clothes. When he arrived at Amman airport he was met by a contact, Abu Ikram Urani. Al-Fadl said Urani spoke with airport officials, and he was allowed to pass through the airport without having his baggage checked; he was then taken to Urani's farm outside Amman, where he handed over the money. Al-Fadl also said that al-Qaeda provided money for the Eritrean Jamaat I Jihad group. The group had a guesthouse in the Riyadh district of Khartoum. Al-Fadl visited the guesthouse with Abu Ubaidah al-Banshiri, an al-Qaeda official who divided his time between Khartoum and the Kenyan capital, Nairobi, and who handed $100,000 in cash to Sheikh Arafa, the leader of the Eritrean group.

Aside from the dispersal of funds to radical groups, funds were also used to build up a business empire through which the terrorist infrastructure could operate. Evidence from bank accounts at Khartoum's al-Shamal Islamic Bank reveals that the al-Qaeda business network extended to an account in Cyprus, where it had a guesthouse. At least one U.S. dollar transfer was to be made to Cyprus, as part of an attempt to boost its business interests there. The aim was to sell sesame seeds and shelled peanuts through the Cyprus free port rather than direct from Sudan, a move it was hoped would bring a higher price as the Sudanese currency plunged. By 1993, al-Qaeda's companies in Sudan employed around seven hundred people, twenty-five at the head office on McNimr Street, and scores more on projects in the north and east of the country. Around six hundred were employed by the largest single al-Qaeda company, al-Hijra Construction and Development Company, which built major roads for the Sudanese government, projects that cost bin Laden around $20 million. Al-Qaeda also created Taba Investments, Laden International import-export company, and Qudurat transport, as well as a bakery and a center for cattle gene technology, all of which were provided with tax-free status by the Sudanese authorities, Jamal al-Fadl said.

Al-Shamal Islamic Bank was founded in 1984 with authorized capital of $20 million. Ismail Mohamed Osman, the bank's acting general manager, said its banking operations started in 1990. According to the bank, its founders were three Saudi investors, as well as the governorate of Sudan's Northern State and the Faisal Islamic Bank. Al-Shamal Bank has denied reports that it was ever part owned by bin Laden. However, a report presented to the French National Assembly on October 10, 2001, by Arnaud Montebourg, an assembly deputy, asserted that al-Shamal Bank was created by bin Laden in concert with Sudan's National Islamic Front. According to Ismail Mohamed Osman, al-Qaeda created two companies that opened accounts in Sudanese pounds and U.S. dollars with the bank. The companies—al-Hijra Construction incorporated in Sudan, and Wadi El

Agig Co., incorporated in Saudi Arabia and a minority shareholder in al-Hijra—were the limit of the bank's relationship with bin Laden, he said. Al-Hijra Construction opened two accounts on March 30, 1992, both of which fell dormant in 1997, a year after bin Laden left Sudan.

In his smart, pleasantly cool office on the first floor of the bank's sparkling new headquarters beside a bus station in Khartoum's bustling Sayed Abderahman Street, Ismail Mohamed Osman went straight to the point. "Bin Laden contacted us as a businessman, and opened a foreign currency account in the name of the al-Hijra company. He never came himself to the bank. The foreign account was replenished from outside Sudan, mainly from Gulf states and from America, through bank transfers," he told me in November 2001. "Over three or four years, probably one million dollars went through these accounts. He also opened an account in Sudanese pounds, to meet his needs for local currency, in which the average balance was around 200,000 Sudanese pounds. Most payments in local currency were made directly from the Central Bank of Sudan, as payment for construction projects undertaken by the al-Hijra company for the government. During his stay he dealt with us as a customer. He was not a founder of the bank, and when he left Sudan he closed the accounts, and there were no funds left,"[13] he said, wiping his hands vigorously together, a sign perhaps of seeking to wash himself clean of the problem.

Details of bank records show that when Sudan was forced, under intense Saudi and U.S. pressure, to ask bin Laden to leave Sudan in 1996, his accounts at al-Shamal Islamic Bank held 554,000 Sudanese pounds and a mere $99.58. This money, according to Osman—apparently contradicting his earlier claim that there are no al-Qaeda-related funds left in the bank—is still there. In view of the scale of investment made by al-Qaeda in Sudan in 1991–1996 and the size of the amounts held at al-Shamal and other banks in Khartoum, it is clear that a large proportion of its financial arrangements did not involve using banks at all, instead relying on informal money transfer companies, *hawala,* which take funds at their offices and then wire authorization for the same amount to be handed over to a beneficiary elsewhere without a physical transfer taking place. Al-Qaeda had, however, been able to move money around the world through al-Shamal's correspondent network of banks, which included France's Credit Lyonnais, Germany's Commerzbank, Standard Bank of South Africa, and Saudi Hollandi bank in Jeddah, in which ABN Amro of the Netherlands has a 40 percent stake. These external links were used in 1993 when al-Qaeda bought an aircraft in the United States with which it planned to move Stinger ground-to-air missiles from Peshawar in Pakistan to Khartoum. The money was wired from the Wadi al-Aqiq account at al-Shamal bank via Bank of New York to a Bank of America account held in Dallas, Texas, by Essam al-Ridi. Al-Ridi, an Egyptian flight instructor who met bin Laden in Pakistan in 1985, flew the plane to Khartoum but crashed it on arrival at the airport.

While al-Qaeda's activities were developing in Sudan, Khaled al-Fauwaz, a Saudi who had fought alongside bin Laden in Afghanistan, had arrived in Kenya and created Asma, an import-export company with authorized capital of Ksh 1 million. The company—the first step toward creating al-Qaeda's Nairobi cell—was created on October 25, 1993, according to company records.[14] Al-Fauwaz employed a Nairobi solicitor, Mohamed Munir Chaudri, to register the company, with himself and two others—a Kenyan and an Egyptian—as directors, each of whom held one share in the company, each worth 1,000 Kenyan shillings. Asma's memorandum of association states its purpose as being the import and export of animal hides, agricultural products, fresh beans, coffee husk, and coffee, and to play the role of "agents, retailers and wholesalers of all commodities, stockists of consumer goods and any other products which may conveniently be dealt with by the company."

Al-Qaeda meanwhile sought to extend its contacts in Tanzania and farther afield to South Africa. Abu Ubaidah al-Banshiri, another veteran of the Afghan war who became the head of the Kenya cell when al-Fauwaz left to open an office in London in 1994, sought to establish a business importing diamonds and tanzanite from Tanzania. The use of precious and semiprecious stones would later become a key part of al-Qaeda's financial structure. A report written by the U.K.-based environmental group Global Witness, *For a Few Dollars More: How al-Qaeda Moved into the Diamond Trade*,[15] details how al-Qaeda made its first contacts with diamond dealers in Liberia in September 1998. A senior adviser to Charles Taylor, the Liberian president until he was forced to leave office in August 2003, and the Sierra Leonean Revolutionary United Front (RUF) rebel force, which at that time controlled the country's diamond area, allegedly met an al-Qaeda operative and opened negotiations. The Taylor adviser, Ibrahim Bah, who fought alongside Islamist forces in Afghanistan and received military training in Libya, discussed diamond deals with Ali Darwish, a Lebanese diamond dealer working with another dealer, Aziz Nassour. In a letter from the RUF rebels, reproduced by Global Witness, Nassour is apparently shown to have had the monopoly of diamond purchases from the RUF, a large part of which was to be bought on behalf of the al-Qaeda operatives. In an interview in April 2003, Darwish told me that the adviser dispatched three al-Qaeda operatives to Liberia's border with Sierra Leone to finalize the buying deal, though he denied knowing the three were part of al-Qaeda.[16] Nassour himself denied that the deal had ever taken place,[17] though Darwish's admission and the existence of documentary evidence to the contrary suggest otherwise.

Both Abu Ubaidah and al-Fauwaz, who had run a similar business in Saudi Arabia before joining the exiled Islamist opposition to the Saudi regime, failed in their efforts to generate substantial income. Azma was closed down, and the Nairobi cell, some of whose members lived in $500-per-month houses while others lived in cheap hotels, lived frugally because money was tight. A sign of how limited their funds became emerged when a $3,000 bribe to police officers, to free al-Fauwaz and another cell member who had raised the suspicion of airport authorities when one was found traveling on a dubious Danish passport, had to be approved by bin Laden's inner circle of advisers in Khartoum. Another cell member, L'Houssaine Khertchou, was told he could not renew the pilot's license for which he had taken fifty-five hours of lessons, due to lack of funds: "Osama bin Laden himself he was talking to us and saying that there was no money and he lost all his money, and he shouldn't extend a lot of things and he reduced the salary of people,"[18] said Khertchou, who would later say that he left al-Qaeda because of its financial problems, which had even led to al-Qaeda's few salaried Khartoum-based staff seeing their salaries cut to around $1,200 a month. "He didn't stay long enough [in Sudan] to get his investment back," Yahia Babicar, the Sudanese intelligence official, told me. "Other than not being paid for his road building projects by the [Sudanese] government, his other problem was that he used the wrong people to manage his investments. He didn't bring qualified people, but people he was associated with when he was in Afghanistan."[19]

For five years the al-Qaeda cell lived quietly in Nairobi, despite occasional official suspicion. Before being told that there was no money to renew his license, Khertchou learned how to fly light aircraft and was a "diligent" pupil, his instructor said. Al-Banshiri was particularly active in developing the commodities side of al-Qaeda's business, traveling throughout East Africa, until one day in 1996 he was drowned when the ferry on which he was crossing Lake Victoria sank. Evidence of the extent of the business side of al-Qaeda's operations emerged when the FBI seized documentation from a

U.S.-based member of the cell, Wadi el-Hage, in whose house were found hundreds of business cards of the East African businesspeople with whom he had struck up contact during visits to Nairobi.

Elsewhere, the individuals who have since helped swell al-Qaeda's ranks were able to draw upon a degree of state support. During the 1992–1995 war in Bosnia, many Arabs who were already associated with or who subsequently joined al-Qaeda fought for the Muslim-led government in a unit known as *el-Mujahid*. After the war, the Bosnian government offered them citizenship. Many took it up, some marrying Bosnian Muslim women whose names they adopted, allowing all traces of their past to disappear. Even for those who had retained their real identities and could not expect state support, al-Qaeda's training during the 1990s included advice on how to overcome hurdles to international travel and bypass immigration restrictions. When Ahmed Rezzam, an Algerian who came close to succeeding in his mission of exploding a bomb at the Los Angeles airport on the millennium, arrived in Canada in 1994, he admitted to immigration officials that his passport was false. He then claimed asylum, alleging persecution in his native Algeria. It took four years to exhaust the asylum procedures, and when he was finally refused entry he simply disappeared, adopting a new identity under the name Benni Noris.

Where necessary, al-Qaeda in the past created relatively open operations to allow a smooth flow of information to would-be recruits. Lawyers for the U.S. government allege that the public face of al-Qaeda emerged in London in 1994 when Khaled al-Fauwaz left Kenya and secured political asylum in the United Kingdom. There, he established an office in the modest suburb of Dollis Hill, opened a bank account, and began disseminating literature critical of the Saudi royal family. He is also alleged to have arranged finance for the purchase of a $7,500 satellite telephone from Ogara Satellite Networks of Deer Park, New York. Company records show that an al-Qaeda operative, Ziyad Khaleel, bought batches of telephone time at four hundred minutes at a time from the company. The billing information from the number—00–873–682505331—shows calls to every country in which al-Qaeda is now known to have had cells.

TERROR'S MECHANICS

Early on the morning of February 26, 1993, a bright yellow Ford Econoline rental van glided down a ramp to an underground car park and slipped unnoticed into a space beneath the New York World Trade Center. A cheap cigarette lighter was used to ignite four twenty-foot-long fuses. Two men inside drove away in a waiting car. Twelve minutes later twelve hundred pounds of explosives and several tanks of hydrogen exploded. Islamist terrorism had hit the United States. The symbolism for America was lost on one of the bombers, Mohammed Salameh. What most concerned him was that he should be able to reclaim the $400 deposit he had paid when he hired the van from an office of Ryder truck rental in New Jersey. Money would lead him to jail, the FBI having learned the serial number of the bomb truck and having traced it back to the New Jersey office. Salameh was arrested when he tried to reclaim the deposit, and the trail soon led back to the mastermind of the attack.

On April 2, 1993. a new face appeared on the FBI's Ten Most Wanted List. His name was Ramzi Ahmed Yousef.[20] Several weeks later, a Pakistan air force C–130 military transport plane landed at a desert airstrip close to Quetta, the main city of Pakistan's southwestern province of Baluchistan. A team comprising two U.S. Diplomatic Security Service personnel and several Pakistani Federal Investigation Agency agents slipped off the plane and made their way to an address in the city. They surrounded the house and broke in. It was the home of Ramzi Yousef. He had disappeared only hours before, apparently tipped off about the plan to capture the man the United States had by then identified as the mastermind of the World Trade Center bombing.

Yousef could rely on protection in high places. A haul of documents found at the house in Quetta led investigators to Peshawar. There they sought Yousef's uncle, Zahid al-Sheikh. But he had fled with just hours to spare. Investigators searched the house and found photographs of Osama bin Laden as a young man fighting in Afghanistan. In the same haul, some investigators say, were photographs of Zahid al-Sheikh with his brother, Khaled Sheikh Mohammed. They were pictured with close associates of Nawaz Sharif, Pakistan's prime minister from 1990 to 1993 and 1997 to 1999. Even with U.S. and Pakistani investigators on his trail, Zahid and Khaled's nephew Ramzi Yousef must have felt confident that he could be protected. His family ties to senior Pakistani Islamists, whose power had been cemented within the country's intelligence service, would keep him out of jail. Yousef made his way to Peshawar and stayed at the *Beit al-Ashuhada*—the House of the Martyrs—a guesthouse created by Osama bin Laden. He was a celebrity, and even then managed to live a semipublic life, attending weddings and recounting how he had committed the most devastating terrorist act the United States had ever experienced. He then moved on to Karachi, where he began to hatch his next plots. It was there that he found his patron.

Operating an import-export company from an office in Pakistan's commercial capital was a man known by a variety of names, including Munir Ibrahim Ahmed, Munir Madni, and Abdul Magid Madni. This list of names figures among the twenty-seven aliases used by Yousef's uncle, Khaled Sheikh Mohammed, the man who has now emerged as the mastermind of the September 11, 2001, attacks. He was the son of Sheikh Mohammed Ali, a respectable man who had taken his family from the barren Pakistani province of Baluchistan to the thriving oil emirate of Kuwait in the early 1950s. A religious man, he had four sons, Zahid, Abed, Aref, and Khaled, and a daughter, and lived in the pleasant town of Fahaheel, south of Kuwait City. In 1952 he took Kuwaiti citizenship, though this is now denied by Kuwaiti authorities, who are trying to erase the family from its records.

Soon after the family's arrival, Sheikh Mohammed Ali became a prominent preacher at the al-Ahmadi mosque in a suburb of the Kuwaiti capital. Then life turned difficult. He found himself entangled in a land dispute with a powerful native Kuwaiti family, the al-Duboos. Details are sketchy, and the al-Duboos deny the dispute ever took place. But by the time Sheikh Mohammed Ali's fourth son was born on April 24, 1965, according to the passport with which he was issued in 1982, the family's comfortable life was in turmoil. Such was the controversy surrounding the dispute that Sheikh Mohammed found himself isolated, possibly even stripped of his Kuwaiti citizenship. This greatly limited his stature and his business activity and labeled the family *bidoon*, meaning residents without citizenship.

It was while in his teens in Kuwait that Sheikh Mohammed's youngest son, Khaled Sheikh—as Khaled Sheikh Mohammed is known to his friends and family—joined the *Ikhwan al-Muslimeen*, the Muslim Brotherhood, the largest international Islamist organization, which had been created in Egypt in 1928 and had an active branch in Kuwait. His membership in the *Ikhwan* was later to give him access to the upper echelons of the global Islamist movement. On December 6, 1982, Khaled Sheikh was issued a Pakistani passport—number 488555—by the Pakistan embassy in Kuwait. He departed Kuwait for the quaint though alien life of small-town America, attending Chowan College in the North Carolina town of Murfreesboro.

The town's history books tell how North Carolina had by the 1800s cornered a profitable trade in agriculture that linked New England and the West Indies. The clinker-built, white-painted homes of Murfreesboro mark the northernmost point of navigation on the Meherrin River, where it reaches into the fertile farmlands of southern Virginia and northeastern North Carolina. Tradition has bored deep into the identity of the prosperous town, which today boasts a famous watermelon festival and the solid education offered by the 155-year-old college.

"Coming to college is a big step in life," says the Chowan prospectus:

> Because we value our students and wish to make their experience at Chowan a success, we have designed a comprehensive orientation program that enables our students to ease into Chowan College socially, academically, emotionally, and spiritually. In order for our students to start their long journey known as college out on the right foot, we promote community, experiential learning, leadership, and personal planning throughout orientation.

It was into this distinctive environment that Khaled stepped in 1983, after a short visit to his ancestral home in Baluchistan, where he spent his time riding a donkey across the desert. While the college has refrained from providing information about the man who has become their most infamous student and is thought to have studied engineering, other Arab students from the time remember him well.

"We lived in one building, had breakfast, lunch, and dinner together—us and thirty Arab students. We all became quite close,"[21] said Mohammed al-Bulooshi, a Kuwaiti advertising executive who attended college in the United States with Khaled. He continued:

Khaled, he was so so smart. He came to college with virtually no English. But he entered directly in advanced classes. He was a funny guy, telling jokes twenty-four hours straight. He was focused. He wanted to get his degree and go home. He was so quiet, there was no indication that he was involved in [religious extremism]. I would never have thought in a million years that he could be involved in these terrorist things—especially such an event as September 11. First of all, he was very smart, but he was not a strategic thinker. Nor did he like American life, and he didn't talk with American students. He was conservative, but so was I. He wouldn't shake hands with women, but neither do I. His conservative attitude was something he brought with him from Kuwait, like me. Not something he learned in the U.S.[22]

But another, more focused side of the man was emerging. Three years before Khaled arrived at Chowan, Saddam Hussein, whom the West backed as a secular bulwark against the radical Islamist regime that had seized power in neighboring Iran in 1979, launched a war against the Tehran regime that was to last eight years. It split the Arab students of Chowan College just as it split the Islamic world. Even among Islam's majority Sunnis the Islamic revolution in Shia, non-Arab Iran was seen as a model. "Khaled sympathized more with Iran in the Iran-Iraq war, and made fun of Saddam Hussein in student plays. The fundamentalist students stood with Iran more than Iraq in the war, because they disagreed with Saddam," said Mohammed al-Blooshi.[23]

But as the war laid waste to areas of Iran and Iraq, the front line of a conflict that was to prove far more significant was opening up among the mountains of the Hindu Kush, where the Afghan *mujahideen* had responded to the Soviet invasion of Afghanistan by invoking their religious duty to rid the country of the invading forces.

I have already examined the emergence and consequences of this phenomenon in my book *Warriors of the Prophet*,[24] and it is not necessary to reassess that earlier account. The focus now is on the consequences of that war with regard to the spirit it engendered, which has today coalesced into al-Qaeda.

Individuals like Khaled Sheikh Mohammed spent the early years of the Afghan *jihad* thousands of miles away, often in the United States or Europe, watching from the sidelines. The extent to which they are in fact the direct heirs of that anti-Soviet war is open to debate. It is clear that the assembling of fighters, the organizational capacity of Osama bin Laden, and the sense of purpose engendered by a charismatic Jordanian-Palestinian cleric, Abdallah Azzam, contributed greatly to the emerging movement. Young Muslims needed encouragement to go there and fight, and it became a badge of honor to have done so. But equally, the Afghan war of the 1980s should be seen as part of a continuum. Islamism of the kind the world is now coming to terms with predates bin Laden. He may, as M. J. Akbar asserts, merely be a maverick, and be far from the real religious figure his infamy and celebrity have portrayed him as. That is part of the crisis the world—the Muslim world, the non-Muslim world, the Middle East, and elsewhere—now faces. The religious root has in many ways been subsumed by circumstance. The fanaticism that has legitimized terrorism in the eyes and hearts and minds of the perpetrators of the September 11 attacks in the United States was spawned in part as a negative; the *jihad* against the Soviet Union brought victory in Afghanistan in 1988, but it did not bring success. After Soviet forces were expelled, the country fell in upon itself. The cleansing process had failed. Political Islam, perhaps, had failed. More likely, however, expectations had simply been far too high.

And into the breach stepped skilled organizers, determined opportunists, disillusioned professionals, malcontents, religious zealots, and a vast pool of impressionable youth—some from the poorest states and communities on earth, others from among the super-rich of the Persian Gulf, others from within the professional classes, whose worldview has become incomprehensible to the West ever since its suicidal sons made history on September 11, 2001. It was from among their ranks that Khaled Sheikh Mohammed emerged. In 1984 he left Chowan College and moved to the North Carolina Agricultural & Technical State University in Greensboro to embark on a mechanical engineering course. As a site of courageous antisegregation protests in the 1960s, the college awards an annual human rights medal to recognize individuals who have "endeavoured to correct social injustice and have significantly contributed to the betterment of the world."[25] It was while he was at Greensboro that Khaled began in earnest to develop his own plans for global "betterment." His ties with the Muslim Brotherhood grew stronger, and his awareness of political-religious issues became more focused. At the same time his elder brothers—Zahid, Abed, and Aref—were forging the family's path into the *jihad* by joining bin Laden's effort in Afghanistan. In 1986 Khaled left the college at Greensboro with a bachelor's degree in mechanical engineering. His old college friend Mohammed al-Bulooshi believes he returned to Kuwait to look for work, but there is no evidence of this in Kuwait's immigration records. Six months later, however, he followed his brothers and made his way to the northwestern Pakistani city of Peshawar.

Among the seven Afghan *mujahideen* leaders of the fight against the Soviet invaders at that time was the man who would launch the young Khaled's career as a *jihadi*, a Saudi-trained *wahhabi* leader by the name of Abdur Rab Rasool Sayyaf. Khaled was recommended to Sayyaf by the Muslim Brotherhood, and he became one of Sayyaf's secretaries.[26] His appointment placed him at the heart of Saudi Arabian influence in the Afghan conflict, his boss being closer to the Saudis than any other of the Afghan leaders. For the next five years,

Khaled lived and worked at the heart of the Arab *jihad*, his experience laying the foundations for the movement that became the organizational backbone of al-Qaeda. It was in 1991, three years after the Soviet defeat, when the war had descended into fighting between the Afghan factions and the Arab recruits had been pressured by Pakistan and the United States to leave, that Khaled is thought to have moved to Karachi and begun to establish a variety of business enterprises with which to finance his next moves.

After spending time in Peshawar as the celebrity who had exploded a bomb in the World Trade Center in 1993, Ramzi Yousef also based himself in Karachi. It was there that he began to hatch his next plots. He turned to his uncle, Khaled Sheikh Mohammed. According to an investigation by the writer Simon Reeve, Yousef's sponsor had established a company importing bottled holy water from Mecca and was operating under a variety of different names.[27]

In July that year, a pilot by the name of Abdel Hakim Murad attended a meeting at Khaled's apartment. On that occasion, Khaled was using the name Abdel Magid. Murad later told investigators that he had been telephoned in March in Dubai by Ramzi Yousef, a friend, whose real name he said was Abdul Basit Mahmoud Abdul Karim. Yousef was present at the Karachi meeting, as was a veteran of the Afghan war, Wali Khan Amin Shah. The subject of flying aircraft was brought up. "Magid is a kind of person who is very much interested in pilot training,"[28] Murad later told investigators. When Murad met Magid for a second time, at a Karachi restaurant, the conversation again revolved mainly around the subject of flying. The third time they met was in the Jinnah Hospital in Karachi during the same month, when Murad went to visit Yousef after the latter had injured himself when an explosive concoction he was making with lead azide and RDX had blown up prematurely. After being discharged from the hospital in September 1993, Yousef went to Iran for eye surgery. On his return to Pakistan, Murad said he went with him to Lahore, where Yousef gave him eighteen days of explosives training. Then they began to hatch their plot, having chosen their destination: the Philippines.

THE EXECUTIONERS

Just before Adriatico Street meets General Quirino Avenue on its long progress from Manila Bay, there is a bar and restaurant with an eye-catching attraction. Perched on the roof of the Unplugged Acoustics bar, a light aircraft has been mounted, as if crashed. Just around the corner, the two men who booked into a small room at the Josefa Apartments might have regarded the crashed aircraft as an apt memento of their visit to the Philippines' capital. It was December 8, 1994. Edith Guerrera, owner of Josefa Apartments, had been laughing with her front desk manager when the two new guests asked for a second registration form to fill out for their room in her small hotel. "Perhaps they have forgotten their names," the women joked, as one of the two men tore up the original form and filled out the new one. Naji Haddad and his accomplice paid 40,000 pesos up front, in addition to a one-month deposit, before taking the elevator to the sixth floor—where a sign on the landing demands "Silence"—and installing themselves in room 603, which had been booked in advance by telephone.

The mistake over the hotel registration forms was untypical. Naji Haddad was the normally meticulous Ramzi Yousef, a man not given to forgetting his alias. Accompanying him was Abdel Hakim Murad, the pilot friend he had contacted in Dubai and met up with in Karachi. They chose the room for its fine view over General Quirino Avenue, the four-lane road that leads down to where the soft hues and ferocious currents of the South China Sea lap against the moored ships off the quayside. "They gave me the impression that they were here to study. They looked like students. They double-locked the door when they were inside or out. They didn't ask the room boy to clear up the room," Guerrera told me.[29] They brought boxes into the building, she said, but never let anybody see inside them. Inside the boxes, it later transpired, were chemicals bought from a variety of suppliers in Manila and Quezon City. In the room, Yousef pursued his lethal fascination with destruction, concocting chemical-based formulas he could use as explosives.

The view from the room allowed the two terrorists to weigh all the options for how best to carry out the plot they had been working on. But their activities in Manila depended on the financial support they received from Yousef's uncle, Khaled Sheikh Mohammed, the man Murad knew as Magid. The actual source of funds was a company called Konsonjaya, an import-export operation dealing in Sudanese honey and other commodities and based in the Malaysian capital, Kuala Lumpur. Among the directors was Riduan Isammudin, better known by his pseudonym Hambali. Until his capture in Thailand on August 14, 2003, Hambali was the operational head of the Southeast Asian regional Islamist network Jemaah Islamiah, whose alliance with al-Qaeda was to become an essential part of the global terrorist network immediately before the September 11 attacks and in the months that followed.

Adriatico Street was the center of the Manila cell's social life. Yousef met his girlfriend, Carol Santiago, at a Seven-Eleven store there. Their favored karaoke bars were the XO on Adriatico Street and the Firehouse on Roxas Boulevard in Pasay City. According to Murad, the one place they never went while they were in Manila was a mosque. According to Philippine police records, Arminda Costudio, the girlfriend in Manila of the fourth cell member, Wali Khan Amin Shah, whom he had met while she was working as a waitress at the smart Manila Bay Club on Roxas Boulevard, remembers Abdul Magid, as Khaled Sheikh Mohammed was known, as

having been always in the company of Ramzi Yousef. He was introduced to Arminda as Salim Ali, a "rich businessman from Qatar."
Her description of him is the same as Murad's description of Abdel
Magid. Both referred to his having "excess meat" on his ring finger.
She remembered specifically meeting Salim Ali twice at the Shangri-
La hotel in the Manila district of Makati in mid-1994, where he
wore a white tuxedo and paid for dinner with a wad of cash while
giving out candies to the gathering. Their experience of the man
was a portent of things to come: the use of aliases, the gregarious
public behavior successfully obscuring hidden aims, and an ability
to network, organize, and operate with total confidence. These
qualities are now at the heart of al-Qaeda's ability to survive.

But Khaled Sheikh Mohammed also spent his money on traveling,
promoting the business enterprises he and the Southeast Asia cell and
the members of the Konsonjaya company were developing as a means
of sustaining the terrorist enterprise. The company was developing the
honey import business with Sudan, where Osama bin Laden was by
then living, though it is not known if they had a business relationship,
and also developed the bottled water business that was operating out
of Karachi. In Kuala Lumpur Khaled was issued a Brazilian visa—
number 194–95 (C0077250)—in an Egyptian passport that named
him as Ashraf Refaat Nabih Henin. It was there that he had also been
issued a new Pakistani passport, number AC113107. He then traveled
at least once to Brazil, either in 1994, while still resident in Manila, or
in 1995. Ramzi Yousef was the key beneficiary of the financial independence allowed by the business enterprises, giving him time to both
play and plot. It was during one of their long discussions, on or
around December 26, 1994, that Murad sparked an idea in Yousef's
mind: Why not crash a plane into the CIA headquarters at Langley,
Virginia? "Okay, we will think about it," Yousef replied, according to
Murad's account, before heading off with Khaled for a scuba diving
course at the resort of Puerto Galera, south of Manila.

But between bouts of enjoyment, Yousef was hard at work. Murad said that Yousef was responsible for a string of bomb attacks in Manila: the Miss Universe pageant and an attack on Roxas Boulevard on May 21, 1994; a blast near a Wendy's Hamburger restaurant on November 13 that year; and the bombing of the Greenbelt Theater on December 1. On December 11, he left a small bomb beneath the seat later occupied by a Japanese engineer, Haruki Ikegami, on Philippine Airlines flight PR434 from Manila to the Philippines island of Cebu. Yousef left the flight during a stopover. Two hours later the bomb exploded. A stewardess used a blanket to cover where Ikegami's legs had been as the aircraft descended to a safe landing, and the twenty-four-year-old man died in agony. Today, Japanese tourists visiting Manila often ask Edith Guerrera, owner of the Josefa Apartments, if they can rent room 603, to get a feel for the man who killed Ikegami. "They say they are curious," said Guerrera.

But the aura of the room could have been much more widely felt if Yousef's major plot—also hatched there and called "Bojinka," meaning "Loud Noise" in Serbo-Croat—had not been foiled. The plot involved placing bombs simultaneously on eleven transpacific airliners en route to the United States. To this plot was added another: to assassinate the pope as he passed by the apartment window.

It all may have happened, had Yousef not been stymied by the smell of fumes coming from apartment 603 on the night of January 6, 1995. Other residents complained about the smell, Edith Guerrera called the fire brigade, and Yousef and Murad, after trying to tell the fire officers to leave them alone, fled the scene. But an alert police officer, suspicious of all the equipment and documents in the room, realized that the smoldering chemicals that had created the smell meant this was no ordinary case. Murad was nabbed when he returned later to try to retrieve a laptop computer from the apartment. Yousef escaped, as did his fellow plotter Wali Khan

Amin Shah, though he was later arrested in Malaysia. But among the array of documents found in the apartment was a letter hinting that while Ramzi Yousef had been obsessively indulging his love for chemistry, another, overlooked player in the group's awful game of terror may have been at work. The letter was signed: "Khalid Shaikh + Bojinka."

After Abdel Hakim Murad's arrest at the Manila apartment in January 1995 following the discovery of the multiple plots, Yousef had made his way back to Pakistan, from where he intended to re-base in Peshawar. But on February 7 a team of FBI, U.S. Diplomatic Security Service, and Pakistani officers swarmed into the Su-Casa guesthouse in Islamabad. They arrested America's most wanted man, who later told a New York court: "I am a terrorist, and I am proud of it." But the man who had signed the "Bojinka" letter, whose wads of cash and white tuxedo had impressed the women of Manila, disappeared. As had become his trademark, Khaled Sheikh Mohammed looked around carefully for a place in which he could feel at home, plan the future, and remain out of the limelight. Following the example of around one hundred other Arab-Afghans—the veterans of the anti-Soviet war—he made his way to the Gulf state of Qatar. There he enjoyed the welcome afforded veterans of the *jihad* accorded by Sheikh Abdullah bin Khaled al-Thani, a relatively benign fundamentalist, a member of the oil and gas-rich state's ruling family who served in the mid-1990s as minister of religious endowments and later held the nominal title of interior minister. His sympathy for those Arab-Afghans who found themselves rootless after the anti-Soviet war was widely known, and he "took it upon himself to give refuge to a large number of non-Afghan mujahideen after the war with the Soviet Union. One hundred of them had no place to go and he took them in," said a senior diplomat with long experience of the country from where U.S. forces throughout 2003 ran the war against Iraq.[30]

Khaled Sheikh Mohammed arrived in Qatar from Manila sometime in the spring of 1995 and was put up in a private guesthouse at the police academy, in which at least one other extremist—Imad Mughniyah, a key figure in the Lebanese Hizbollah organization—is thought to have been housed. He was given a post in the Ministry of Public Works, though under an assumed name, while continuing to travel, including visits to the Czech capital Prague in 1996 and 1997, according to intelligence sources.

But the net was closing in on him. The FBI learned of his presence in Doha, the Qatari capital. Despite so little being known about him, and his role in the "Bojinka" plot being vague compared with that of Ramzi Yousef, he had still been indicted by a New York court. The FBI made known to the Qatari authorities in 1996 that they wanted to arrest him and sent a team to bring him to justice. But when a squad of Qatari police was dispatched on behalf of the FBI to the police academy where Khaled had been staying, they arrived to find it had been cleaned, tidied—and emptied. Their quarry was meanwhile flying west on a private jet, bound for his next destination, tipped off in good time that the law was about to catch up with him. Intelligence sources say his journey ended in Kandahar, among the massed ranks of the Taliban, at the heart of the extremist movement's power base in the southern Afghan city.

As he had always done, and would continue to do, Khaled arrived at an opportune moment: just as the Taliban regime was poised to assert its tyranny over the vast majority of Afghan territory. The period 1996–2001 saw the emergence of what is in essence the *new* school of political Islam, *jihadist-salafism*, though it has deep roots and has been very long in its formation. Political failure had been matched by catastrophic disarray in the religious life of the Middle East, which was matched by the depth of the crisis in Afghanistan, where hundreds of Arabs had fought less than a decade before. The Taliban emerged to represent the medieval *ideal* of the

Taliban fighters, Afghanistan.

salaf—literally, the forefathers—practicing brutally coercive religious strictures, isolating themselves from all forms of modernity, reducing women to chattels, and practicing the age-old Afghan art of buying political influence and establishing flimsy, opportunistic alliances that allowed their influence to expand.

It was into the midst of the Afghan tragedy that Osama bin Laden flew in mid-1996, having been expelled from Sudan shortly after Khaled Sheikh Mohammed arrived from Qatar. Bin Laden was in the area around the northeastern town of Jalalabad until the Taliban seized Kabul in October. Khaled had already ensconced himself in Kandahar, the Taliban stronghold. Like previous Islamist leaders in the last hundred years, bin Laden began laying the groundwork for his emergence as the figure who is—history has shown—*required* by a sizable number of despairing, indignant Muslims. Bin Laden's success in drawing together refugees from the failed Islamist conflicts of the Muslim world from 1996 onward; his ability to forge ties with Shia Muslims—Hizbollah in Lebanon and the conservatives in Iran—who had traditionally been the outcasts of the Sunni-dominated Islamic world; his attraction for Western converts; and his ability to attract cross-class support among Arabs are vital to his influence and the significance of al-Qaeda. Bin Laden began riding a wave that others had created, and which will grow as a consequence of global political circumstances. What he required to implement the emerging vision of a global terrorist campaign were ready recruits, the tools of global warfare, and time and space in which to plan. Within weeks of the Taliban seizing Kabul in October 1996, his plans began to take shape.

BROTHERS IN ARMS

The war had come again, after a week or so of silence.[31] It was December 1996, and I had traveled to Afghanistan to witness the Taliban's power at first hand. Kabul cowered—a frozen shell of a city, spread like a lake of rubble on a high plateau just beneath the sky. Beyond the northern suburbs, snow draped the soaring peaks rising above the Chakadaria Valley. Tangled grapevines had lost their leaves. Over the brow of a hill a herd of goats bleated as they were driven along the road by old men fleeing the frontline fighting a few miles ahead. City buses had been sent to bring civilians from the battle zone. Households wrapped in colored cloths teetered on the roofs of vehicles packed with young and old—women covered, children bewildered, men ponderous, unmoved but anxious, clinging to the steps and windows and roofs of the buses taking them away from the conflict.

Farther on, the plateau seemed the most silent place on earth. The sun was bright. The land was pale brown where the vines lay in their tangled winter dormancy. The mud-walled compounds of the Kabul elite's weekend retreats lay deserted in the shelter of leafless

Hindu Kush Mountains, Afghanistan.

trees. All was silent, until the vast valley screeched with the sound of rockets searing the frozen air between the mountains, then shook as the missiles pounded the hills near the former *mujahideen* government's stronghold at Jabal es Saraj, where the Chakadaria Valley meets the Pagman range and the Hindu Kush scrapes the sky.

A truck carrying a multiple rocket launcher was parked on a slight rise beyond a walled compound where the Red Cross had set up a hospital. Another rocket launcher, its barrels pointed skyward like the pipes of an organ, was parked farther along the rise. There was no movement around the vehicles, and no obvious signs of preparation. Just the silence, then a roar, as a missile surged into the icy air. From over the hill a tank rattled along the road toward the battlefront. A pickup truck sped down the slope just behind it, overloaded with young men, Kalashnikovs, rocket-propelled grenade launchers, and mortar firers.

"It is the way to Allah," one shouted, as the truck went past. The Taliban were on the move.

Commander Hafez Abdirashid peered from the small open window of his Russian-made jeep. The engine turned over noisily as he spoke. The driver of the tank sent blasts of black smoke into the air. The young fighters sat silently in the back of the pickup where they had stopped at a rope slung across the road to mark a checkpoint.

"We are going to apply Islamic sharia. The *mujahideen* were raping and looting and throwing up illegal checkpoints where they were troubling the people. This is why we're going to annihilate all these things and apply Islamic sharia all over the country," said Hafez.

The rope was lowered at the checkpoint and the tank roared across the plateau toward the distant Pagman. Hafez turned his jeep and followed. The pickup truck with reinforcements followed, as another searing volley from the multiple rocket launcher splintered the air. At the checkpoint three of the Taliban raised the rope and asked to have their photographs taken. A group of old men leading a herd of goats approached from the direction of the mountains.

"We came from Kalikan. The Taliban told us to leave, and they took the women and children on the buses, but told us to walk with our goats. The alliance were bombing from an airplane, from just after dawn. They launched the attack, and so we fled."

They talked on the roadside. Both Kalikan and Estalef had been bombed that morning. Some of the injured had been brought to the Red Cross hospital nearby. An Afghan official there talked about what had happened, saying that three seriously injured Taliban had been brought in. He was silenced by a European who arrived to assess the situation. Farther along the road toward Qarah Bagh there were no signs of life. The road descended steadily. A jet fighter circled high above the mountains. The village was empty. The forces of the *jihad* had moved north.

By midday the battle had died down, though it was to restart the following day. On the hill outside Kabul to where the people from the villages had fled, a few now remained, as the sun reached its midday heat but failed to lift the cold. In the suburbs it was as if there were no war. Or perhaps these were merely the suburbs of a war, market stalls offering the wares of wartime, bulbous vegetables transported from some peaceful part of the country. The stump of a huge tree was being slowly chopped with blunt axes, its branches being weighed on a massive pair of scales to ensure that every drop of heat was paid for by weight.

In the bazaar the eyes of an old woman set in a thin, haggard face caught mine. She was the only woman whose face I had seen since my arrival in Kabul. She passed three other women who were completely covered in their flowing *byrkas*, cloaks falling in faded blue, green, or indigo from their heads down to their feet, broken in their flow only by an intricately woven grille across the eyes and nose and mouth, through which nothing could be seen from the outside. The covered women's hands were gloved, their pace rapid, their world hidden from view. But this other woman was different.

"We have become very poor. Our property was robbed by the last army which came. That's why I'm forced to beg. When the army came to town they looted everything. My house is in southern Kabul and it was completely destroyed, though things are a little better since the Taliban came, only food has become very expensive, for me and my seven children," she said. Poverty completely dominated her life. She stood on the roadside talking to me, breaking all the rules. A woman should not have been seen alone on the street. She should not have revealed any part of her body to any man other than her husband. She should not have spoken with a man who was not known to her. But she talked, while other women scuttled past, the gaze from behind their woven grilles seeming to fall upon her where she stood talking.

"I don't have money to buy a *byrka*," she said. "But nobody creates any problems for me because my face is showing. They think I am weak and poor, so they don't disturb me."

Her presence was a relief from the Taliban's excesses. I had seen a succession of lampposts in the center of the city from which the city's new rulers had hung smashed televisions, which were condemned as agents of decadence and were destroyed in the street by the young zealots and then strung up by their cables. Women had been beaten in the streets for failing to cover themselves completely, while all women had been suspended from work and female students told that they would no longer be allowed to attend Kabul University. The leadership was about to start debating whether two fifteen-hundred-year-old standing statues of Buddha at Bamian—the tallest in the world—should be pulled down, as they contradicted Islam's ban on statues. Five years later, the statues were decimated by a mixture of tank shells and dynamite.

Across the road, beyond a maze of market stalls, was the Ariana money market, a two-story building surrounding a muddy courtyard, where men in groups of two or three stood counting piles of ragged bank notes as they discussed exchange rates and converted foreign currency into Afghanis. From somewhere within the market a loudspeaker crackled into life. The call to prayer drowned the talk of business. Transactions were rapidly concluded, and some of the men drifted into a room in one corner of the courtyard set aside as a mosque, while others drifted out of the gate onto the street.

There, swinging a long, knotted rope, was the representative of the government department responsible for assuring Islamic morals are upheld. With a lunge he brought the heavy knot down onto the back of a man attempting to ignore the call to prayer. A man beside him started to flee but was caught on the back of the head by the lash. The man wielding it then began to round up all those trying to leave, swinging the rope over his head as he forced twenty or thirty

Afghan man.

men back through the gate and into the courtyard. Then the road outside was empty, the money market quiet, but for the occasional murmured responses of those at prayer inside.

Mawlawi Abdarab Akhunzada fumbled with a gold pen as he sat at a table large enough to seat thirty or forty people. The thirty-two-year-old second deputy chairman of the central Da Afghania Bank was surrounded by the civil servants who had, until a few weeks before, served the Rabbani government as loyally as they were now being expected to serve the young men whose seizure of Kabul had overturned every institution in the city. Akhunzada was discussing whether or not the 250,000 bank accounts held by women would be forcibly closed, taken over by the women's husbands, or left dormant. It would be a decision taken by the High Council of the Ulemas, he said, referring to the religious council whose decisions would forge the new Taliban government's religious identity.

"We are going to take special measures for this. First, we are going to see whether we can organize for women to stand in separate queues in the banks. We have a commission which will decide this. Right now the conditions are suitable for that, but for various reasons we aren't in a position to make a decision about this. It will be a decision taken by the higher authorities, and we will do what they say," he said, with calm certainty.[32] Akhunzada said he had spent twenty-three of his thirty-three years before joining the Taliban movement at a religious school. His education, he said, had not included economics, and it was unclear why he had been chosen to reform the central bank.

"It's not only the Holy Koran which must be followed on this, but the other words of the Prophet, the *fiqr*. It needs a lot of scholars who have specialized knowledge to make a decision. It's not clear in the Koran. But the high council will make any decisions in the light of Islam, because in Islam a person can't give his own views."[33]

Our conversation ended. He silently returned to his adjoining office and his team of male advisers. The bank's four hundred women employees had been suspended on full pay of 200,000 Afghanis per month while it was decided whether they should be allowed to continue to hold jobs, the religious system having decreed that women should remain at home.

But the bank official with Akhunzada lingered, gathering his papers. It would be difficult, he said in a low voice, once his youthful and heavily bearded boss had left the room, to Islamize the banking system. Such a system would have to comply with the koranic ban on the payment or charging of interest on loans, which would significantly reduce bank profits and thereby reduce their ability to lend.

"There's no evidence that it works. It's not a simple task. If they allow women to keep their accounts, then they will have to employ women to serve them in the banks. I was asked to participate in the consultation to make it an Islamic bank. But it will be very difficult.

The main difficulty is that, if there is no interest paid by the bank then people won't put their money in it."[34]

Kabul was now under a strict dictatorship. The men of the city smiled as they discussed how well they were doing in growing the beards the government had instructed them to wear. Woolen cloaks and embroidered hats replaced jeans and jackets. Behind the smiles, the change became entrenched.

"Afghans had always experienced economic poverty. Now we are moving toward cultural poverty, which is very dangerous."[35] Dr. Amir Hassanyar was witnessing the end of his attempts to use his chancellorship of Kabul's sixty-three-year-old university to safeguard Afghanistan's intellectual life and prevent its isolation from the outside world. The university was largely rebuilt and then reopened under *mujahideen* control in 1995, with a student population of ten thousand. In February 1997 it was reopened after the Taliban takeover, though only to male students.

"When we reopened the university in 1995, some students came back from Pakistan who had grown up there, in the Pakistani culture. Others came back from Iran. Others were ex-Mujahideen. They are all part of the cultural crisis in Afghanistan," he said.[36]

> We are losing our Afghan cultural heritage, because they returned with no national pride. Then [when the Taliban arrived], the university was closed, which was a catastrophe. Even before they came, when the [Mujahideen] were in control in Kabul, we had problems. They wanted to separate boys and girls and to influence the subjects we taught. But I knew some of the people in the government, and we were able to overcome.
>
> But the problem for intellectuals remains. We are in a minority. We believe that we cannot live outside human civilization. We believe that the world is moving. But we are not even one percent [of

the population]. Since 1978 the intellectual stratum has left the country. In this country and society there's no place for them. They are out of place and out of time. We stay out of politics, because it's dangerous for us, but we want an elected government. We want the people of Afghanistan to participate in creating their own destiny. We don't have a nation. It's a tribal society. But we are very proud of our past heritage. We are brave and hospitable. But in the past two decades we have lost what we had.[37]

Outside Hassanyar's office the remnants of Kabul's intellectual elite had gathered under the leafless trees, waiting to see if the university would be reopened. Hassanyar had said that most of the professors were now to be found in the market, selling potatoes. They all had to report to work once a week, to sign for the pay that they had been told would eventually arrive but that they had not received for the previous two months. A feeling of isolation, of being forgotten, of slipping irretrievably into oblivion, prevailed.

It was into this ghost of a country that Osama bin Laden had stepped in May 1996, deserting his onetime allies among the *mujahideen,* with whom he had fought against the Soviet Union, but who by then were the sworn enemies of the Taliban, and throwing in his lot with the young zealots from the southern city of Kandahar who had seized Kabul.

AN AGE OF TERROR

On August 23, 1996, bin Laden staked his claim to the leadership of the new, global war by issuing a "Declaration of Jihad on the Americans Occupying the Two Holy Places."[38] It was two months since his expulsion from Sudan and arrival in Afghanistan, and he intended that his declaration would eventually force American troops to leave the Muslim Holy Land of Saudi Arabia.

By the time he arrived in Afghanistan, many of the elements of al-Qaeda's global network had already begun to coalesce into the structure that is now, in 2004, operational worldwide. Contacts built up by Ramzi Yousef and Khaled Sheikh Mohamed in southeast Asia were to become a key part of the new structure. In 1997, Khaled moved into the al-Qaeda inner circle, more or less in tandem with the arrival of a band of wandering Egyptians led by Ayman al-Zawahiri. The leader of the Egyptian Islamic Jihad (EIJ) movement, which had carried out the assassination of Egyptian President Anwar al-Sadat in 1981, al-Zawahiri arrived in Afghanistan in May 1997. There he sought to build up the by then beleaguered, fractious, and impoverished EIJ faction he had led, by drawing closer to bin Laden and providing him with the political vision that is the foundation of al-Qaeda today.

Their joint efforts coalesced into a *fatwa* issued on February 23, 1998, signed jointly with the leader of a breakaway faction of Egypt's al-Gama'a al-Islamiyya and the heads of Bangladeshi and Pakistani Islamist groups. The "Fatwa Urging Jihad against the Americans," which was first published in the London Arabic daily newspaper *al-Quds al-Arabi,* was a turning point. It refocused al-Zawahiri in particular away from his original goal of bringing Islamic government to Egypt, and instead identified that government's "infidel" supporters in Washington as the main enemy. The *fatwa* made clear:

> The ruling to kill all Americans and their allies—civilian and military—is an individual duty for every Muslim who can do it in any country in which it is possible to do it, in order to liberate the al-Aqsa Mosque and the holy mosque from their grip, and in order for their armies to move out of all the lands of Islam, defeated and

unable to threaten any Muslims. This is in accordance with the words of Almighty God, "and fight the pagans all together as they fight you all together," and "fight them until there is no more tumult or oppression, and there prevail justice and faith in God."[39]

Six months later, the "vision" of the *fatwa* and the planning skills al-Qaeda had developed at their Afghan base but had also dispersed in East Africa provided the opportunity to turn the theory into practice. The Nairobi and Dar es Salaam bombings of August 7, 1998, which killed hundreds and destroyed the U.S. embassies in the two cities, allowed al-Qaeda's operatives to fully reveal their expertise and organizational skills. Meanwhile, other plans were being hatched at camps established in various parts of Afghanistan—notably in Kandahar and Herat—where experiments were carried out that would lead to the development of chemical and biological weapons programs. Recruitment also continued apace, and plans began to take shape that focused on attacking targets in the West. Terrorist cells emerged that evolved into the network of like-minded radicals who had long been based in various parts of Europe, from the United Kingdom, France, Spain, Italy, and Germany, as well as in the United States, central Asia, Canada, southeast Asia, and east and southern Africa.

Al-Qaeda is now as ubiquitous as all the major global Islamic movements that have preceded it. But it has achieved this presence much more quickly than any other movement, due to both careful planning and the impact of its violence. Its influence is unlikely to diminish just because large parts of its leadership have been captured since the attacks of September 11, 2001. Its ability to continue its attacks will be dependent upon both the resilience of its organization and the strength of conviction among its current and future activists. Despite up to three thousand alleged al-Qaeda and former Taliban fighters having been arrested worldwide since September 11, most academics, intelligence services, and others agree that the network has already found ways of surviving the global campaign to destroy it. Up to thirty thousand militants passed through al-Qaeda's Afghan camps in 1996–2001, and the movement is reckoned to have a presence within the Muslim populations of ninety-two countries. As a mark of its continuing operational capacity since September 11, 2001, it has directly or indirectly been responsible for the deaths of some six hundred people in attacks ranging from Bali to Yemen, Tunisia, Riyadh, Casablanca, Jakarta, Istanbul, and then Madrid on March 11, 2004.

The Madrid bombs exposed both the flaws in Europe's security apparatus and the resilience of the terrorist network in the heart of a region that had devoted vast resources to destroying it. The attacks were the most ambitious the network had undertaken up to that point, and were aimed at achieving the goal of expelling non-Muslims from the Islamic world by pressuring Spain to withdraw its forces from Iraq. To achieve this, the strategy has been to attack the West in Muslim countries as well as in Western countries themselves.

The pattern of attacks since the outbreak of the war in Iraq has revealed a strategy with several facets. One has been to create chaos within Muslim countries, with the aim of creating conflict, fear, and insecurity, which would drive non-Muslims from these countries. A second aim has been to encourage Muslim support for and recourse to al-Qaeda's violent brand of conservative Islam— *jihadist-salafism*, which has turned violence into a religious creed. A third aim has been to create turmoil in Muslim countries—particularly Morocco, Yemen, Turkey, Saudi Arabia, and Iraq—which will in turn create a political vacuum into which al-Qaeda's adherents may then seek to step.

The signs that these different elements had coalesced into something resembling a strategy emerged most starkly after four bombings in Istanbul in November 2003. "The only way to weaken this government is through violence or through the military," Cengiz Çandar, a prominent Turkish political commentator, told me. "If this wave of attacks continues, the military might manipulate it to their own ends. I don't think the extremists are trying to get into the political fabric of the country. They want to create instability."[40] However, the terrorists' ambition of exploiting the chaos they could create, by inserting themselves into the political vacuum, may also be emerging. As Mohamed Darif, a Moroccan academic who has closely followed the emergence of the new terrorist threat in Islamic countries, told me after the March 2004 Madrid bombings: "The priority among these groups that are the constituent parts of al-Qaeda, is to attack Muslims that they see as miscreants. . . . They can't overthrow the Arab regimes without first confronting the Western powers. But the real targets are the Muslims they regard as irreligious."[41]

The political and religious sentiments upon which al-Qaeda has been built will sustain its ideological support. But without the major acts of violence with which it is associated, al-Qaeda could lose its aura and appeal, because its use of violence is a key plank of the *jihadist-salafist* doctrine, distinguishing it even from other Islamic groups that have used violence. Thus, new conflicts will be sought. Since March 20, 2003, this has not been difficult. In an address to Egyptian forces during a military parade in Suez on March 31, 2003, Egypt's President Hosni Mubarak gave a stark warning of the consequences of the war which by then had started in Iraq: "When it is over, if it is over, this war will have horrible consequences. Instead of having one [Osama] bin Laden, we will have 100 bin Ladens."[42] It can be argued that al-Qaeda brought the fight to the United States on September 11, 2001. Now the United States has taken the fight back into the Muslim heartland. The battleground that has now united Muslims—whether they are al-Qaeda diehards, or simply invigorated by the rage to which Osama bin

Laden have given voice—is now very much closer to home, being fought in a country that is a key part of the Muslim heartland. Afghanistan was a distant war, which did not stir up the real enemies of U.S. hegemony, the Arab Muslims. The new arena, the new *jihad*, in one form or another, has now refocused back onto the Middle East, a region now dominated by the U.S. presence in Iraq.

4

BY THE RIVERS OF BABYLON

ARABS, MUSLIMS, AND THE INVASION OF IRAQ

ON THE AFTERNOON OF APRIL 9, 2003, A U.S. MARINE LIEU-
tenant in the center of Baghdad yelled from the turret of his M1
Abrams battle tank at a British opponent of the invasion of Iraq
who had just told him to "go home": "I was at the Pentagon September 11. My co-workers died."[1] He handed a Stars and Stripes to
a Marine corporal, who climbed up a vast copper statue of ousted
Iraqi president Saddam Hussein and with it covered the fallen dictator's face. A steel hawser was roped around the statue, and the edifice was torn from its pedestal and fell to the ground. The statue had
dominated Baghdad's Paradise Square for years. A few hundred
Iraqis had gathered in the square when it became clear that Saddam's rule was over and had begun hacking at the statue with ham-
mers, before it became clear that more muscle would be needed to
bring it down, and the tank was used to topple it.

It was a symbolic moment in all ways: the Marine lieutenant thinking that by overthrowing Saddam Hussein he was somehow avenging the deaths of those who had died at the hands of Osama bin Laden on September 11, 2001; the British protester against the war and the American soldier, both of them thousands of miles from home, arguing about a war in somebody else's country; the Iraqis themselves, lacking the power—literally—to pull down Saddam, having to rely on a U.S. tank to do it for them.

The adorning of Iraqi towns the entire length of the country with U.S. flags was consistent with the sentiments expressed by the Marine lieutenant. There is no connection between the September 11 attacks and the Iraqi regime that the Marine had helped overthrow, but the overthrow of another Arab figure—Saddam—was a means of exacting revenge on the one who had evaded capture—Osama bin Laden. Meanwhile, the British opponent of the war arguing with the American participant in the war was symbolic of what a small distance Iraq had come since the carving up of the Middle East in the wake of the Ottoman defeat in the First World War. Foreign meddling was still vibrant, and the readiness of a crowd of wild looters and vandals to lend themselves to a Western propaganda machine, which required scenes of jubilation in Baghdad's Paradise Square to dominate television screens, was a stark reminder on that day of "liberation" that while Saddam's demise was welcome, deep reservations kept millions of other Iraqis off the streets. Huge anxiety swept through much of the country, as rapidly as the mechanized whirlwind that saw tanks enter Paradise Square after twenty-one days of war. A relatively modern and sophisticated country that was also one of the wealthiest and most developed in the Arab world had been revealed for how weak it really was. Its Republican Guard forces—the pride of Saddam's regime, and perhaps of other Arabs—had crumbled, despite putting up resistance all along the route of the U.S. and British advance through the country.

A U.S. convoy is ambushed in Najaf, early April 2003. Photo courtesy of Charles Clover.

Infantryman from the 101st Airborne watches a field west of Najaf. The plume of smoke is from an airstrike on a clothing factory in the city. Photo courtesy of Charles Clover.

The conventional Iraqi forces were either pulverized by intensive bombing or shed their uniforms and ran.

The invading armies—one the country whose support for Israel is as objectionable to Iraqis as it is to most Arabs, the other the old colonial power that had run Iraq until the late 1950s—had done as much to reveal the weakness of the country as Saddam Hussein had done to hide it. Just as Egyptians are humiliated by the fact that it took Israel only six days in 1967 to defeat the combined Arab armies and grab Sinai and the West Bank, so the Iraqi consciousness is deeply sensitive to the fact that history will say that it took only twenty-one days to annihilate a regime that had spent billions of dollars building up a military machine that represented the kind of autocratic power to which many Arabs cling as a desperate source of pride.

Despite this pride, Saddam Hussein was nevertheless widely reviled not only within Iraq but also across the region. His divisive impact on Arab affairs throughout the 1990s undermined regional efforts to pressure Israel to pursue dialogue with the Palestinians. His brutality was widely known, particularly after his expulsion from Kuwait in 1991, after which emerged vivid accounts of how his invading forces had behaved. But the power he represented—in a region that has been humiliated by foreign invasion for centuries—was not in itself the cause of the loathing with which he was regarded. It was his and his family's abuse of that power and the extreme cruelty he used to retain it that were obnoxious to Iraqis and Arabs. Abuse of power, which has encouraged the rise of Islamist movements across the region, has been at the core of the political and military conflicts dogging the Middle East for much of the past hundred years. But power in itself is regarded as a vital component in the struggle to build an Arab region whose influence reflects its wealth, strategic importance, and historical and cultural riches. The defeat of the widely loathed Saddam Hussein is a defeat for many Arabs, because it has revealed how weak they are. American and

British tanks were not greeted with euphoria by Iraqis, because being "liberated" by an army that sides with one's enemy—Israel—and plans to effectively colonize one's country, after decades during which nationalism and independence had been entrenched ideals, can produce nothing but deep anxiety.

As Arab states watched helplessly from the sidelines while the United States geared up for war, their awareness grew that the threat of "alien domination" that the historian Bernard Lewis had warned was on the horizon in the wake of the September 11 attacks[2] was manifesting itself. "Anglo-French rule and American influence, like the Mongol invasions, were a consequence, not a cause, of the inner weakness of Middle Eastern states and societies,"[3] Lewis asserted. The suggestion is that whatever systems of government emerge from within Middle Eastern society, they will inevitably clash with the West and its interests; its interference will be a "consequence" of whatever emerges from the region. The two, Lewis appears to be saying, are incompatible, and by implication only Western colonization of the Middle East can protect its interests in that region and—due to the perceived global reach of terrorist groups associated with al-Qaeda—around the world.

This perception has set back any gains made by the end of the Cold War, because it has fundamentally undermined the real prospect of freedom that emerged at the end of the East–West conflict. The slow and painful process of nation building, which took root globally in a multiplicity of ways after the end of the Cold War, has been set aside in favor of building up the new hegemonic power centered on Washington. The Marine who raised the Stars and Stripes over Baghdad in the mistaken belief that he was avenging the deaths of colleagues in fact killed by somebody with no ties to the regime in Baghdad is setting the tone for this shift. The readiness to impose rule in an area of the world that—if Egyptian president Hosni Mubarak's warning is right—now has the dangerous potential of creating "one hundred Osama bin Ladens" as a result of the foreign invasion, is a

Hosni Mubarak, president of Egypt.

mark of how far the evolution of nations has been taken from the hands of the people who live in those countries. In a November 12, 2002, statement broadcast by al-Jazeera, in which he highlighted the plight of Iraqis and Palestinians, bin Laden sought to drive a wedge between the United States and its Western allies. Porter Goss, chairman of the U.S. Senate Intelligence Committee, told me that the tape "is a total admission of the linkage [between Iraq and al-Qaeda]. I think that we don't need to release any more information about Iraq [and al-Qaeda] because Bin Laden did it on al-Jazeera last night."[4]

THE LIVES OF A DICTATOR

"It would be a mistake, I think, to reduce what is happening between Iraq and the United States simply to an assertion of Arab will and sovereignty versus American imperialism, which undoubtedly plays a central role in all this. However misguided, Saddam Hussein's cleverness is not that he is splitting America from its allies (which he has not really succeeded in doing for any practical purpose) but that he is exploiting the astonishing clumsiness and failures of U.S. foreign policy,"[5] wrote Edward Said, the Palestinian-American writer, in 1999. Said asserted that by that point in the war of attrition against Iraq, which had been ongoing since the end of the Gulf War in 1991, 567,000 Iraqi civilians had died "mostly as a result of disease, malnutrition and deplorably poor medical care."[6] In a devastating critique of the plight of the Iraqi population, Said unequivocally explained the readiness of the United States to induce such suffering as part of its disdain toward Arabs and the Arab world. The refusal of U.S. policymakers to pursue any kind of balance in their Middle East policy has fed the fire of a more general potential "Arab/US crisis,"[7] the conditions for which are exacerbated by the fact that "the notion of an Arab people with traditions, cultures and identities of their own is simply inadmissible in the United States."[8]

Said's view that "clumsiness and failures" are intrinsic to U.S. policy verges on the charitable. In fact U.S. policy is direct and successful, if seen from the perspective of U.S. interests. The mistake of many commentators is to believe that U.S. foreign policy is intended to respond to the interests of the targets of that foreign policy. It is not, and as are all foreign policies, U.S. foreign policy is intended to extend the interests of the United States alone. The terrorist attacks of September 11, 2001, convinced the United States—rightly—that reliance on Saudi Arabia was unwise, as the country was bound at some point to fall victim to its internal political shortcomings. The U.S. need for oil—though not, as has been widely claimed, simply the need for U.S. oil companies to find new and captive markets—certainly lay behind the readiness to risk a

full-scale invasion of Iraq, inspired by a lack of confidence in Saudi
Arabia and a strong suspicion of Saudi attitudes toward the United
States. But long before American tanks rolled into Baghdad in April
2003, U.S. policy also required that the Middle East be rid of all
leaders capable of opposing Israel. Washington had long ago shifted
from the policy of containment to the strategy of overthrow, called
"rollback" by policymakers. The announcement of this policy, the
passing of the Iraq Liberation Act by the U.S. Congress in October
1998, and the allocation of $97 million for military supplies to the
Iraqi opposition drove in further the wedge between the United
States and its Arab interlocutors in the region.

There is little doubt that efforts at containment of Saddam Hussein had not brought Iraq any closer to the end of the tunnel into
which it had entered when it invaded Kuwait. The impact of the
sanctions imposed on Iraq at the end of the 1991 Gulf war had
been to strengthen the political status quo, rather than achieve the
U.S. intention of delegitimizing President Saddam. The impact had
been to isolate the majority of Iraqis from both the regime that op-
pressed them and the Western powers whose strategy failed to ame-
liorate their condition. "There were originally many Iraqis who
agreed with Western policy," a senior Iraqi relief official opposed to
the regime told me in Baghdad in 1998. "Now, there's a silent majority who feel they have no chance to decide their fate. And they
feel misled by both sides."[9] Meanwhile, the spurious U.S. aim of
protecting its allies in the Gulf was exposed as such by adoption of
a policy to which no Arab leaders—other than the Kuwaitis—sub-
scribed. While many—in fact most—Arab leaders long regarded
Saddam Hussein as a menace whom they would rather be without,
none could have justified the practice of rollback to their own populations. "I told Albright: Please don't make the attack now. We
have to deal with Arab public opinion. If the people aren't prepared,
we will face a whole lot of problems. Give room for a diplomatic

solution," President Mubarak of Egypt told me at the height of the Iraq crisis in March 1998, when war seemed imminent. "The double standard [on the issue of weapons of mass destruction], of Israel versus Iraq—we feel it. And I am very sincere. There are extremists who are ready to act. You will not find any leader who will say they are in favor of the air strikes."[10]

During its preparations for the bombing of Iraq in February 1998—a bombing campaign eventually prevented by the successful intervention of Kofi Annan, the UN Secretary-General, on February 23—it became clear how dangerous U.S. policy in the region had become. A public relations exercise was launched intended to pacify Arab public opinion. The U.S. State Department sent Ambassador David Newton, a retired diplomat, to the region, to face a growing welter of criticism that can have left him in no doubt about how unpopular the U.S. threat against Iraq had become. When asked at a press conference in Cairo why the United States insisted on going ahead with a strategy for which it had not received any public support in the region, his response was as disdainful as U.S. policy had always been: "There is in some countries a difference between public and private support. This is a part of the world where people are cautious about getting involved."[11] The United States was pursuing a policy that no leaders in the region could support and that public opinion vehemently opposed, and was a precursor to a longer term policy of rollback, which found neither support in the region nor even informed support in the United States. "To divide Iraq is not in the interests of peace in this region," said President Mubarak. "If there was a division of Iraq, part of it might join Iran. That would create another big problem. If Saddam is removed, whoever leads the country would be worse."[12]

Kofi Annan's determined diplomacy in the face of intense hostility from the United States, and from Madeleine Albright in particular, denied the United States and its British allies the opportunity they were looking for to bomb Iraq. President Saddam agreed to open up presidential sites to inspection by teams from the United Nations inspection teams, UNSCOM.[13] But it was not long before alleged infringements of the agreement made with Annan were identified by the chief weapons inspector, Richard Butler. Determined not to be subject to the diplomatic delays that had thwarted the launch of their campaign the previous February, the U.S. and British military machines were gearing up within hours of Iraq (on October 31, 1998) denying UNSCOM the right to carry out spot inspections of its military sites until the United Nations lifted the embargo on oil sales imposed after the Gulf war.

During the buildup to the 1991 Gulf war, the potential for a negotiated Iraqi withdrawal from Kuwait had been quashed by the United States, because "pursuing that was too dangerous, given Washington's fears that it might lead to Iraqi withdrawal, undermining the opportunity to smash a defenseless country to bits and teach a few lessons about obedience."[14] Noam Chomsky's damning critique of the motives behind U.S. action in Iraq leads ultimately to the frightening conclusion that even before the election of George W. Bush, the end of the Cold War had created a situation in which—rather than creating greater opportunities for peace—U.S. supremacy had reduced the inhibitions that have prevented war. The United States sought to avoid discussion of solutions during George Bush senior's tenure in the White House, just as Madeleine Albright gave a frosty and dismissive response to the potential for UN diplomatic success when Kofi Annan went to Iraq in 1998. The United States has always sought an excuse to bomb Iraq. "The most interesting feature of the debate over the Iraq crisis is that it (the debate) never took place. True, many words flowed, and there was dispute about how to proceed. But discussions kept within rigid bounds that excluded the obvious answer: the United States and Britain should act in accord with their laws and treaty obligations," Chomsky wrote at the time.[15]

As air strikes erupted in November 1998, Palestinians burned the American flags that just a day earlier had decorated their streets to mark the visit of President Clinton to the Gaza Strip. While Palestinian Authority leaders did not say they supported the Iraqi regime, they, like other Arab leaders, highlighted the impact of the bombing on Iraqi civilians. But for them, as for others directly involved in the Middle East peace process, the strikes that the United States says were intended to destroy Iraqi weapons of mass destruction sent a different message, centering on the U.S. acceptance of Israel's retention of similarly powerful weapons and the double standard this implied. Most Arab states rejected the view that disarming Saddam Hussein's regime would bring regional security. President Mubarak issued a statement on December 17 blaming Richard Butler, the UN chief weapons inspector, for having "pushed the situation to the current crisis."[16] Most Arab states, including Syria, nevertheless held the position that as long as Iraq refused to comply with UN resolutions, it would have only itself to blame for military strikes, even though few accepted that air strikes were a solution. Meanwhile, the legality of the strikes was raised in a statement issued by the Organization of the Islamic Conference (OIC), which asserted that: "Iraq is target again to military strikes, carried out in vague circumstances and with unknown intentions."[17]

But still Saddam survived. The regime had sought to improve relations but had generally misread the regional mood. "Regional states have been waiting for a moment at which they could say 'enough,'" Riad al-Qaysi, Iraq's deputy foreign minister, told me in Baghdad in March 1998. "Iraq will not [again] invade Kuwait. You learn from your mistakes. We have turned a page. What other choice do we have? If you lift the external pressure immediately, the Arabs will put aside their differences. They will see that the danger does not come from Iraq."[18] Having survived war, sanctions, international opprobrium, and attempts to unseat him, President Saddam came to be regarded domestically and regionally as likely to continue adorning the streets of Baghdad with his ever-smiling image. But his intentions—denied the weapons capability built up over fifteen years—still remained unclear. "President Saddam hasn't changed," said al-Qaysi. "I don't think that he has ever lost the conviction that he was right. The man is the same man. The qualities are the same qualities. The ideas are the same ideas."[19]

But it was the belligerence of a violent dictator who really had very little to show for his long, violent, and war-racked years in power that really isolated Iraq from the Arab states, as it failed to attract support for its case. President Mubarak announced that Iraq's "ruling regime there is the cause of all problems. Egypt, of course, does not support that regime." While rejecting U.S. and U.K. strategies to precipitate the overthrow of President Saddam, Mubarak said in 1999: "It is high time the Iraqi regime took responsibility for the suffering it has brought Iraqis."[20] The estrangement of the Iraqi leadership from regional states was cemented when Arab leaders sought to prevent Iraqi participation in Arab League discussions on the crisis, believing Baghdad would seek to divide Arab opinion. Foreign ministers from Egypt, Syria, Saudi Arabia, Yemen, and Oman met on January 14, 1999, to prepare a common strategy in advance of an Arab League foreign ministers' meeting in Cairo on January 24, intended to clarify the distinction between Iraq's government and the Iraqi population, whose suffering had inflamed public opinion throughout the region. "Saddam misjudged Arab opinion when there were protests against the bombing of Baghdad in December," was how one senior Egyptian official dismissed Iraq's strategy.[21] Thus was the U.S. military action against Iraq allowed to filter into the Arab popular memory, as a devastating show of military force in the face of which Arab leaders could only watch from the sidelines, refusing to support, unable to prevent, and ultimately incapable of resolving through negotiation.

Despite Saddam Hussein's undoubted unpopularity across the region, as well as the loathing with which he and his cruel regime were regarded in Iraq itself, nobody was strengthened by the U.S. and British military action of 1999. Nobody ultimately drew comfort. The Arab world was left simply wondering where its real interests lay. Meanwhile, the United States did not help its allies, nor did it end Saddam's rule. Small wonder then that a far more decisive plot was being hatched in Washington, by people who were at that time not even in power.

A TWENTY-FIRST-CENTURY PROJECT

President George W. Bush's ultimatum to Saddam Hussein on March 17, 2003, to leave Iraq within forty-eight hours or face a military onslaught was the culmination not only of months of argument but also years of waiting. Eighteen months after the terrorist attacks on New York and Washington, Bush finally transformed the administration's vision of the global role of the United States into action, for reasons he made clear: "The [Iraqi] regime has a history of reckless aggression in the Middle East. It has a deep hatred of America and our friends. And it has aided, trained, and harbored terrorists, including operatives of al-Qaeda. . . . Instead of drifting along towards tragedy, we will set a course toward safety. Before the day of horror can come, before it is too late to act, this danger will be removed."[22]

To the critics of U.S. policy as it manifested itself in the hours before the invasion by U.S. and U.K. forces, the evolution from the threat revealed by al-Qaeda on September 11, 2001, to the throwing down of the gauntlet to the "axis of evil" in the State of the Union address four months later was both surprising and baffling. But to the architects of U.S. foreign policy it was a shift that had been long in the making. Paul Wolfowitz, the U.S. deputy defense secretary, had been the driving force of the Bush administration's policy of regime change in Iraq. As far back as 1977 he had predicted that Iraq would invade Kuwait. In 1992, as the Pentagon's undersecretary for policy, Wolfowitz had authored the Defense Department's post–Cold War strategy document. In an early draft, which was later modified when it was deemed overly provocative, Wolfowitz had proposed building a "New World Order" based on "convincing potential competitors that they need not aspire to a greater role or pursue a more aggressive posture to protect their legitimate interests."[23] In 1998, during the presidency of Bill Clinton, he complained to Congress: "The heart of the problem is that the . . . United States is unable or unwilling to pursue a serious policy in Iraq, one that would aim at liberating the Iraqi people from Saddam's tyrannical grasp and free Iraq's neighbors from Saddam's murderous threats." This did not, he asserted, mean a call for U.S. troops to invade: "The key lies not in marching US soldiers to Baghdad, but in helping the Iraqi people to liberate themselves from Saddam."[24] But days after the September 11 attacks, Wolfowitz was the first to link state sponsorship with the attacks, defining a policy of "ending states who sponsor terrorism."[25] Even before it became clear that the 2003 war in Iraq would be launched, in May 2002 John Bolton, the U.S. undersecretary for arms control and international security, linked arms control agreements to the necessity for action against terrorism: "Global terrorism has changed the nature of the threat we face. Keeping WMD out of terrorist hands must be a core element of our non-proliferation strategy."[26] His view, and that of Wolfowitz, were crystallized in the U.S. National Security Strategy issued in September 2002, in which it was made clear that the United States would "prevent our enemies from threatening us, our allies, and our friends, with weapons of mass destruction."

"The realists became convinced that September 11 was the warning of what could happen. 9–11 reminded us how dangerous the world is, and Iraq was the obvious place to start,"[27] said David Frum, the presidential speechwriter who had coined the phrase "axis of evil" for Bush's State of the Union address of January 2002, in which he cited an apparently unified threat from weapons of mass destruction emanating from Iran, Iraq, and North Korea. The "realists"—dominated by the "neoconservatives" of the Bush administration led by Wolfowitz—had long identified Iraq as a major threat. But it was the devastating blow delivered at the heart of America by al-Qaeda that gave Washington's policymakers the opportunity to turn the "war on terror" into the centerpiece of a far broader foreign policy, one that had been forming ever since the humiliation of George Bush senior's defeat in 1992.

"There's never been a shift in policy, as Iraq has always been in the gun sights of the key advisers," Charles Peña, senior defense policy analyst at the Cato Institute in Washington, told me. "Linking weapons of mass destruction to terrorists is not new. The thing that is new is that after 11 September you can prey on fear."[28] The target—indeed, the "axis of evil"—derived its menacing unity primarily from possession of weapons of mass destruction, not from its specific identification with support for terrorism. "The only way you see Saddam as a threat is if he is in bed with terrorists, because he is not a direct military threat to the U.S. The proposition that he will give WMD to al-Qaeda is pure suspicion," Peña said.[29] For both the Bush administration and U.K. Prime Minister Tony Blair's government in London, the linkage would always be different. For Bush—his analysis articulated by Colin Powell to the United Nations—Iraq was a threat because of its alleged WMD arsenal, and because it harbored terrorists including those linked to al-Qaeda, and—to cap it all—had harbored terrorists linked to al-Qaeda who had developed their own chemical weapons capability. For Blair,

Saddam Hussein was a menace who should be dealt with because "it is the right thing to do." For David Frum, evidence was less important than appearing to have a grip on policy: "The Iraqis have all this poison, but it would be mad for Saddam to deliver this with a missile. Terrorism would be the obvious way. It's logic that you have to fear. As for terrorist sponsorship, Iran had provided most sponsorship until that point. And once you have come up with a definition, you can't leave North Korea off."[30]

Thus, a policy was born, with President Bush declaring that "states like these, and their terrorist allies, constitute an axis of evil, arming to threaten the peace of the world. By seeking weapons of mass destruction, these regimes pose a grave and growing danger."[31] The assumption within the administration was that in the short or medium term Iraq—at least until the start of the war that began on March 20, 2003—was more likely to use its WMD capacity via a terrorist surrogate than of its own accord, but it necessitated finding a tie between the regime in Baghdad and the threat that Americans knew: al-Qaeda. Prevention, preemptive action, and a wholly new assessment of the character of the threat would dominate policymaking. For critics of the Bush administration, the details upon which the war may or may not have been justified have provided little ammunition. The policy of preventing threats left the administration room to maneuver on a large and as yet ill-defined scale, intensifying the concerns of skeptics; the alleged terrorist links provided the administration with an almost limitless range of military policy options. "There's been basically a hijacking of U.S. national security policy, by a small group of revolutionaries in the government," Joseph Cirincione, director of the nonproliferation project at Washington's Carnegie Endowment for International Peace, told me. "What they are advocating is completely unprecedented in American history."[32]

Cheerleading, or perhaps leading, in reality, was the group of right-wing republicans led by Wolfowitz, who had long been preparing for the return to office of an administration they could mold in their own image. These neoconservatives—so-called because several of their leading lights had been political liberals during their formative political years but had subsequently veered to the right—had been nursing the wound inflicted by Bill Clinton when his victory in 1992 put paid to their dreams of a second presidential term for George Bush Sr. Throughout the 1990s they had balked at the foreign policy of the Clinton White House and had herded their views and political soul mates into a close-knit body of conservative thinking that emerged on June 3, 1997, as the Project for the New American Century (PNAC). In its statement of principles, the PNAC made clear that, as a consequence of what it described as the "incoherent policies of the Clinton administration" in the areas of foreign and defense policy, there were four pressing imperatives:

- we need to increase defense spending significantly if we are to carry out our global responsibilities today and modernize our armed forces for the future;
- we need to strengthen our ties to democratic allies and to challenge regimes hostile to our interests and values;
- we need to promote the cause of political and economic freedom abroad;
- we need to accept responsibility for America's unique role in preserving and extending an international order friendly to our security, our prosperity and our principles.[33]

The PNAC was the biggest political winner from the September 11, 2001, terrorist attacks. The power of the hawks within the Bush administration clearly soared when a response to the al-Qaeda attacks was required. The architecture of that response had long been discussed within the world of the PNAC. The signatories to the

Statement of Principles of 1997 read like a list of those who are now the most powerful men in the world: Dick Cheney, the vice president; Donald Rumsfeld, the defense secretary; Wolfowitz, now Rumsfeld's deputy; and Zalmay Khalilzad, President Bush's envoy to the Middle East. Since the September 11 attacks, the PNAC has widened its attraction, issuing statements to which academics from the respected Brookings Institution, as well as ultraconservative newspaper editors, have seen fit to attach their names in support of administration policy. The consequence has been to give an academic aspect to the militarism that brought the overthrow of Saddam Hussein.

But it was an academic exercise characterized by a shallowness that is likely to haunt the Bush administration. The most pressing part of the neoconservative agenda was the need to explain why an administration that had passed its first nine months in power turning its back on the world now required that the entire world change its attitude to suit U.S. interests. There is no doubt that al-Qaeda is a global threat. There is also no doubt that a global effort is required to contend with this threat, and that a U.S. role—and even U.S. leadership in contending with the threat—is essential. But for the ideologues lying behind and within the Bush administration, the leap from isolated sole superpower to global leader required a display of diplomatic and political gymnastics that has been far from successful. It is not in the pursuit of bolstering U.S. power that countries from Kenya to the Philippines to Indonesia have joined the "war on terror." It is clearly in those countries' own interests to exploit American offers of help. But when it came to the Bush administration calling in its credit and demanding global support for its plan to overthrow Saddam Hussein, the support was shaky. The reason was simple: The intellectual backing for the war and the intelligence information used by the administration to link Saddam Hussein to al-Qaeda and portray Hussein's regime as a threat to *world* security due to its alleged possession of weapons of mass destruction were unconvincing.

The rationale was portrayed by leading lights within the PNAC such as Richard Perle, an adviser to the Pentagon who later had to resign following a scandal over his business interests, as an act of self-defense. "At the end of the day, the United Nations, Article 51, recognizes the inherent right of self-defense. It doesn't confer that right," Perle said on February 13, 2003.[34] He continued:

> [W]e want support in the UN, we want the approbation of the UN, but no American government can allow the defense of this country to depend on a show of hands at the United Nations or anywhere else. . . . The fabric of the UN, of the international community, is just not strong enough now that we would be ready to abandon our sovereign right of self-defense in the hope that some other structure is going to protect us.[35]

The pursuit of unilateral interest on the multilateral stage, which has characterized the Bush administration's foreign policy since the September 11 attacks, has been a major flaw in the administration's thinking. It has left the administration with few real friends in the world, led to accusations of militaristic imperialism, and engendered deep suspicion of the links between the business interests of administration officials and the awarding of contracts for the reconstruction of postwar Iraq. But this has not deterred the PNAC and the neoconservatives, as William Kristol, editor of what is in effect their in-house journal, the *Weekly Standard*, wrote in *The Washington Post* on October 12, 2002:

> What accounts for the president's success [in winning support for a war in Iraq]? Primarily it's the clarity, toughness and straightforwardness with which he has marshaled his arguments. . . . So the

president has succeeded in explaining why Hussein must go, why time is not on our side, why deterrence can't be counted on, and why war is necessary.[36]

On all counts, Kristol was wrong. But the war went ahead anyway. Bush's arguments failed to convince the United Nations, and millions around the world—including in the United States—marched in protest against the impending conflict, many of them more in anger at the way that a steamroller had been driven down the road to war than because of even the slightest sympathy with Saddam Hussein or a belief that he had any rights. But aside from the damage to international relations the war created, the absence of a political blueprint for postwar Iraq, coupled with the failure to confront the looting and violence that erupted in Baghdad in particular in the wake of the military campaign, exposed the paucity of ideas and inappropriateness of the military-political theorizing of the PNAC and its adherents when its principles were tested on the ground in one of the most fractious countries in the Middle East. It was hardly surprising that within days of the war starting, the PNAC had apparently started to moderate its U.S.-centered views and was robustly calling for the U.S.-Europe alliance to be repaired in the wake of the successful French-led campaign to prevent UN endorsement of the war, and also calling for a strong UN role in the postwar reconstruction of Iraq.[37] To have adhered strictly to the anti-European views of Donald Rumsfeld would have diminished the intellectual credibility of the PNAC project and exposed how little thought had been given by the broadest swath of Washington power brokers to what should happen in Iraq once the fighting was over. It was in part this lack of planning for the postwar period that inspired the condemnation of the war even before it started, as Edward Said, writing in the *London Review of Books* on April 17, 2003, made clear:

This is the most reckless war in modern times. It is all about imperial arrogance unschooled in worldliness, unfettered either by com-
petence or experience, undeterred by history or human complexity,
unrepentant in its violence and the cruelty of its technology. What
winning, or for that matter losing, such a war will ultimately entail
is unthinkable. But pity the Iraqi civilians who must still suffer a
great deal more before they are finally "liberated."[38]

CAPED CRUSADERS

It is Osama bin Laden who unleashed the military whirlwind that
has now overthrown Saddam Hussein's regime. But he achieved this
at a time when his influence in the Arab world was uncertain and
his fate unknown. He brought the wrath of the United States down
onto the Middle East by precipitating a war in a country that he is
not known to have visited, bringing the overthrow of a regime with
which he had no ties, and leading to the widely filmed deaths of several thousands of Iraqis during the course of a war that brought
some 150,000 "infidels" to a country that had since the eighth century been an intellectual powerhouse of Islam and Islamic art and
culture. On November 12, 2002, the al-Jazeera satellite television
channel broadcast a taped message from bin Laden in which he
highlighted the plight of Iraqis and Palestinians and sought to drive
a wedge between the United States and its Western allies. It was addressed "to the people of the countries that are allied with the unjust
American government" and specifically mentioned Britain, France,
Italy, Canada, Germany, and Australia. The voice warned: "You will
be killed just as you kill, and will be bombed just as you bomb.
. . . And expect more that will further distress you."[39] But even while
his focus has been on the West, bin Laden's key aim has been to turn
Muslim against Muslim: to turn Muslim populations against the

leaders of their countries, to overthrow regimes within the Islamic world and replace them with Islamic governments, trying to use the foreign presence in the region as the catalyst for this change. On February 11, 2003, he warned leaders who assisted the United States in its war in Iraq:

> [W]hoever helps America . . . either if they fight next to them or give them support in any form or shape, even by words, if they help them to kill the Muslims in Iraq, they have to know that they are outside this Islamic nation. Jordan and Morocco and Nigeria and Saudi Arabia should be careful that this war, this crusade, is attacking the people of Islam first. It doesn't matter whether the socialist (Ba'ath) party or Saddam disappear. . . .
>
> We want to ask the good Muslims to help in any way they can to join the forces and . . . overthrow the leaderships that work as slaves for America. . . . And it doesn't harm in these conditions the interest of Muslims to agree with those of the socialists in fighting against the crusaders, even though we believe the socialists are infidels. For the socialists and the rulers have lost their legitimacy a long time ago, and the socialists are infidels regardless of where they are, whether in Baghdad or in Aden.[40]

It was on the basis of this message in particular that officials in the Bush administration bolstered their argument that by attacking Saddam Hussein, they would be hitting al-Qaeda, even though the message seemed to make clear that bin Laden had no sympathy for Saddam Hussein's Ba'athist regime—a regime that had persecuted Islamists and that despised Saudi Arabia's *wahhabism*. But the foreign policy challenge—possibly even *crisis*—facing the Bush administration was dominated by the absence of decisive means at hand to deal with a non-state actor like al-Qaeda. The attacks of September 11, 2001, not only transformed U.S. foreign policy but also transformed terrorism, by drawing on the power of faith to inspire a *global* conflict.[41] For decades, localized disputes usually confined terrorist campaigns to the states or regions from which they emerged. Moreover, terrorism rarely had the power to decisively shift the political landscape. Governments have generally refused to negotiate with terrorists, leading either to campaigns being abandoned or political structures being developed as a means of facilitating negotiation. Al-Qaeda broke this pattern, and stirred a superpower that even at the height of the Cold War had considered itself largely immune from the terrorist threat on the home front. Meanwhile, al-Qaeda did not—and has not—sought to keep a path open for dialogue, another feature distinguishing it from "traditional" terrorist organizations. The relative lack of experience in the United States with the kind of terrorism that plagued much of Western Europe from the 1970s onward, and the trauma of September 11, combined to forge a U.S. response that reflected the self-image George W. Bush had been seeking—and had largely failed to find—prior to the transformation of his role that the September 11 attacks facilitated.

The decision of the Bush administration to use the September 11 attacks as a trigger for the revolutionizing of U.S. policy in the Middle East emerged within hours of the Twin Towers falling. Administration hawks had for months—and in some cases years—been seizing on any signs that Iraq and al-Qaeda even had thoughts about each other as proof that they were operationally connected and that hitting Iraq would therefore undermine al-Qaeda's ability to strike. On June 15, 2003, the former NATO commander in Europe, General Wesley Clark, told NBC's *Meet the Press* that within hours of the aircraft hitting the Twin Towers on September 11, 2001, he had been called by a Bush administration official and told that he should link the terrorist attack with Saddam Hussein if asked about it by the media. "There was a concerted effort during the fall of 2001, starting immediately after 9/11, to pin 9/11 and the terrorism problem on Saddam Hussein," Clark said.[42] When asked who had carried out this effort, he replied:

> Well, it came from the White House. It came from people around the White House. It came from all over. I got a call on 9/11. I was on CNN, and I got a call at my home saying, "You got to say this is connected. This is state-sponsored terrorism. This has to be connected to Saddam Hussein." I said, "But—I'm willing to say it, but what's your evidence?" And I never got any evidence.[43]

As the prospect of war in Iraq loomed in the early weeks of 2003, evidence to substantiate the claim that al-Qaeda had ties with Baghdad was requested from the Central Intelligence Agency. It largely failed to provide what the political leadership had asked for. In his January 28, 2003, State of the Union address, President George W. Bush repeated the assertion that "evidence from intelligence sources, secret communications and statements by people now in custody reveal that Saddam Hussein aids and protects terrorists, including members of al-Qaeda."[44] According to U.K. intelligence officials, al-Qaeda had sought to create ties with Baghdad on at least three occasions; al-Qaeda operatives were reported to have met Iraqi officials in Cairo and Jalalabad, Afghanistan, in 1997 and 2000; and an al-Qaeda delegation had traveled to Baghdad from Tehran in 1999 to try to build ties. These efforts, however, were rebuffed by Iraq. Hours before the launch of U.S. bombing on Taliban and al-Qaeda targets in Afghanistan on October 8, 2001, senior officials from the Taliban regime said they would provide the United States with detailed information showing links between Iraq and terrorist groups, including al-Qaeda.[45] The offer came from Alhaj Abdul Salam Zaeef, the Taliban ambassador in Pakistan, who appeared at that time to have become the leader of a group within the movement that was opposed to the al-Qaeda presence in Afghanistan and was aware—far too late—that al-Qaeda's activities were about to bring an end to Taliban rule. An unofficial delegation of U.S. businessmen, led by Mansoor Ijaz, a Pakistani-American financier, and including James Woolsey, the former CIA director, arranged to meet the Taliban officials on the understanding that they release eight foreigners being held there on charges of spreading Christianity, and discuss the issue of Iraqi links with terrorist groups. In a letter to Ijaz and Woolsey dated October 7, 2001, faxed to them in a hotel in Copenhagen, Zaeef agreed to "expand on your expressed interest to provide us with information about the nature and extent of relationships between Iraq and terror groups in the region, including potentially bin Laden's al-Qaeda organization."[46] Interestingly, the terms of the discussions agreed to by Zaeef were also intended to give the Americans an insight into whether allegations of Iraqi support for terrorist groups "represents a uniform opinion within the Taliban leadership or a factional view," as Zaeef wrote, suggesting that elements of the Taliban leadership— possibly even a majority of it—were seeking to accommodate U.S. concerns on security issues rather more enthusiastically than they had in the past.

The overthrow of the Taliban, and the dispersal of its leadership, meant that the planned meeting never took place. It has yet to become clear whether Zaeef—who is now in U.S. custody—has subsequently convinced the U.S. authorities that he had something sincere to say about Iraq and al-Qaeda. Anyway, the Bush administration's thirst for a decisive step against Saddam Hussein was not going to be influenced by information from an extremist theocratic regime that had harbored al-Qaeda. Even so, when the full story of al-Qaeda is one day written, the truth of its relationship with the Taliban will be a key element, and is likely to reveal a far more fractious relationship than previously thought.

Any evidence drawing upon interrogation of Taliban officials seemed absent when Secretary of State Colin Powell delivered the administration's detailed evidence against Iraq to the UN Security Council. His presentation on February 5, 2003, was intended—ultimately—to justify a strike on Iraq as being consistent with the global "war on terror" launched in the wake of the September 11, 2001, attacks. For while Tony Blair, the U.K. prime minister, stressed the potential threat from Iraq's alleged possession of weapons of mass destruction as the justification for a war, the Bush administration had to seek closure on September 11 by attacking a regime it had to present—largely for U.S. domestic consumption—as in some way responsible for it.

Powell's evidence centered on the presence in Baghdad of Abu Musaab al-Zarkawi, an al-Qaeda poisons expert who had worked on its weapons of mass destruction program in Afghanistan and was implicated in the murder in October 2002 of a U.S. diplomat in Jordan. Intelligence services had long known that in May 2002, al-Zarkawi had left Afghanistan injured and had traveled via Iran to Baghdad for treatment, during which he had had a leg amputated. Powell told the United Nations that while there al-Zarkawi had been accompanied by up to twenty-four other "al-Qaeda affiliates" who were able to operate "freely in the [Iraqi] capital."[47] Al-Zarkawi had also spent time in an area of northern Iraq not under Baghdad's control, from which U.K. and French intelligence services had traced a flow of Islamists who had traveled via Turkey to Western Europe. The area they had come from bordered Iran and was under the military influence of the Ansar al-Islam, an Islamist group linked to al-Qaeda, and in whose territory it was thought experiments with chemical weapons—in particular ricin poison—had been carried out. In his speech to the United Nations, Colin Powell sought to tie the Ansar al-Islam with the regime in Baghdad by saying that not only had al-Zarkawi shuttled between the two, but a member of Iraq's security police was officially responsible for liaising with "the most senior levels of the Ansar al-Islam."[48] Powell said this liaison was the latest in a series of contacts that amounted to links between al-Qaeda and the regime in Baghdad, and that while at least four such communications had been known, there had been at least eight high-level meetings. In addition, he said Osama bin Laden had met an Iraqi intelligence officer while al-Qaeda was based in the Sudanese capital, Khartoum, in 1996, and that an al-Qaeda operative, Abu Abdallah al-Iraqi, had visited Baghdad several times in 1999–2000, with a mission to develop cooperation on weapons of mass destruction.

Powell's claims were generally not substantiated by the information he had received from the CIA, though this had more to do with the agency's analysis of the facts than with a dispute over their veracity. While the Bush administration preferred to argue that any minor sign that al-Qaeda operatives had rubbed shoulders with the Iraqi regime was sufficient grounds to overthrow Saddam Hussein, analysts and others within the intelligence service were advising that unless the "alliance" amounted in itself to a real security threat, then it was inconsistent with the facts that a war was the correct next step. On October 7, 2002, the CIA director, George Tenet, wrote: "Our understanding of the relationship between Iraq and al-Qa'ida is evolving and is based on sources of varying reliability,"[49] with the implication from the detail that while Iraq and al-Qaeda had had contacts, there was no evidence of an operational relationship, and that by attacking Iraq the Bush administration would not be addressing the terrorist threat head-on.

Both the United Kingdom and the United States have sought to portray the future threat from al-Qaeda as derived in part from its possible possession of weapons of mass destruction. Ample evidence exists of al-Qaeda's determination to obtain or develop a WMD capacity. But no evidence exists that Iraq was prepared to share its WMD capacity—about which it was highly secretive even within its own military and scientific hierarchies—with anybody, least of all terrorists. Meanwhile, other U.S. intelligence officers have been more direct. "If the presence in Baghdad of al-Zarkawi had been of major significance then it's something that would have been put out before now. There is an inferential leap being made between his presence there and any ties with the regime," a senior U.S. intelligence official told me in January 2003, adding that he regarded al-Zarkawi's presence in Baghdad as insufficient evidence of official Iraqi ties with al-Qaeda.[50] His view was shared by U.K. and French counterterrorism officials I spoke with. "We have not found any link between al-Qaeda and Iraq. Not a trace. There is no foundation—according to our investigations—for the information given by the Americans," Jean-Louis Bruguiére, France's leading counterterrorism investigating magistrate, told me.[51] In the United Kingdom, while the government of Tony Blair sought to stress the threat from Iraq's alleged weapons of mass destruction as a reason for going to war, the prime minister did broaden his claims to include the possibility that Saddam Hussein might give WMD technology to terrorist groups. He thus drew slightly closer to the Bush administration, though the U.K. intelligence service, MI6, held firmly to the view that there was no operational link between al-Qaeda and the Iraqi regime.

But the Bush administration's focus on bin Laden's public statements highlighting the Iraq issue—messages that did not give any substantive reason for asserting that links existed between the terrorist network and Iraq—obscured other elements in the broad tapestry of the Middle East that throw a much more accurate light on the true nature of any ties that may have existed. In his February 11, 2003, statement, bin Laden made clear that al-Qaeda's support for Muslims in Iraq was a religious ideal and "not in the name of national ideologies, nor to seek victory for the ignorant governments that rule all Arab states, including Iraq." It is a fact yet to be incorporated into analyses of Western countries' relations with al-Qaeda and its affiliates, that Osama bin Laden's opinions of Middle Eastern dic-

tators like Saddam Hussein are not entirely dissimilar from those of
Western governments. Extreme Islamism of the kind practiced by al-
Qaeda was in part born out of the cruelty of such regimes. Their
overthrow and replacement by systems of justice along Islamic lines
are at the core of the doctrine al-Qaeda purports to hold dear.

Clearly there is no likelihood of such common ground amount-
ing to anything between the United States and al-Qaeda. However,
it has amounted to something within the region in the past, and the
pragmatism of the region's political leaders—rather than the sim-
plicity of the "for us or against us" attitude expounded by President
Bush—is closer to reality and therefore a necessary aspect of any
sound analysis. Bin Laden's criticism of Iraq's secular Ba'athist
regime did not preclude ties with people who would later join him
when it was necessary. Since the arrest of alleged al-Qaeda operatives in Spain in the wake of the September 11 attacks in the United
States, evidence has revealed that ties between senior individuals
who became al-Qaeda operatives in Europe and Saddam's regime go
back as far as the early 1980s, when Iraq was a Western ally against
Iran. Many of those arrested in Spain are former members of the
Syrian Muslim Brotherhood (SMB), ties between whose members
in Spain and Germany extended to the inner circle around Mohammed Atta, the Hamburg-based terrorist who led the September
11 hijackers. Key figures within the SMB trained up until 1986 at
the al-Rashdiya camp near Baghdad, where they were provided with
lessons in sabotage and basic combat techniques, according to testimony from detainees being held in Arab countries. Intelligence officials say Iraq intended to use the SMB as a lever over the Syrian
leadership, with whom its bilateral relations were often poor.

One key figure in the SMB, who trained in the Iraqi camp and
has subsequently been identified as an al-Qaeda operative in Europe,
is Imad Yarkas, also known as Abu Dahdah. He was arrested in Spain
in November 2001 and is known to have trained SMB members in

Iraq in the early 1980s. He spent time in Germany, where he shared an apartment with both Mohamed Atta and Ramzi Binalshibh, the coplanner with Khaled Sheikh Mohammed of the September 11 attacks. Another former SMB member is Mohamed Haydar Zammar, now being held in Syria, who developed close ties with al-Qaeda in Sudan in the mid-1990s, according to one of his former associates.

STATESMEN AND SPIES

By the time a cruise missile strike on a Baghdad residence in which Saddam Hussein was thought to be present marked the launch of the war on the night of March 20, 2003, Colin Powell's specific assertions justifying the war were still highly dubious. Much of the doubt and suspicion his words aroused stemmed from the validity of the intelligence information gathered by the U.K. and U.S. governments, and upon which both governments drew their authority to act. In two U.K. government dossiers—one on Iraq's alleged WMD capacity, the other on its efforts to hide that capacity from UN weapons inspectors—intelligence gathered by MI6 and allied services was used for the first time ever as the sole justification for war. "This is the preemptive war. We had good information about the Iraqi weapons program. It's been difficult to come by, in conjunction with close allies, and now there is a huge weight of responsibility that is foisted on us," a senior U.K. official told me.[52] When Tony Blair gave the U.K. Parliament details of Iraq's alleged WMD capacity on September 26, 2002, he forced previously unseen aspects of the secretive world of intelligence into the open, raising the specter of intelligence becoming politicized. It also opened to scrutiny secret intelligence information that could later be publicly verified—and possibly proved wrong.

When the problem of defending information became insurmountable, the case for war as it had been argued started to unravel.

The U.K. government claimed in September 2002 that Iraq had sought to secretly buy "substantial quantities of uranium from Africa"[53]—later said by Colin Powell to have been Niger. Mohamed ElBaradei, director general of the International Atomic Energy Agency (IAEA), to whom copies of letters allegedly from the Niger government to Iraq confirming the deal were given, told the UN Security Council on March 7 that: "Based on thorough analysis, the IAEA has concluded, with the concurrence of outside experts, that these documents—which formed the basis for the reports of recent uranium transactions between Iraq and Niger—are in fact not authentic. We have therefore concluded that these specific allegations are unfounded."[54] The U.S. government faced similar embarrassment when aluminum tubes, which it alleged Iraq had sought to buy for use in the uranium enrichment program, were said by Dr ElBaradei to have been the wrong specifications for use in a nuclear program and therefore likely to be useful only in a rocket program,[55] which is what the Iraqi government had claimed all along.

The controversy over the alleged uranium purchases from Niger blew the lid off both governments' cases and began a process that is likely to culminate in both being forced to accept that the strategy of using intelligence to justify preemptive war in Iraq has failed. Ultimately this failure is not explained by a faulty or misplaced conviction on the part of the two governments that something needed to be done about Saddam Hussein, or necessarily by the CIA and MI6 harboring doubts about the veracity of most of the information—aside from the uranium issue—they had assembled at the time they had gathered it. The failure was in transforming the intelligence into a credible and enduring political argument. Secret intelligence is a potent weapon, which by the outbreak of war in Iraq had become a veil used to obscure the shortcomings of a strategy based on secrecy rather than openness. "Intelligence," a senior intelligence officer told me at the height of the war, "is that crucial 5 percent that can make a picture whole."[56] Rarely is it so substantial as to constitute the entire picture. But by falling back on intelligence to justify war, both the U.S. and U.K. governments had sought to transform that "crucial 5 percent" into 95 percent of the reason to fight. The dangers of doing so emerged rapidly after the war, because information that intelligence agencies may feel comfortable using as the basis for action is wholly inadequate when thrown into the political arena. A crucial but over-looked element in the debate about the credibility of the secret intelligence used to justify the war is that information accepted by the CIA was often rejected by MI6, and vice versa. The different views of the U.S. and U.K. intelligence services on the issue of Iraq's alleged attempts to procure uranium, for example, are consistent with the way intelligence agencies work but at odds with the way governments work. The United Kingdom continued to insist that it had solid information that Iraq had indeed sought to buy uranium, and that its evidence was not the documents later proved to be forgeries. The United States, however, sought to trash the entire idea that Iraq had tried to make deals with Niger, and did little to assist its ally—the United Kingdom—as it struggled to retain the credibility of its arguments.

But the Niger issue was in many ways less important than the much more pronounced and important—though largely over-looked—difference between the two allies: Iraq's alleged ties to al-Qaeda. Throughout the lead-up to war, the rationale pursued in Washington held the September 11, 2001, terrorist attacks in New York and Washington as the starting point. In the United Kingdom, this link was never accepted by MI6, despite the issue being at the heart of the U.S. rationale for war in Iraq. Other significant differences existed. In the immediate prewar period, the CIA concluded that, if left unchecked, Iraq could build a nuclear weapon within one year, while the United Kingdom assessed that it would take two years. With the outbreak of hostilities, the coalition partners' vastly different assessments of Iraq's military capability and strategy quickly became clear. The United States claimed that a "red line" existed around Baghdad that—when crossed by coalition forces—would be the trigger for Iraq's use of chemical weapons. This theory was rejected by U.K. intelligence. To convince their doubting publics of the correctness of war, the governments in London and Washington had at all costs to highlight the common ground and breadth of agreement that existed between them. But to achieve this they used material from intelligence agencies whose positions differed on crucial issues, and whose often opposing views are a normal state for intelligence agencies. What has become clear is that the contradictions in intelligence—a normal state of affairs in the intelligence community—are clearly untenable as the building blocks of a political and diplomatic alliance intended to bolster the case for the invasion of a sovereign state.

On July 17, 2003, the U.K. government's vulnerability to accusations that its case for war had been based on deeply uncertain premises was intensified when a government scientist, David Kelly, committed suicide. Kelly, a highly experienced virologist in the Ministry of Defence Proliferation and Arms Control Secretariat, had been identified as the source of a story broadcast by the BBC that appeared to question the validity of U.K. government claims regarding the threat from Iraq's WMD. Throughout the 1990s, Kelly had been closely involved in UN weapons inspections in Iraq and Russia, and was one of the most senior such scientists in U.K. government service. The furor that had preceded Kelly's exposure as the source of the BBC story—in which it was reported that he had questioned government claims that Iraq's chemical weapons could be deployed within forty-five minutes of an order being given, and that the prime minister's communications director had "sexed up" the government's September 24 dossier to make the case stronger—obscured the real issue of whether Iraq had been an imminent threat, as claimed in the dossier, and whether Saddam's removal had made the world a safer place. It became a battle between the government and the media.

But in the process of an inquiry into Kelly's death, internal government documents were released showing the extent of doubts within the government over the claims included in the September 24 dossier. One key e-mail, from Jonathon Powell, Tony Blair's chief of staff, addressed both to Blair's communications director and his political adviser, stated:

> The dossier is good and convincing for those who are prepared to be convinced.
>
> I have only three points, none of which affect the way the document is drafted or presented.
>
> First the document does nothing to demonstrate a threat, let alone an imminent threat from Saddam. In other words it shows he has the means but does not demonstrate that he has the motive to attack his neighbours, let alone the west. We will need to make it clear in launching the document that we do not claim that we have evidence that he is an imminent threat. The case we are making is that he has continued to develop WMD since 1998, and is in breach of UN resolutions. The international community has to enforce those resolutions if the UN is to be taken seriously. Second, we will be asked about the connections to Al Quaeda. The document says nothing about these. . . [the remainder of this sentence is blacked out].
>
> Third, if I was Saddam I would take a party of western journalist to the Ibn Sina factory or one of the others pictured in the document to demonstrate there is nothing there. How do we close off that avenue to him in advance?[57]

Such skepticism within Tony Blair's personal staff about the way the United Kingdom was presenting its case is revealing, and probably encouraged the editing process that led to the highlighting of the two issues—the claim of 45 minutes deployability and the assertion that Iraq was an imminent threat—that caused the furor. The witch hunt within the government, and the readiness of the Ministry of Defence to identify Kelly when it should have kept his identity confidential, led to the truth about both issues being entirely lost. The major casualty of the row was the truth about what Kelly believed: While he had been used as a source by a BBC reporter to apparently doubt government policy, his views in fact remained almost identical to the government's. In a letter to his superiors within the Ministry of Defence, written after he realized he may have been the source of the BBC report, Kelly wrote:

> I did not discuss [with the BBC reporter] the "immediacy" of the threat [from Iraq's weapons]. The discussion was not about the [September 24] dossier. Had it been so then I would have indicated that from my extensive and authoritative knowledge of Iraq's WMD programme, notably its biological programme, that the dossier was a fair reflection of open source information. . . .
>
> I most certainly have never attempted to undermine Government policy in any way especially since I was personally sympathetic to the war because I recognized from a decade's work the menace of Iraq's ability to further develop its non-conventional weapons programmes.[58]

The controversy into which Kelly was thrust, with little support from his employers, who saw him as a scapegoat the sacrifice of which could have helped their case had it not led to his suicide, would perhaps never have happened had the weeks after the war produced the evidence of WMD both the U.K. and U.S. governments had sincerely expected to find. Months later, they have found nothing to suggest that the evidence people like Kelly—who had been a UN weapons inspector in Iraq—had provided was accurate. Had the entire world been duped?

AMONG THE INVADERS

Saddam Hussein's presence had been neatly erased from the al-Qaim fertilizer factory. While elsewhere in the country his portraits have had their eyes gouged out, or had horns painted on his head, the employees of Iraq's largest fertilizer producer instead took a can of red paint and carefully coated the larger than life image that stood at the factory entrance. For al-Qaim's employees, erasing the past was a duty, a necessity, and an obsession. But for Sensitive Sight Team Five (SST5)—a group of U.S. and U.K. soldiers trained in unconventional warfare—the mission was the opposite. Its role was to painstakingly go over old ground in the hunt for the evidence of Iraq's weapons of mass destruction, which had brought the downfall of the Iraqi dictator. Tumbleweed blowing in the teeth of a violent sandstorm sped past the concrete bunkers in a fenced-off inner site of the factory, a few miles from the country's border with Syria, and within which Iraqi scientists in the 1980s had extracted uranium oxide—so-called Yellow Cake. The "cake," if produced in quantities Iraq never in fact achieved, could have been used in the development of nuclear fuel and weapons. The bunkers were ordered closed and encased in concrete by UN inspectors after the 1991 Gulf war, and UN inspectors had regularly visited the site, most recently in early March 2003, days before the U.S.-led invasion. But beneath a building partly destroyed by bombing in 1991, sixteen blue plastic barrels lay coated in a thin film of dust. A British specialist with the U.K. Nuclear, Biological, Chemical Regiment, seconded to the U.S.-led SST5, surveyed the barrels with an Exploranium chemical detector. Its indicator ticked rapidly, and words on a screen described the contents of the barrels as "industrial uranium 238"—Yellow Cake.

A few weeks before, when advancing U.S. forces were regularly proclaiming that they had unearthed evidence of Iraq's WMD, this find would perhaps have been called a "smoking gun" by the excitable invaders. Instead, by mid-May 2003, when I visited Iraq, expectations of such finds had evaporated, and suspicion was mounting around prewar claims that major WMD finds made at sites identified before the war would provide justification for the invasion.

"Our best information is going to come from human sources: Iraqis, when they feel comfortable enough, will come forward," said Lieutenant Colonel Keith Harrington, the U.S. Special Forces officer heading SST5. "The new approach will be: piece it together from the human intelligence. We probably won't find the big smoking gun."[59] The first detail provided to the SST5 by Ismail Ibrahim, al-Qaim's production manager, was that the site had already been visited by other coalition troops, and it was later confirmed to me that the U.K. Special Air Service—the SAS, equivalent to the U.S. Special Forces—had visited the factory several weeks before. Ibrahim said that the troops had kicked down doors and used explosives to crack open the company safes, leaving one internal office wall standing at a precarious angle, knotted and broken cables dangling from the ceiling. Undeterred by the possibility that they may have traveled for several hours by helicopter from Baghdad only to be duplicating others' work, the twenty-strong SST5 team spent seven hours painstakingly testing chemicals, photographing laboratories, and examining mineral crushers and scores of other facilities. The team had not been provided with details of al-Qaim's activities included in previous UN inspections—some of which are available on the Internet—and it was Ibrahim who volunteered information that Yellow Cake had once been produced at the site.

His readiness to provide details exposed both the dependence of the new WMD inspectors on well-informed Iraqis prepared to share information and the prospect of investigations being started from scratch when extensive information already lies with the United Nations. "The UN inspectors knew everything," Ibrahim told me,[60]

resigned to the fact that the reluctance of the invading armies to engage the United Nations in a task for which it was far better equipped
and about which it already had a vast amount of data meant that
months were likely to be wasted in gathering information that was already available. The dependence of the SST teams—of which there
were seven until the entire WMD investigation operation was re-
formed in July 2003 and brought under the auspices of the Iraq Sur-
vey Group—on Iraqi officials, factory employees, scientists, and
others, left the U.S.-led teams with little likelihood of unearthing
much that the UN inspectors, whose own failure had been used as the
excuse for going to war, had failed to find.

The chaplains of the V Corp headquarters—from where SST5
was dispatched on its missions—set the tone of the elaborate palace
out of which the invading force was conducting its affairs. They
were sitting behind their laptop computers discussing an electronic
sermon that would be distributed to thousands of troops whose
Humvee military vehicles crawled around the grounds of the vast
presidential estate out of which much of Iraq was being ruled. There
were five chaplains, chatting, half-smiling, beneath the only working chandeliers on the sprawling estate. Walking into the operations
room seemed—on a first visit—to be like stepping into the evil vil-
lain's headquarters on the set of a James Bond movie. While outside
it was Iraq—hot, dusty, desperate, haunted by the legacy of Saddam, a Middle Eastern country—through the door of the captured
palace was another world. An enormous electronic map on the wall,
surrounded by screens showing CNN and Fox TV, caught the eye,
while hundreds of uniformed officials dispatched orders, planned
operations, and conducted warfare and nation building via e-mail.

In their villa, in the shadow of another, apparently unfinished
palace beside one of the estate's man-made lakes, where the unex-
ploded bomblet of a cluster bomb—one of the small bombs dispersed when the main incendiary device explodes and distributes

hundreds of smaller, lethally dangerous bombs—lay in a few inches of water ready to go off, the troops of SST5 were wondering whether their task was a waste of time. They had traveled hundreds of miles, examining sites that had provided no evidence of the weapons whose alleged existence had given the United States and the United Kingdom their reason for going to war. "The sites are so far gone that you can't tell whether they have been looted or sanitized," said Major Ron Hann, deputy head of SST5, whose degree in chemistry had earned him a place on the team. "We just haven't seen a laboratory or a [scientific] setup that allows us to be clear whether we are looking at things that have been well-concealed. We were trained to look at U.K. and U.S. production techniques. Before, we were looking for an obvious smoking gun. We thought we would find major indicators [of WMD]. So we had big WMD teams who were trained to look for these indicators. Now we have to go into detective mode. In our country we got far too far away from human intelligence and much too overreliant on technology. We are facing the intelligence gap that we saw develop over the past few years."[61] This was a criticism of the Clinton administration echoed by the Washington neoconservatives whose war he—and others like him—had been sent to fight on the battlefields between the Tigris and Euphrates Rivers.

At the V Corp headquarters, the major's views were reflected by Colonel Tim Madere, the Corp chemicals officer, and the man overseeing the seven Sensitive Sight Teams. He had been hauled onto the battlefield when it was realized that his Cold War expertise in chemical weapons—expertise that had become rare since the United States banned chemical weapons from its arsenal in the 1970s—was essential to the WMD hunt. "I'm a dinosaur. I was still testing the chemical binary weapons in the 1970s. That experience is rare. I have the understanding of how to operate in dirty environments," he told me, with an odd mix of humor and distaste at the grim skills that continued to make him employable. "When the intelligence community started all this, they probably had good intelligence. But what we didn't realize at the time was that after that the Iraqis got an opportunity to hide it and move it around. I always said that in a lot of sites there was probably a lot of information. But 90 percent of the intelligence has been compromised. You go to these sites and you find nothing. Now you find places where things have been burned. But perhaps it was by looters," he said, with more than a note of exasperation.[62]

Before the war had even ended, both the U.K. and U.S. governments were preparing their populations for the probability that the hard evidence they had claimed existed as justification for the war would not be found. Among the intelligence services that had been used to provide the governments with their arguments, there was an assertion that it was not the case that there was no evidence, but that it had been moved, concealed, altered, or in one way or another made unavailable. It was not the case that they had been lying, that what they knew to be true before the war was not true after it, but that the situation they had described prior to the war had been accurate at that time. This was not—of course—what the political leaders in both countries had argued. To justify the war post factum, they had to provide the evidence they had publicly said existed before the war. It was on the basis that they would do so that they had gathered support for the conflict. But in both countries, as it became clear that the evidence was simply not available—whether or not it had ever been—ministers and officials began a stealthy campaign intended to dilute expectations and refocus public opinion on the benefits to their own national interests of getting rid of Saddam Hussein. To most residents of the United Kingdom and the United States, however, these benefits are difficult to discern. Saddam was never a threat to either country, and the links to al-Qaeda his regime was alleged by Colin Powell to have had have proved as impossible to substantiate as the proof of his illegal weapons programs has been to find. In short, nothing that either government argued as justification for the war—in terms of specifics, as opposed to the general view that Saddam's regime was violent and repressive—was bolstered by proof delivered after the conflict was over.

With the Bush administration's motives so riddled with ambiguity, it is hardly surprising that the Iraqis being asked to assist the weapons hunters have voiced suspicion, some perhaps aware that the United States has a success rate of zero as an architect of nation building, in countries ranging from the South Vietnam of the 1960s to Somalia and Haiti in the 1990s. At the al-Qaim fertilizer factory, Ismail Ibrahim reflected the uncertainty: "We know which is right and which is wrong. Iraqis believe that the Americans are going the right way. But we are thinking about the results. The Americans are not saying what their plans are for the future. So, can I say how things are really going? No."[63] His conclusions throw light on a much larger reality than the weapons hunt, one that is ultimately more important to Western policymakers and their constituencies than it is to Iraqis. As the United States embarks on a plan to remodel the Middle East and create a democracy in Iraq that it claims will be a model for the rest of the region, what hopes of success does it have if even the Iraqi population that it has "liberated" remains so deeply uncertain about its role and motives? Moreover, what is it in the region—both in its past and in the present—that has created the urgency for change the Bush administration sees as *its* role, rather than as the role of Arabs, to bring about? The democratic model the Bush administration envisages Iraq becoming for the region is a fantasy, not because Arabs do not want democracy, but because democracy cannot be implanted; it evolves, as the experiences of other new democracies, many in sub-Saharan Africa, have shown since the end of the Cold War.

By invading Iraq, the Bush administration has exacted a catastrophic revenge on the Arab and Muslim world for the September

11 attacks. The democracy that the administration romantically envisaged may emerge from the wreckage is no closer, crippled by the
violence and insecurity that now rack Iraq. The idea of democratic
models—one example leading others to follow—is itself a highly dubious one, as each country has its own history; democracy is not an
infection, but a system of rule that emerges out of historical, cultural,
and political circumstances. The extraordinarily naïve assumption,
coming at a time when the Arab and Islamic worlds are in the throes
of the crisis created by Islamic extremism, that Iraq would embrace a
democracy imposed by an invading force sent by a country that has
never before been so unpopular in the Arab world and whose troops
have taken months to even make the lights work, is breathtaking.

But even if there were no chaos in Iraq, no threat of "one hundred Osama bin Ladens" emerging, and no Israeli–Palestinian conflict to dominate attitudes toward the United States, there would
still be huge mountains to climb. At the very least, the Arab world's
leaders would have to reconcile themselves with their own peoples.
To achieve this the violence at the core of dictatorial rule would
have to be recognized for what it is, and new rules governing the behavior of leaders would have to be established, accepted, and implemented. This debate is not going to happen while U.S. forces
colonize Iraq, as the contradiction between the United States as
democratic model and the United States as invading force is too
stark. But, left to evolve without the foreign meddling that has only
ever wrought havoc worldwide, recognition of the primacy of
human rights may emerge from within Arab society itself.

5

BRUTAL TRUTHS, FRAGILE MYTHS

HUMAN RIGHTS AND THE LEGACIES OF TERROR

Torture, massacres, repression, undemocratic practices: this
is what we Arabs have become known for.
    —Edward Said, *Al-Ahram Weekly*, January 29, 1998

THE TAPPING OF A HAMMER INSIDE A BRICK OVEN STOPPED WITH
the sound of military boots on the broken glass and smashed tiles. A
wild dog howled outside, pigeons cooed, and the wrinkled, soot-
caked face of a man appeared from a hole in the wall in which the
cooks of Abu Ghraib prison used to bake their bread. The ransack-
ing of Iraq's most notorious prison—the man in the bread oven was
stealing bricks, which he had neatly piled in the center of the prison
kitchen—had left much of the vast complex in pieces. But it had
left its atmosphere intact. Mounds of partially burned prison

records and faded photographs of inmates holding up their prison numbers littered the floors of offices, cells, corridors, and offices in which the deposed Ba'ath Party regime institutionalized its brutality. The cell doors, hundreds of them, all painted in bright blue not long before I visited, lay open; the cells onto which they opened were empty, evidence of redecoration suggesting that the regime had plans for the place that hardly countenanced its overthrow. On the walls, the misery and fear seemed compounded by fantasies of what life could be like. Brightly colored murals along the corridors depicted a swan and its signets gliding along a pleasant stream, a horse galloping across open grassy plains, a sailing ship plunging through the sea without a crew, a boy washing his donkey in a fast-running river watched by a stag and a family of deer.

The confidence Saddam appeared always to exude is most cruelly acute in the jail where dissenting voices, common criminals, and those who had the misfortune to fall from grace with the regime were thrown together. A U.K. government report drawing upon several accounts of human rights under Saddam Hussein's regime said that 4,000 prisoners at Abu Ghraib were executed in 1984 alone.[1] In February and March 2000, 122 political prisoners were executed there, and in October 2001 a further 23 political prisoners were either hanged or shot. And if those who remained alive but incarcerated ever forgot whose rules they had broken, they could strain their eyes to the end of every one of the cell blocks and see the face of the dictator—smiling, shooting his shotgun, laughing with children, dressed as a peasant—his image always there, compounding their punishment by reminding them daily who it was had put them there.

"The last time I saw him was here." Abdul Jaber Mutashir unrolled a piece of white paper. On it was the photograph of a man in a head scarf and *jelabia*. "It was this cell."[2] He was not talking about Saddam Hussein, and he was standing outside a two-story building that was the only one in the hundreds of acres within which Abu Ghraib sprawls on which trees gave some shade. There was grass, and bougainvillea grew up a wall. The shadow of the trees would have shaded the building had it not been midday. "Then he was taken here." Abdul Jaber pointed to a heavy metal door painted gray, opened it, appearing to know his way, and walked inside a room that rose through the two stories of the building. Inside, there was no bright blue paint, just gray. A mezzanine at the top of the ramp was bare but for a metal box with two handles. Above it, two large metal brackets were welded to the ceiling, and directly beneath them in the floor, two rectangular holes opened onto the concrete floor below. The two ceiling brackets, two holes, two trap doors— all was clinical. Prisoners were hanged side by side. Abdul Jaber Mutashir wondered who had been hanged beside his brother. He wondered if they had spoken together before the handles were pulled, the trap doors swung open, and they fell.

Saddam released thousands of prisoners in an amnesty in the autumn of 2002, though nobody could understand why. Hardened criminals, petty thieves, some political prisoners: All were suddenly told they could go. The event was filmed, the sight of bewildered and ecstatic convicts filling the television screens. Saddam was perhaps trying to appear beneficent, though his gesture also succeeded in putting back on the streets some of the more unsavory characters whom it might have been better to keep behind bars. But the gesture—like the message implied in the lurid murals that to this day adorn the now empty cell blocks at Abu Ghraib—was essentially aimed at showing the absence of law. The law was Saddam, not even the regime, which itself cowered beneath the anger and brutality of the nation's leader. At one extreme, tales of the arbitrary power of Saddam were legion throughout his rule, and have emerged in even greater detail since his overthrow, tales of cruelty and obscene violence. A story often told about his son Uday tells how he would sit of an evening on the balcony of his rural residence, armed with a shotgun, taking shots at whoever might fall within his sights. Nobody ever complained, not even the owners of a holiday camp situated next door, where Baghdad residents went to escape the pressures of the city. Who was there to complain to?

Despite references to the readiness of Saddam Hussein's regime to use its weapons of mass destruction against Iraq's Kurdish population, the arguments used by the U.S. and U.K. governments to justify the war in Iraq centered upon the threat to *world* security—in other words, to the United States—as a reason for forcing regime change in Iraq. It is small wonder that when U.S. and U.K. forces invaded, they were met with popular emotions ranging from anxiety and doubt to outright condemnation by Iraqis. The issue of the deposed regime's real relationship with its own people was not a central part of the equation of war, because that relationship did not threaten *world* security. Indeed, one can even argue that Saddam's autocracy was the sole guarantee that the fractious makeup of Iraqi society was assured against instability and collapse, of a kind that could have had resonating security implications had his iron rule flagged. The war was fought for global rather than local Iraqi reasons; it was an invasion pure and simple, since which the victors have claimed the spoils. The challenge facing the Shia majority, the Sunni minority, and the Kurdish population, as well as distinct sections of the population such as the marsh Arabs, is dominated by the need to both rebalance political power in a manner that reflects national realities and also prevent the invaders' perception of what Iraq is from forcing settlements that have more to do with revenge on behalf of constituencies in Washington and London than the *realpolitik* of Iraqi political relationships. The decision in late May 2003 by U.S. administrators to dismiss all Ba'ath Party members from civil service positions, and to follow this move by banning them from the fledgling armed forces, was a case in point. This decision excluded upwards of one million of the country's most experienced administrators from positions for which few others were trained. It revealed both administrative ineptitude and strategic shortsightedness on behalf of the invaders. To have a government job under Saddam Hussein, Iraqis had to be members of the Ba'ath Party. The extent to which they believed in Ba'athist principles—principles that Saddam had largely dispensed with in the late 1990s—was of no consequence to the invaders.

As well as being a wholly impractical decision, it was also an odd one for the U.S. administrators to make, because it assumed that Ba'athism and Saddam Hussein's regime were inextricable, when in fact it was relatively easy to see that they were not. At least by the end of the regime, there was little that was political about the regime, its main aim being survival, its main practice being theft of state funds, its main practitioners being relatives of Saddam rather than individuals with a Ba'athist political identity that in any way distinguished them from Saddam. What Saddam had was an apparatus of repression that was exercised through the machinery of the Ba'ath Party, which had an organizational aspect through which the regime's violence could be practiced. The main victims of this machinery were members of the population, among them Ba'athists who signed up because that was the only way to get along in Saddam's Iraq. So, come the invasion, people who were punished until they became members of the party out of necessity then found themselves being punished by the invaders for having been part of the party machinery.

The blanket ban on Ba'ath Party members holding government office after the invasion did not involve any kind of investigation into the actual activities of individual members. And it was with this ban that the political remodeling of Iraq was launched. On this foundation, the meeting of Western-style democracy and Arab political culture, which had been tested unsuccessfully in many parts of the region during the mid-twentieth century, was engineered. The ambition, widely discussed within the Bush administration, of creating a democratic model in Iraq, whose influence would spread across the region, was thus launched with a process of cleansing, of banishing the past, of attempting to bury history, of isolating thousands of small symbols of the old regime, of forcing the cleaning of the slate, and the petty symbolism of tearing down statues of Saddam Hussein or disfiguring his image. Most ineptly, this process then led to the entire Iraqi army—350,000 men—being dismissed. The decision created a ready-made militarily trained opposition to the foreign military presence, manned by extremely angry and unemployed soldiers, whose potential to destabilize Iraq was huge. It took weeks before the stupidity of this decision was realized, and each of the soldiers was promised a small pension. But by then the damage had been done, eventually forcing a reversal of the decision when a former regime general was sent on April 29, 2004, to relieve embattled U.S. forces in Fallujah.

ARTICLES OF FAITH

The process of deconstructing and rebuilding in Iraq has raised a vast array of questions. But one of the most important is whether it is bound to fail because it was not inspired from within Iraq but was solely a result of foreign invasion. Efforts by the United States at nation building elsewhere in the world have had a success rate of zero, ever since the fledgling state of South Vietnam was invented and left to die. To focus such ambitions among the harsh and fractious communities living between the Tigris and Euphrates Rivers, after a war whose primary purpose was to lift a supposed security threat to the invaders rather than primarily to free a downtrodden population, requires a level of understanding of not only why Iraq found itself festering in a mire of political stagnation and militaristic brutality, but also how the region within which it sits has remained similarly slumped. While few of the region's regimes today compare in their brutality with that led by Saddam Hussein and his family, the fear that is the chief tool of dictatorship hangs like an ever-present shadow over much of the Arab world. Any profound shift in political direction would require a wholesale reassessment of the rights of individuals, a transformation of the relationship between the state and the nation, the leaders and the led, on a scale that none of the region's regimes could survive. Any such change would take place against a background of Islamist political activity, much of the popular support for which is a reaction to brutality, in particular the torture of political prisoners in the 1980s and 1990s. With the Islamist voice the strongest opposition voice in the region, and its adherents at their most virulent when condemning the cruelty of the regimes they seek to overthrow, the emergence of a politics based on individual rights—human rights, the right to organize outside the state structure, the right of the media to operate without harassment—has in fact taken on a tone that is essentially indigenous, anti-Western, and fundamentally Arab, and has a relevance to regional political realities that the invading armies now present in Iraq will barely influence beyond the boundaries of their territorial possessions. Their presence in the Arab world is alien, and even if their aims are to bring democracy, the means by which they have sought to bring it is of greater significance than the ideals themselves. Ultimately, their ideas are as invasive as the troops that have sought to run the lives of Iraqis, and their presence has probably set back the process of democratization substantially, as few Arab reformers will find a responsive audience for their calls for reform if these calls appear to resemble the ideas forced by a foreign invasion onto the Arab soil of Iraq.

Such calls long predate the invasion of Iraq, and the challenge facing the region's reformers is how to pursue their ambitions without losing that which must always remain at the heart of any reform: the evolving Arab identity. For all countries in the Arab world the rigid political structures have had the effect of restricting the right to define that identity to those who are in power. Foreign critics of Arab governments generally argue that the cultural impact of Islam lies behind the rigidity of the region's political life. Such claims are usually made as a way of seeking to portray Israel as the region's sole democracy, and as a vehicle for arguing that Arab resistance to Israel is too deep—culturally and religiously—to countenance the possibility of a Palestinian state living peacefully alongside Israel. This argument—usually put by pro-Israel lobbyists in the United States—is at best disingenuous, at worst vindictive propaganda. It rests upon the assumption that there is a uniformity to Arab life that is truly represented in the statements and claims of the undemocratic leaders ruling Arab states. Islam is not intolerant of other religions, which is why the Arab world—the heartland of three religions—has not experienced the expulsion of Jews as experienced in fifteenth-century Spain, nor has it seen pogroms of the kind suffered in Czarist Russia, nor in more recent years has it seen the religious violence of the Indian subcontinent.

However, as in all regions of the world that in the past were the colonies of European states, the intense political necessity to represent the "true" indigenous identity is an article of faith at the heart of the political lexicon for any regime seeking to retain its credibility and authority. In the Arab world, the task is complicated by the huge variety within Arab society making it impossible to identify a single pillar of that identity, beyond the powerfully unifying bond of the Arabic language. Centuries of Arab–European contact have meant that aspects of European culture are also embedded within Arab culture, as befits a region that is a geographical crossroads. Equally, the Arab world is the heartland of three world religions, all of which remain vital parts of Arab life, whatever may be the attitudes of incumbent regimes to the variety over which they rule.

For me, it was late one August afternoon that the weakness of the state and the failings of its rigid structure as a mechanism for responding to this variety became all too obvious. The night train from Cairo stopped just before dawn at Sohag. The sky was just turning steely gray. I had never been there before, to this town at the heart of Egypt. Huge American cars dating from the 1950s served as taxis, hauling their great hulks through the waking streets, taking the drowsy rail passengers off into the neat tree-lined fields that spread out from the town in a lush sea of irrigated crops.

Mohamed Saleh, my colleague, and I drove out of town toward el-Kosheh, stopping beside a two-thousand-year-old temple to eat a breakfast of sweet tea and falafel. The ubiquitous police officers, even at 6:30 A.M. in a rural backstreet, were curious and asked questions about my presence. We had arranged to meet with Amba Wissa, Bishop Wissa, the Coptic bishop of Sohag, at the bishop's palace, which stood back from the road midway between Sohag and el-Kosheh. But when we arrived, we were told he had already gone to el-Kosheh, so we followed him.

The Coptic church at el-Kosheh has a pleasant courtyard enclosed on three sides by long buildings. A large group had gathered to hear Wissa, whose outspoken criticism of the clumsy way the government and the brutal way the police handled religious affairs in the country had raised his profile. He was far more popular than Shenouda, the Coptic pope, who barely dared speak out on behalf of Egypt's six million Copts in any manner critical of the government, preferring to discuss things discreetly with government officials in a manner that may well have had a positive impact but did little to raise the morale of Copts who saw themselves as the victims of discrimination. At el-Kosheh, during that summer and autumn of 1998, the full scale of the government's failure to instill a sense of humanity into the police force that was its iron fist was laid bare:

They took me on Saturday, 15 August. I was in my house. They took me without reason. They took me from the house to the police station. In the police station they asked me if I knew the dead. I told them I didn't know anything because I had been in my house. I was in the police station for seven days. They tied my hands behind my back. They blindfolded me. They attached electric shocks to my ears. They did it only one time. They didn't want to let me go home, and each day they let me out they rearrested me.[3]

Rifaat Kamel was one of the first to be arrested when a riot had broken out following a dispute between a Coptic woman and a Muslim market stallholder in the town. The woman had not been satisfied with what she had been sold and wanted to return it. When the stallholder refused to take it back, violence erupted. But very quickly the issue became less about the relationship between Muslims and Christians and more about the way in which the Egyptian state—in particular the police in el-Kosheh and the nearby town of Dar el-Salaam—waded into the violence in its efforts to establish who was responsible for the deaths of two Coptic men during the disturbance. The strategy of the police was clear from the start. To try to preserve the religious harmony that had existed as the norm in el-Kosheh for as long as many people could remember, despite occasional friction, the police were determined that the killer or killers of the two men would not be found to have been Muslim. They feared—probably genuinely—that if the men were found to be Muslim, it would serve to heighten the religious divide. It was of course never stated that this was their strategy. Instead, it became obvious from the way in which they went about interrogating and threatening the Copts in the weeks after the killings in the hope that one among them would admit to the killings.

Sitting among the crowd in the cloistered calm of an el-Kosheh church, Michael Milik told me:

At the beginning they took me and my wife to the police station. They kept us there for three days. Then we were taken to the main police station in Dar el-Salaam. I was tied and blindfolded. I was tied upside down from the window with my son, for three days. Then they let my son go. He is in the army, and they let him go back. Then they took another of my sons. I was there for another three days, without water, without food. They brought my other son back from the army. They put a cup of water in front of me and said that my son could drink it if he wanted to. In all I spent thirty-four days in prison. They took my fourteen-year old daughter to the fields. They placed her in front of her brother, and threatened to put her brother up like Jesus Christ.[4]

The arbitrary arrests of around twelve hundred Copts in the weeks following the murders in August 1998 then evolved into more brutal police actions, as they failed to find the killers, as Boktar Abel Aymeen told me:

The police took me. Then they took my sons, Michael and Amir. They hung me up, with my children. I spent thirty-four days in prison. They hung me up by my feet from the window frame in the police station, and demanded to know if I had killed the two men. Then they took my wife from the house. Then they threatened to rape my children.[5]

He went on: "Now there's a feeling of hatred. And the government is with them. The police are waiting for my children to do something wrong. They are always harassing my children." His wife added: "The feeling now is one of hate, because the police accused my son of being a criminal when he is not. For five days I was hung up. The police insulted the Christians. They insulted the church. They said that there's no religion among the Christians. Generally, the police are like donkeys, not men. The police are there to apply the wrongdoings."[6]

Their deep distrust of the police and the motives of the authorities was made even clearer by Adel Asel, whose brother Karam was one of the two men whose murder had led to the police investigation and the ill-treatment that followed: "During the period the police brought me and my wife in order for us to accuse Boktar. The police found a woman—Nadia Abdesalam Rawi—who knew the truth, but they hid her in order to blame a Copt. The truth about my brother? I don't know why he is dead. The police cursed our religion, saying that we had no religion."[7]

Adel's flow of words was stopped when a group of police officers barged into the room and began staring at the crowd. Everybody remained silent. The most senior of the officers then saw Bishop Wissa, in full religious regalia, and had little choice but to back off, saying he had only come there because he wanted to make sure that everything was calm. "My authority is here. I'm the bishop," Wissa told me after the police officers had left, adding that he had written to every minister in the government after the violence, appealing for them to raise the issue, but had had no response to his letters. "There are legal ways. But I can't do anything. I can give comfort to my people. I try to comfort them." He continued:

> It's not going to create a problem between the Muslims and the Copts, because all the people lived together. The entire police have contributed to this. This action is anti-humanity, but not anti-Christian. I shall try. But I feel sad. The human rights organizations come and do their reports, and then they do nothing. The church is going to the government to express the problems the people are facing. But there's no response. Now we know very well how to continue: to stop the police through the lawyers. There will be trials of the police. Why not?[8]

Several of those in the church took me on a tour of the town. We drove, followed by two police cars a few feet behind us. We dropped the Copts back at their church, then drove to the police station where Boktar had been hung upside down by his feet in the hope that he would confess to something he had not done. In his stifling office, Police Commander Abdel Hafiz sipped tea from a mug painted with a large male toad telling a female toad: "I toad you that I loved you." The commander denied everything. Nobody had been suspended from the ceiling fans. No electric shock torture had been carried out. There had been no beating of children, and nobody had been strung upside down by their ankles from the window frame. Nor had anybody been threatened with crucifixion. He would not clarify whether the Copts who had been interrogated had been insulted for their religion, deeming it a matter beyond his remit.

We left his office. It was already midafternoon, and the train from Sohag back to Cairo would be leaving in less than two hours. We drove back along roads that passed through the lush fields, tailed all the way by Commander Hafez's officers. The impact of the distance between the nervous population of el-Kosheh and Egypt's power center in Cairo became ever more clear. Only in October 1998 was the violence being committed by the police in the town first reported. That report had been in a Coptic newspaper and had no impact beyond the Coptic community. It took six weeks before testimony from those—like Boktar—who had been the victims of the police action began to filter through to Egypt's human rights organizations. But most revealing was the way in which the authorities then began to handle the issue, once they realized that they had failed to keep it out of the media. When I went to el-Kosheh with my colleague from Cairo, the police were taken by surprise, as no other foreign journalist had followed up on the reports by visiting the town. Commander Hafez said he had never seen a foreign reporter in the town before, and it became clear that the distance—it took nearly eight hours to reach el-Kosheh from Cairo—was something the authorities used to their advantage.

But the news did filter out. And in consequence of their failure to keep the issue out of the press, the Egyptian government adopted the clumsiest possible approach to crisis management. Instead of publicly lambasting the police for their brutality and offering an apology to those who had suffered, they turned on the human rights organizations that had taken up the issue. The Egyptian Organization for Human Rights (EOHR) had—like many of the people in el-Kosheh itself—early on identified the issue as being one of police brutality rather than religious strife. As Mustapha Zidane, EOHR's director, told me: "The issue is one of the relationship between the authorities and the people. Events like el-Khosheh: These incidents occur often. Police officers see that it is easy to get information from people by torturing them. The victim is happy just to leave the police station. There's no direct complaints procedure for citizens."⁹

But this was not what the authorities wanted to hear. In the weeks that followed, the government—specifically the interior ministry—responded to the increasingly intense focus on the events in el-Kosheh by accusing those who were highlighting the issue of doing so at the behest of foreign interests, notably Christian groups in the United States. This came to a head when an article appeared in the Egyptian newspaper *al-Osbour* accusing the EOHR of receiving money from the British embassy in Cairo to finance its investigation into the events at el-Kosheh. The newspaper's editor, Mustapha Bakri, had never been known for the high quality of his journalism, and was grouped even by government ministers with what were called the yellow press—journalists who would write what they were told by anybody they got along with. Bakri obtained evidence that the British embassy had paid EOHR the sums of $17,000 and $25,000 at around the time the organization had been investigating el-Kosheh in late September. In a front-page article Bakri condemned EOHR's readiness to accept money from what the newspaper called "an enemy foreign embassy." The fact that the money was specifically earmarked to finance a women's center, which had previously been financed for two years by the Dutch embassy with the full knowledge of the government, was not an issue for Bakri. More revealing was his own history. Until shortly before he wrote the article, he had actually been on the board of the EOHR. He then left, but shortly afterward the existence of a secretly taped meeting of the board at which he had been present emerged, when the issue of overseas finance for EOHR was discussed and Bakri had not raised any objections. The British embassy denied that it had anything to do with the EOHR report on el-Kosheh, but Bakri insisted to me that "the linkage between the embassy check and the al-Kosheh report was based on the length of time between the two, and the fact that it was the first time the British embassy had issued [such] a check."[10] A weak link indeed. But it was enough for the government, which on December 2 arrested Hafez Abu Saida, the EOHR secretary-general, accusing him of treason.

Abu Saida was later released, having had his head shaved—a factor that resonated powerfully when he arrived shortly afterward in the Netherlands for a human rights conference at which the state of human rights in Egypt was discussed. The full combination of circumstances that had led to el-Kosheh becoming a tragedy of such significance was soaked up by the Egyptian authorities as rapidly as it was by the organizations of civil society—in particular the human rights organizations. El-Kosheh was proof that the economic liberalization program that was under way in Egypt during that period was not being matched by any meaningful liberalization in the political arena. Throughout the 1990s, and up to today, the gulf between Egypt's political theory—embodied in a multiparty parliament and secular constitution—and its institutional practice has, continued to be exposed most starkly by issues in which the government has either deliberately or by default sought to maintain a large degree of uncertainty, as it juggles with political, security, and cultural concerns. Pressure for political reform, and hopes for an end to the political stranglehold of the National Democratic Party, mounted with the advance of economic reform from the mid-1990s. Among academics, the two were seen to go hand in hand. But the connection was never clear when seen from the perspective of those less closely involved in the economic liberalization process, in particular the hawkish interior ministry, the security police, the information ministry, and the small of group of advisers around President Mubarak—dominated by the shadowy figure of Omar Suleiman, the head of security—whose calls for caution in reform remain extremely influential.

It is Egypt's preoccupation with Islamic fundamentalism that has been the litmus test by which most other political decisions have been made—from aspects of foreign policy to the drawing up of university reading lists. The plight of the Copts has been obscured by the greater violence of the conflict with the Islamists. The direct and indirect power of the Islamist trend has been pervasive in deliberations over issues as diverse as organ transplants and the freedom of students to read the classics of Arabic literature. Equally pervasive, and in part connected to the growing influence of the Islamist trend across the region, has been a growing conservatism within the establishment itself. Despite associating with the forces confronting Islamism, ruling elites in Egypt, as elsewhere—in the form of ministers, influential journalists, academic pressure groups, and others—have clearly been influenced by the Islamists' campaign. This has manifested itself in a conservative backlash, to which governments have attempted to give succor while trying to contain the Islamist challenge. Reflective of this trend in Egypt is the fact that by year

2000 there were around sixty books poised for banning or already proscribed from the bookshop and course texts of the American University in Cairo (AUC), on the basis that they offend cultural sensibilities. The university is the preserve of those who can afford the high fees. A tiny minority of students, asked to read texts that have been on the AUC curriculum for decades, have led the invariably successful campaigns to have the books banned by the Ministry of Higher Education. The politics of book banning, coupled with a reactionary trend within Egyptian society that has been inspired by Islamists, has led some to conclude that Egypt's love-hate relationship with the United States lies behind this defiance of the teaching practices in what is after all the "American university."

Even so, the condition of civil liberties in Egypt is increasingly subject to the immediate political needs of the government, as it seeks to maintain stability and control through the flawed and inadequate institutions at its disposal. Chief among its fears is that the security forces, upon whom it has relied to fight the rise of Islamic militancy, will suffer severe problems of morale if they are made to answer for the routine and unpunished abuses of human rights of which they are regularly accused. Incidents like that at al-Kosheh essentially reflect the impunity of the security services, to which the rest of the government is beholden for its ultimately successful campaign against the Gama'a al-Islamiyya, Egypt's largest Islamist militant organization. However, the issue of human rights has yet to rise up the agenda within the broader context of civil liberties. The government is both reactive and proactive. Pressured by reactionaries who for different ends flaunt the threat of the Islamist bogeyman, the government is beholden to a security service that it is loath to punish for its excesses. Four officers were moved to other posts following the al-Khosheh incident. The government then decided that it would end the incident by allowing several new churches to be built in the town—after decades during which licenses for new churches had been almost routinely rejected—and then suggested that the name of el-Kosheh be changed. It suggested *al-Salam,* "peace," which was rejected by the townspeople, who instead favored *al-Mahaba,* "friendship." Neither name made much difference, as violence erupted in the town again in January 2000, forcing a long reappraisal of what lay beneath the surface. This time it appeared the violence erupted when several Muslim shopkeepers built new shops in front of shops owned by Copts. Yousry Mustapha, by then the director of EOHR, told me:

> The problem is between the citizens and the state institutions. The officers in the police station don't solve problems. So the people try to solve the problems themselves. This means that the Muslim majority can always win a fight. It is exactly the same as violence against women. People don't go to the state. The violence is because of the absence of the state, not due to the state. The police can't solve cultural and economic problems in such areas, and the violence escalated quickly.
>
> There's a problem of citizenship in society: the fact that there's no voice for the Copts except the church. They have no voice in the state. There's a big gap between the people and the state, which means that everybody reverts to family, tribe, and church.
>
> We have a very terrible bureaucratic system. They try to solve the problem through very false solutions, like changing the name of el-Kosheh.
>
> All the time we feel that we are in a religious race between Muslim and Copt. But solving the problem is a question of having civil rights and law.[11]

Egypt had experienced robust attempts by civil society groups to assert their influence over the process of changing state institutions to force them to accept that they could no longer expect to be all-powerful. But, as Diaa Rachwan, an expert on Egypt's religious affairs at the al-Ahram Centre for Political Studies, told me after the new outbreak of violence in el-Kosheh in early 2000: "There isn't a clear policy. They don't know what the best position is. The decisionmaking is paralyzed. The state for at least twenty years has refused to represent any social current. They don't have social inter-action. The ability to study situations before making a decision is something that is seriously lacking. The majority of the people in the government who work on the south are not from the south. For most people, being sent to the south is a punishment. Also, there's an absence of relations between the state and the networks of local politicians." He added: "The problem there is this weak-ness of local networks and civil society. The religious division can continue in the absence of the state."[12] Saad Eddin Ibrahim, the so-ciologist arrested in 2000 on an array of charges (see Chapter 1), cited his public response to the recurrence of violence in el-Kosheh as a reason for his subsequent arrest, detention, and trial. In a lec-ture Saad had blamed the state security for what became known as "el-Kosheh 2," listing fifty-five incidents of sectarianism and detail-ing how difficult it remained for Copts to get permission to build churches, despite assurances that licenses would be granted. "This infuriated the state security, and I began to receive death threats,"[13] Saad told me in April 2001, while awaiting his sentence. He went to see Salah Salama, the head of internal security, and reminded him that when he had been threatened by Islamists in the past, he had been offered police protection. But instead of offering Saad protection again, Salama had been told by the security chief: "'Why don't you stop infuriating the fanatics with the things you write and say, like the things you say about the Copts. Why are you concerned about the Copts?'" But when Saad was arrested, the threats stopped "as if the Islamists had gone," Saad told me. The message was clear: The threats had come from the regime all along. "Saad had the impression that he was permitted to go beyond the limit. But he couldn't," Mohamed Sid Ahmed, one of Egypt's most prominent political commentators, told me. "Saad was at the limits of the regime's capacity to tolerate, and will be given a harsh sentence and then pardoned."[14] He was right. Three years later, on March 18, 2003, Saad was acquitted of the charge of "defaming the nation" and freed, despite two previous court appearances having led to his being found guilty.

LOOKING FOR LEADERS

Saad Eddin Ibrahim's experience at the hands of a regime that once sought his advice on religious and social issues was a clear message from the regime to its critics abroad. His dual American-Egyptian nationality brought with it inevitable U.S. engagement in the whole affair. But it also brought a greater sensitivity to and resentment of that engagement. The threat that U.S. financial assistance to Egypt—which amounts to $2.1 billion annually and has reached nearly $35 billion since 1978—would be capped if Saad Eddin were not seen to have been treated correctly by the legal system, was brushed aside by the regime. The issue ultimately served to prove not only that U.S. influence, born of its financial clout and diplomatic power even with its supposed closest ally in the region, was apparently limited, but also that the assumption that U.S. influence had become entrenched was itself a chimera. Until the war in Iraq that overthrew Saddam Hussein in April 2003, U.S. attitudes had— in general—been dominated by the view that because it was a major player in the Middle East peace process, American attitudes had entered the veins of the region and that it was only a matter of time before its ideological stance on issues ranging from democracy to human rights, economic reform, and religious affairs would find currency in the region. The opposite has now become the case. Revealing this most starkly was a poll of sixteen thousand people in twenty-one countries taken in May 2003 and published on June 3, 2003, by the Washington-based Pew Research Center.[15] The Center found that, despite general acceptance that Western-style democracy of the kind espoused by the United States could work in the Middle East, anti-American feelings had ballooned across the Muslim world. Favorable ratings for the United States had fallen to 15 percent in Indonesia and to 38 percent in Nigeria, while in Jordan and Palestine the United States was favored by fewer than 10 percent of the population. In the wake of the war in Iraq, a growing number of Muslims regarded the United States as a potential military threat, while nearly half of Moroccans and Pakistanis and 71 percent of Palestinians polled said they had confidence in Osama bin Laden to "do the right thing regarding world affairs." According to the poll, Israel is the only country in the Middle East where U.S. policies are regarded as contributing to greater stability.

It is startling that the gulf between the United States and the Arab population of the Middle East could have become so wide, when the United States ought to be regarded as an ideological bastion against autocracy and corruption. Instead, these abuses of power have thrust large sections of the region's peoples into the arms of the Islamist groups that articulate most clearly the anger at the abuse of power by the region's regimes. Successive U.S. administrations have found that their association with these regimes has daubed them with the same brush as the regimes themselves. But the Pew poll also shows that the negative reputation of the United States has become widespread because of its perceived antipathy toward Muslims more generally. The extent to which the United States is regarded as a potential military threat, in light of the Iraq war, is revealing of how deep the distrust of the United States, which had already become entrenched by its one-sided support for Israel, now is. The United States is not regarded as the champion of many of the political aspirations that many Arabs nevertheless share with Americans. The kinds of societies Iraqis or Egyptians seek to build can never be created in the image of the Western-style democracy that the policymakers of the Pentagon envisaged when they were planning the overthrow of Saddam Hussein and the redrawing of the map of the Middle East. The reason for this is straightforward: The United States is not trusted, and Arabs across the region regard its relationships with the leaders of the region as substantiating their belief that it should not be trusted.

When, on August 1, 2000, *New York Times* columnist Thomas Friedman published a spoof letter from President Clinton to President Mubarak of Egypt,[16] he revealed—once again—the motivation behind U.S. policy. The letter laid bare the establishment view in the United States that—far from any intrinsic identification with the Arab world—there is really only one reason to be at all interested in the region, and that is the importance of Israel:

> Where do I start? You just arrested Saad Eddin Ibrahim, an American University of Cairo democracy specialist who has a U.S. passport and whose crime seems to be that he was working for democratic elections in Egypt. I say "seems" since you've been holding him without charges while your press smears his name. (Your press seems to be free only to spew hate at Israel or spin conspiracy theories about the U.S.) In 19 years as president of Egypt you've never visited Israel, save for Yitzhak Rabin's funeral. And you were just re-elected in a one-man election by 94 percent of the vote. Not as good as Hafez al-Assad used to get, but close.
>
> I have started to realize, Hosni, that Israel is to Egypt what oil is to Saudi Arabia—a hugely distorting factor. Ever since Camp David, we in the U.S. have judged Egypt on only one yardstick—

how nice you were to Israel. And as long as you were not totally hostile, we made excuses for you and turned a blind eye to your regime's corruption and lack of democracy. In doing that, we've done you no favors.

The U.S. role in the Israeli–Palestinian conflict, and the ways it affects the Arab world, are examined in Chapter 7. For now, what Friedman's letter revealed was the depth of the gulf that existed and exists, not between the ruler of the Arab world's largest country and the United States, but between mainstream American attitudes and Arab public opinion—the "Arab street." There are many reasons why Hosni Mubarak has only once visited Israel. One is certainly that to do so would increase the risk of his own assassination at home. A second reason is that—ultimately—Israel needs Egypt more than the other way around. Israeli leaders can make the journey, while Mubarak sends Osama al-Baz, his political adviser, or Omar Suleiman, his intelligence chief, to do the talking. No Arab leaders have ever gained anything by visiting Israel. Those that have made the trip have ultimately done so to please the United States, returning empty-handed from an Israel that seeks nothing but their acquiescence in its process of land grabbing, evictions, and the illegal occupation of Arab land. Why should Mubarak appear to condone the daylight robbery of Palestinian land?

It is in this climate of widespread Arab suspicion of Western "liberal" motives, as espoused by the United States and its mainstream media, that Arab countries have nevertheless sought to address the issues that are the heart of that liberalism. Human rights issues are central to both the Islamist and liberal agendas among Arabs across the region. But such is the complexity of the Arab relationship with the West, that it has followed paths toward reform that leave no doubt that its pace, character, and result will not build Western society in the Arab world. Thomas Friedman's criticisms of Mubarak reveal an irritation with the Egyptian leader and his regime. The readiness of such a high-profile newspaper as the *New York Times* to voice such irritation reveals how little is understood about the region. Using such a format—a spoof letter—created a sense of insult that went far beyond the ruling regime. It further alienated the human rights movement and was widely seen as an attempt to scold the Egyptians for their way of doing things. It was as if the United States generally was saying: We give you $2.1 billion in foreign aid annually, and you still don't do exactly what we tell you to do. Egypt's response has been, "Keep your money," though there is no doubt that it has benefited from this finance. Even so, it serves no Arab leader to be seen to be kowtowing to the United States, nor is it prudent to be seen to be American in one's political style. This was Saad Eddin Ibrahim's problem. His dual Egyptian-American nationality made him appear less than loyal to the ideal of Egyptianness. He spoke to an audience that barely supported him during his three-year travail with the regime—not because they disagreed with what he advocated, but because his vocabulary and manner were alien to the reality of Egypt's highly conservative society.

In Algeria, by contrast, demands for redress for crimes committed against civilians during the horrendous civil war that erupted in 1992 have been forced to the forefront.

The solemn photograph of a young man depicted against a studio backdrop is probably all that remains of Dalila Kouidri's son Jellal. The image she carries has frayed since he disappeared in 1996, but the memory she keeps is stark. Her living nightmare is shared by the families of those who have disappeared since Algeria collapsed into violence. "For me the horror is to live all these years without knowing if he is alive or dead, if he is eating, if he has clothes," Mrs. Kouidri said, unable to admit that the truth is she will probably never see her then twenty-three-year-old son again.[17]

By mid-2000 there were 7,023 disappeared being dealt with by the National Association for the Families of the Disappeared (ANFD). However, lawyers believe twenty-two thousand vanished at the hands of the Algerian government's various security forces after violence erupted. "They picked him up outside his favorite pizzeria," said Safia Fahassi, whose husband Djamil had worked at the national radio station until he disappeared in May 1995. "I thought he had been taken by one of the armed groups. But then we received an anonymous telephone call saying he had been taken by military intelligence. I think he perhaps disappeared because he was seen as a little dangerous by the state. Everybody who didn't say things in favor of the state was assumed to be against it."[18] "It all started in 1994 when Redha Malek, the former prime minister, announced that 'fear must change sides,'" said the father of a twenty-two-year-old man last seen in 1997. He was referring to the infamous statement by the former Algerian prime minister, who had given the green light for the armed forces to create the same sense of terror as that being created by the Islamist opposition groups. "That was when they began taking people away. Now, we are the living dead. It's a suspended death. We are dangling. My wife has more or less abandoned our other children, in the search for information about our son."[19] he said. As he talked, caring little whether his comments were being noted down by the policemen who accompany all foreign journalists, a tiny, aged woman arrived from the eastern city of Constantine. "My husband died as a martyr in the war against the French. Now, I have sold the house to get the money to look after my six grandchildren. My son was an accountant, and he was taken away six years ago. I am sure he did nothing wrong; and if he did, let him go before the court. All I want to know is if he is alive or dead," she said.[20]

The ANFD persisted with campaigns and sit-ins with such determination that the authorities have had little choice but to allow it to operate, despite curtailing its activities and ignoring its accusations of state brutality. "We know who the authors of this situation are. It's a daily nightmare. Here, in this room, we can show our tears, but most people are too frightened even to cry in their sadness," said Layla Ighil, the ANFD president.[21] The pressure the organization has built up has exposed the rigidity of political life. Most striking has been the sidelining of the issue by most news outlets, many of which are either loosely attached to factions within the security establishment or allied to political parties. "The disappearance of people amounts to a crime against the citizenry. There is a group of criminals who are exercising public functions in the Algerian state, whom the state is protecting. The state institutions have the mandate to protect us. Instead, they have stolen our children," said Mahmoud Khelili, the ANFD's lawyer.[22]

Change without upheaval in countries that know they need it but are facing stagnation and autocracy can only be brought about if those in power discern that their survival depends upon it. No amount of foreign pressure has yet been successful in bringing this process about, hence the invasion of Iraq: an act of frustration based on a series of half-truths from the U.S. and U.K. governments. In Morocco, the process of loosening the shackles of royal domination has been due to the realization by the monarchy that its claims of popularity could unravel. The cruelty of King Hassan was more subtle and calculating than the clumsy repression practiced in Egypt. But the personalization of his rule meant that when his son Mohammed became king on July 23, 1999, the wide abuse of power that had so characterized Hassan's rule could be addressed by seeking to resolve the issues that were inextricably linked to Hassan himself. Burying Hassan would mean burying the past itself, as well as all the excesses and cruelty that went with it. For King Mohammed, however, the challenge is to shed the past without shedding the power that went with it.

Shortly after Mohammed became king, a photographic essay about the Moroccan monarch appeared in the French magazine *Paris Match*. Among several large color portraits was one of the king in jeans and leather jacket striding with his friends through a Paris park, dark glasses covering his eyes, a packet of Marlboros in his hand. The image was clear: This was the new Morocco—young, fashionable, and Westernized. The belief was that by changing the image, the reality behind it could be seen to have altered, and the monarchy could be portrayed as moving with the times in a manner that would help retain its relevance. "There's a new concept of authority, and a new rapprochement with the people and an appreciation of civil society. It's necessary that the state involve itself in the situation of the underprivileged," Hassan Aourid, the young king's spokesman and adviser, told me in December 1999. "We are in the process of turning the page, without *complexes*. There were the disappeared. The state will compensate people who were victims. If we look too much at the past there is the danger of creating revenge."[23] Aourid sought to portray the moves made to resolve the human rights issues accumulated by Hassan as consistent with the dead monarch's own strategy. It is true that Hassan had freed political prisoners from Tazmamart and had allowed the Oufkir family a growing degree of liberty (as discussed in Chapter 1), until they were finally free to travel abroad. In October 1999, Ibrahim Serfaty, the leader of Morocco's leftist party who had been jailed for sixteen years before being forced into exile in 1991, was allowed to return. Then, on November 9, Driss Basri, the interior minister who had been the architect of King Hassan's repression, was fired. Two weeks later, nine members of the family of Mehdi Ben Barka were allowed to return to Morocco. In October 1965, Ben Barka, a vocal critic of the king who had fled to France, was kidnapped from the terrace of a Parisian café and never seen again. A French court later found General Oufkir, the interior minister who would later die after

President Bill Clinton with Prince Moulay Rachid of Morocco.

attempting to seize power, responsible for Ben Barka's kidnapping and death.

The freed prisoners of Tazmamart are now rebuilding their lives. The Oufkir family has steadily done the same. But the cruelty King Hassan meted out to them was never likely to stir popular feelings. The young cadets sent to rot in the High Atlas did not generally identify with the aspirations of the socialist political prisoners incarcerated in better conditions at Khenitra for equally long periods, and the Oufkir family were seen as a part of the elite, whose nightmarish story was ultimately a tale of palace intrigue that was unlikely to affect the lives of ordinary people. These were King Hassan's personal victims, people who were an embarrassment or threat or were paying the price of betrayal. Their very existence was emblematic of how far apart were the two worlds of Morocco: the royal court and the reality of daily life. "The new king is completely at one with the changes that are taking place. He does represent hope, by taking on the issues that trouble the people. Now, the question of the political prisoners is definitely finished. There should be no settling of accounts," Raouf Oufkir, son of the dead general, told me in 1999.[24] It was a view shared by Mohamed Rais, an army colonel who had been one of the organizers of the attack on King Hassan at Skhirat, and who had been incarcerated at Tazmamart: "It's all finished with the death of Hassan," he said. "The new king wants to change Morocco. He wants to lift the taboos. Morocco has changed. The mentality has changed. People speak. They won't accept this kind of thing anymore. The young king has understood that it's necessary to win people over."[25]

SECRET WARS

The issues facing King Mohammed are those that Hassan's autocratic power allowed him to keep at arm's length. Just as he had the power to devise the punishment of those who crossed him, so he had the power to give them their freedom when he chose. He had called Tazmamart a "secret garden," which every king has the right to own, he claimed. But the real issues facing Morocco as a country are those Hassan could not resolve by a switch in personality. Whether there is any profound change in Morocco will be seen in the way that the monarchy addresses the growing Islamist challenge to its rule and in how it eventually resolves questions over its claim to the Western Sahara, the territory to the south of Morocco seized by the kingdom when Spain decolonized in 1975. For Morocco, the loss of the Western Sahara is unthinkable. The so-called Green March led by King Hassan when he occupied the territory was his attempt to unify Moroccans around him after more than a decade of listless rule and several attempted coups. Hassan needed credibility and to stamp his authority on the country. Guided by Driss Basri, Hassan encouraged thousands of Moroccans to relocate to the territory, lured by cheap land and financial grants, as Spanish forces retreated. A resistance force emerged—the *Frente Popolare de Seguir el-Hamra et Rio de Oro*, known as the Polisario Front—to confront the Moroccan occupation on behalf of the native Sahraoui people in the territory. Supported by Algeria, the Polisario launched guerrilla raids into the territory, to which Morocco sent thousands of troops, until a stalemate was reached. But even with the death of King Hassan, the issue has not become any less significant as a source of national pride for Morocco, whose territorial claim to the area is part of a much wider claim to land extending into Mauritania and as far to the southeast as Mali.

In the dim light of a backroom office near the main square in the Western Sahara provincial capital of Laayoune, a table strewn with the faded photographs of 526 people who had disappeared without a trace in the territory between 1975 and 1993 is a reminder that the country remains haunted by and vulnerable to the legacy of past abuses. "We are the disappeared who came back," a Sahraoui former detainee told me. "We know the others are gone forever, but we can still dream that one day they will come through that door." He continued:

> I was in prison from 1986 to 1991. My family had no information. My parents lived forever in a nightmare. I have nightmares. Every day my hands were tied behind my back. My eyes blindfolded. The day I disappeared the guards said: You have come here to die, not to live. They said that we were killers; that we weren't civilians. I had prepared a list of the disappeared, and that was why I had disappeared myself. On 30/12/1987 my friend was beaten to death by a guard as he lay beside me. Now, we are fighting for our friends who died with us. The people of Tazmamart received Dh5,000. The Sahraouis have nothing. We can't share the same flag and the same government with the Moroccans.[26]

For the Sahraoui activists in Laayoune, the arrival of the new king did little to satisfy their demands for either a resolution to the conflict or recognition of the injustices done to those who had disappeared: "It's not just a question of changing one king for another, or that Morocco is a country where there's no democracy and where there's a totalitarian monarchy. The Sahara problem is historical," said another of the Sahraouis who was hoping for redress. "Morocco is opening the human rights issue in a way that is negative for the Sahraouis. There were heavy prison sentences for demonstrators. The Moroccan authorities say that all movements here are political movements. So the penalties are very heavy. The torturers have been pardoned, and the violation of human rights hasn't changed since the end of Basri. There have continued to be arbitrary arrests and detentions."[27]

The government has yet to provide a full account of what happened to any of the hundreds of Sahraouis missing since the late 1970s. Moreover, the robust debates over human rights taking place elsewhere in the country have yet to apply to the thorny question of control of the territory. A UN plan to hold a referendum among the Sahraoui, allowing them to vote for independence or unity with Morocco, is now more than a decade behind schedule. United Nations officials regard any shifts in the search for a solution as ultimately dictated by the fragile relations between Morocco and Algeria, whose senior army officers are keen to retain a state of tension with Morocco, by supporting the Algeria-based Polisario Front. "In the Maghreb there is still a Berlin Wall, and these past ten years have been a total failure in terms of seeing a change in the political environment. The expectations were probably too high. These things, which are so entrenched in the political life, can't be changed just because of a change of political leadership," a Moroccan official told me.[28] The Polisario Front remains determined to see the referendum held, in the expectation that it would win in a fair vote. Its Algerian backers remain equally determined that the vote should go ahead. The growing concern now is that if Morocco were to lose, it would not accept the result and would refuse to withdraw from the territory in which it now has stationed up to 100,000 troops.

"There's no Morocco without the Sahara. Nor has there ever been a Sahraoui people," Allal Saadaoui, the governor of Laayoune, told me in November 1999, in a statement strangely reminiscent of the early Israeli view that there was "no such thing as a Palestinian people." "There's not a single Moroccan who wants to lose one square meter of this land. So, the solution is very simple: The Sahara must remain Moroccan."[29]

The sensitivity of the authorities to any pressure for a change in the government's attitude—and therefore to any suggestion that the monarchy had in any way shifted its position on the issue—was starkly revealed when the country's leading independent newspaper, Le Journal, published an interview with Mohamed Abdelaziz, the Polisario leader. The newspaper was impounded, and two executives from the state-owned 2M television channel, which showed the newspaper's front page, were fired. The ban flew in the face of much that had been expected of King Mohammed, and even palace officials admitted that the measures had been excessive. What the response showed, however, was that even without Driss Basri in charge, the authorities were not prepared to tolerate negative publicity over issues that directly affected royal rule. King Mohammed cannot afford to be the king who lost the Western Sahara. To secure it, Morocco has routinely added thousands of names to the list of potential voters in the UN-sponsored referendum, to ensure that a vote—if it ever happens, which is highly unlikely—will go Morocco's way. Thousands of these voters have been rejected by the United Nations and have gone through a tortuous appeals process, which is years behind schedule. Morocco's aim, ultimately, is to outlast both the United Nations and the Polisario, exhaust all patience, and force the United Nations to give up and the Polisario to capitulate and join Morocco, with promises that Sahraoui rights will be respected. The Moroccan strategy is a clear sign of how fragile the monarchy really is: It can only retain control over the issue of the Western Sahara by refusing to apply the modernizing outlook it seeks to project in other areas. King Mohammed has overseen the resolution of some aspects of his father's cruel abuse of power, but in the end he is faced with the fact that the Moroccan monarchy is an autocracy dependent upon a mixture of myth, fear, and the claim of religious divination—the Commander of the Faithful—that cannot change without losing its authority. The Western Sahara is an issue the monarchy can keep at bay for a few more years, denying the inevitable day of reckoning. It can do so because there is no challenge to its position coming from within Morocco itself.

Where it must tread the reformist path far more carefully is in the face of the challenges that question the religious authority of the monarch, which emanate from *al-Adl wal-Ihsane*, the Justice and Charity Islamist movement, whose supporters are in the midst of Moroccan society.

"We are not utopian. Nor are we idealists. There wasn't perfection during the time of the Prophet. In fact there were many imperfections. But even with them there can be a workable society, with all its imperfections,"[30] Nadia Yassine, the outspoken daughter and key confidante of the *al-Adl wal-Ihsane* leader Sheikh Abdesalam Yassine, had told me when we first met in July 1996.[31] She sat demurely on a carved and cushioned armchair in the corner of the sitting room of the small groundfloor apartment where she lives with her husband and children in a district of the Moroccan town of Sale.[32] "The world is becoming foolish. It's going too fast, and if it's not slowed down there will be fewer and fewer people who can keep up with it. Economic inequality is monstrous. At the same time, we want to return to our spirituality. The Islamic movement is essentially spiritual. And the great chaos we are living in is essentially spiritual. We don't know who we are. Are we Arab, African, or members of a deprived economic group? There are social causes. Poverty is a determinant. But the social situation doesn't explain the Islamist influence, because the middle classes are in the movement. It is because religion alone can give people a new life."[33]

Nadia Yassine was at that time living in the twilight world of the Moroccan Islamist movement. Her father had been under house arrest—in a house a few muddy streets from his daughter's—since 1990. Late one evening in December 1995, outside a newspaper shop on a near-deserted street off African Unity Square in central Rabat, an aging Mercedes Benz stopped beside the postbox agreed to as a meeting place from which I would make my first contact with the clandestine movement. Through the car's open window the middle-aged driver asked me my name, opened the door, then beckoned me in. We drove through the elegant Moroccan city, out past the great walls, south toward the new suburbs that line the road to Casablanca. In a modern apartment *al-Adl wa'l Ihsane's* official spokesman, Fathallah Arsalan, waited in a brightly lit room lined on three sides by a modest *salon Marocain*, the embroidered settee that serves as seating for guests and beds for children and has a symbolic importance as the first item of furniture bought for a new home.

"Our current strategy is bound up in safeguarding our existence. Ensuring our existence is our man preoccupation, to ensure our position in the political life of the country," he began by saying. "We are not authorized to play our role in social life. We are waiting for the day when we will be able to play our role. We are now preparing for that period, by educating people, and propagating our vision secretly, by publishing books and secretly circulating them, and videos of Abdesalam Yassine, at meetings in people's houses. We cover the entire country, and we're present in all social groups. The loss of confidence among people with regard to the political life means that people are spontaneously coming to us."[34] The organization was closely watched by the Moroccan security services. Its leaders had their telephones tapped and were denied passports to travel, even to participate in the Muslim pilgrimage to Mecca, the *haj*. "We constitute a threat, not because we advocate violence. We are against violence," Arsalan told me. "But we constitute a threat because we are popular. The state of siege we face, and the trials [of our supporters], have given us publicity. We think that the situation will become truly explosive, and everybody will become desperate for change."[35]

Dominating the strategy of *al-Adl wa'l Ihsane* is the need to forge a new religiously inspired identity without directly confronting the king's claim to being the rightful leader of the country's Muslims as a direct descendant of the Prophet Mohammed and bearer of the title *Emir al-Mumineen:* Commander of the Faithful. "If he was only head of state, that would be fine," said Arsalan. "But as Commander of the Faithful there are many contradictions. He doesn't apply true Islam because he doesn't apply the *sharia*, and he doesn't give an example of the Islamic way of life. His hypocrisy is visible. He maintains non-Islamic traditions."[36] Under King Hassan, contradictions were the essence of Moroccan political life. Nadia Yassine was able to visit her father in his home, despite his house arrest: "Morocco is a great waiting room," she had told me. "The politics of the *makhzen*[37] is always to do what is unplanned. The most successful repressive regime is here, because it's a very intelligent repression. It's very original and successful."[38] For the Islamists the ultimate goals of the regime, as much as the goals of reform, were unclear, confusing, and ill-defined in the Moroccan context. "The Islamists don't have a significant role in Morocco because we are not free. If the state allowed us to operate, then that would change," said Mustapha Ramid, an Islamist lawyer who has since become a legislator in the country's national assembly and has defended Islamic activists charged with organizing activities on behalf of *al-Adl wa'l Ihsane*, told me in 1995.[39] "The state controls religion. The authorities have left the Islamists between the earth and the sky. And the situation for the Islamists is worse than that of the political opposition parties.[40] The Islamists are marginalized, so we are not influential in society in a way that is [practically] effective. Even so, the Islamists are present in all areas, while the left-wing parties have a very limited presence, and the right-wing parties have no presence at all among the population. The government has no solutions regarding the political and economic crisis, and we Islamists can arrive at our goals, because of the force of Islam. Islam will find its origins."[41]

It is the apparent reluctance of Morocco's main Islamic movement to stir up their politically stagnant country that has *allowed* the ruling elite to treat them with caution and a degree of restraint. "We are the only [real] opposition in Morocco. And we are silent," Nadia Yassine said. "We can't do much else. [King] Hassan II doesn't want my father to be a martyr. He had the intelligence to understand that a martyr would be much more influential."[42] So, Morocco remains what she aptly described as a waiting room. The question therefore arises, what is being awaited? Explanations of what may happen in the future were more pertinent among Islamists within the country, even those not associated with *al-Adl wa'l Ihsane*, than among any of the secular parties, whose role was essentially to give a pluralist gloss to monarchical absolutism. "Public opinion isn't politicized. So the political parties don't represent public opinion. They represent the political elites of Casablanca, Fez, and Rabat,"[43] Mohammed Yatim, president of the moderate Islamist organization the *Mouvement de la Renaissance et de Renouveau*,[44] which functions mainly as an editorial body for the newspaper *al-Arraya, The Flag,* told me at that time. "The [secular political] parties don't have ideology. They have only regional and personal allegiances. These lie at the heart of the political crisis in

Morocco. These parties haven't brought the masses on board. And the process has excluded the Islamists. There's no stability without mass participation in politics, and meanwhile there is general discontent. We will see how it develops. Tomorrow, or the day after."[45]

During the declining years of King Hassan's rule, however, Morocco's political stagnation was less of a problem for the Islamist movement than it first appeared. The absence of immediate change, the apparent reticence of *al-Adl wa'l Ihsane* to force a change in its own status, and the readiness with which its leaders were prepared to await that change at a point in the future were all elements of a decidedly long-term strategy, derived from the basic assumption that change was inevitable. "Those who are opposed to change are simply afraid to lose their privileges. That is why they tend to equate change with heresy. . . . The Prophet Muhammad always looked to the future and very rarely looked back on the past. It is even said that, when he walked, he always looked ahead and never turned his head," said Mahdi Elmandjra, a professor of social science at Rabat's Mohamed V University and one of the Muslim world's leading writers on the future of Islam and its relations with the non-Muslim world. "When young Muslims return to their cultural sources, it is because they are seeking guidance from their endogenous values. The future that the Arab-Islamic world is looking for depends on the revival of Islam in its innovative acceptation, not an Islam of blind imitation which led to the fall of a once brilliant civilization."[46]

The death of King Hassan was the moment *al-Adl wal-Ihsane* had been awaiting, though it remained secretive about what it really expected to happen. "There are no real changes. The Makhzen can't change overnight," Nadia Yassine told me in February 2000,[47] shortly after her father had written a thirty-five-page open letter to the new king, in which he openly doubted the readiness of the *makhzen*—the political elite—to allow the new king to innovate, saying "we cannot expect to counterbalance sly old foxes with innocent goodwill."[48] He called upon King Mohammed to use the royal fortune to pay off the country's $20 billion foreign debt, invest in projects for the poor, and prove that his appointment marked a real break with the past. "The system can't change. To change it's a matter of revolving the pillars," Nadia Yassine said, continuing:

It's not a question of joining in with the *makhzen* system. We are in favor of political contest. But in Morocco there is a political game, not a political life. The way we could play political suicide would be to play the game of the *makhzen*. If there were elections tomorrow, all the people in Morocco would say they are in favor of the monarchy. Our view is that in Islam there is no monarchy. Mohammed VI can't get out of the protocol of the *makhzen* without losing his own status.

We refuse to enter into the political game. But I think the Islamic movement will become more and more involved in the first rank [of political life]. Our aim is to inform the people. Why? To forge a Morocco that is informed and is in touch with its spirit and which is able to think freely. We are against violence. And when you are against violence you have to be patient. We are not in a hurry. We know that we are a minority. We are in favor of multilateralism, democracy, and transparency. But we are against secularism.[49]

But three months later it was the game of the *makhzen* that Sheikh Yassine had little choice but to enter into when the authorities decided they could afford to release him from house arrest on May 17, 2000. Stepping serenely into the sunlight of the street outside his home, the sheikh launched a new phase in the opening of political life in his country by praying at his local mosque—which he had visited only once previously during his eleven years under house arrest. The following day Ahmed Midaoui, the interior minister, said he was free to go where he liked. "We are happy, because it's the first time for so long. The Friday prayer is crucial to all of us," Nadia Yassine told me as we walked with her father to the mosque. "But really we think it's another sign that the authorities are in the process of tightening the screws on all of society. It's a strategy of diversion: to allow some freedoms as a way of preventing future freedoms."[50] Outside the Ben Said mosque there was a heavy-smoking huddle of plainclothes policemen. Chanting boomed from the speakers perched on the crenellated top of the mosque's tall, square minaret. Giggling children dressed in ragged tracksuits played in the courtyard until they were chased away by the policemen, who also took down the names of all the foreigners—mostly journalists—present. "Sheikh Yassine, he's very rich, like all Islamists," said the policeman who took my name. "He has a farm and lots of property. You can quote me if you want." A few stooped old men lingered at the gate to the courtyard hoping for alms, until they were swept aside by the tide of eager young militants and sagely elders surrounding the sheikh as he left.

Among analysts of all political shades there was and remains the growing concern that unless the population starts to feel tangible results from the new political direction being sought by King Mohammed, the high expectations of the new monarch will turn to disappointment and strengthen Islamist support against a background of economic problems. Persistent drought and the slow pace of economic reform failed throughout the 1990s to break a cycle of low and sometimes zero economic growth followed by years of high growth, largely dependent upon good rain. "The problem for the king is that there isn't a government capable of carrying out what he wants. He doesn't have the money, nor does he have the people," said Ahmed el-Kohen, a professor of sociology at Casablanca University and a strong critic of both the secular opposition and Abdesalam Yassine. "Yassine is fanatical and doctrinaire. He does think that only the extremist path is the profitable one, and he is against compromise. So, short-term politics doesn't interest him." He continued:

The traditional political parties have forgotten what it is that makes them political parties. They aren't in the poor areas helping people. But the Islamists are doing this. The real militants of al-Adl wal-Ihsane number 20,000. But their force lies in their energy.

Morocco is in a phase of change. The provincial governors were given the guidelines by Basri. Now that is no longer happening. Hassan had mastered the political control of the parties. The opposition parties are now orphaned. They don't know what to do, and there is a young king who wants to give them power. Meanwhile, the masses are angry, and the Islamists are in a position where they can scoop up this anger. I think it's a crisis that will last another ten years.[51]

Despite being well-organized, *al-Adl wal-Ihsane*'s aims vis-à-vis Morocco's political life initially focused on drawing in a wide range of opponents of the traditional political elite. "Morocco has always had a political void, which has left the field open to the Islamists," said Mohamed Darif, an expert on the Moroccan Islamist movement. "The rise of Islam should be placed within the context of a crisis of identity. The social and economic crises and the absence of democracy have contributed to the birth of opposition movements. But it doesn't explain their ideological color. It's the same social and economic crises as in the 1960s, which then gave birth to the radical left. Why is it now a religious movement, not a civil movement? The Islamists' support is among people who have not benefited from the fruits. The administration is largely francophone. There is a Westernized elite which has excluded everybody. It's the revenge of history, that the particular kind of opposition has now emerged with the Islamist color."[52]

For King Mohammed, the goal has been to try to build—and rebuild—a direct link between monarch and people, as a means of confronting the growing voices of dissent that have emerged from outside the *makhzen*, and over which the traditional power structure has little influence, as a leading industrialist told me: "The poorest Moroccan no longer accepts the injustices of yesterday. There's an awakening. There's no longer that inhibition. People are not any longer accepting to live as before. Mohammed must assert his power within the *makhzen*. The kings of Morocco aren't automatically accepted in power. They have to assert their power. Hassan was contested."[53]

The success of rebuilding the frayed strands of Moroccan society on the basis of mutual interests rather than royal autocracy, and thereby distancing himself from the brutal truth of his father's legacy, will depend upon how successfully King Mohammed retains acceptance of the monarchy's role while also reducing its oppressive influence over everyday life: Will Mohammed's reformism deem the monarchy itself unnecessary? Quite possibly, though a popular attachment to the fragile myth of tradition is likely to sustain his credibility, lingering as it does in the minds of those with no influence over the elite but who, like Aisha d'Afailal as she smiles out of the cold gloom of her casbah house near the square where the villains of Tetouan used to be hanged, remain part of the royal firmament. When we first met in March 2000, d'Afailal was enjoying a resurgence of the fame she once had as the favorite cook of Morocco's first king, Mohammed V. In October 1999, his grandson Mohammed VI had broken a thirty-year royal absence from the north of the country by visiting Tetouan, the Spanish- and Arabic-speaking town that for his father Hassan had been the bastion of opposition to his French- and Arabic-speaking rule ever since he had been sent to suppress a rebellion in the north soon after independence in 1960. Repairing the rift was seen as a priority for the new king and as essential to revitalizing the country's economic prospects owing to the impact on the rest of the country of the neglect of the north. "King Mohammed especially liked the *bastilla*," said d'Afailal, referring to a pastry dish filled with almonds and chicken.[54] After eating her *bastilla* during his visit to Tetouan, he had invited Aisha to cook for him at the royal palace in Rabat. The cultural division between north and south extended to the food: in the northern part of the country, *bastilla* is a sweet dish, covered in sugar and lemon; farther south it is a savory dish. Throughout Hassan's rule, Aisha was never invited to cook northern sweet *bastilla* in the royal kitchen. But that changed when Mohammed succeeded Hassan. Nevertheless, the power he is seeking to build is rooted in foundations that are likely to be far more fragile than those he inherited, as the future of both Morocco and the wider Arab world come to be determined increasingly by events both in the region and the wider world over which its leaders have diminishing influence. The divisive impact of these global issues will eventually force the region's leaders to choose whether it is the aspirations of their own people they should represent, or those of a region whose future development and prosperity are dependent on diluting extremism, promoting harmony, and creating democracy. As anger and frustration have grown, the region's leaders appear to have little choice but to try to keep the lid on an explosive combination of circumstances. It remains to be seen whether any of them can take the lead in finding solutions. But few are likely to try until there is a marked change for the better in the one area whose crisis affects them all: Palestine.

6

ROADS TO JERUSALEM

ISRAEL AND PALESTINE

We must do everything to insure they never return. The old will die and the young will forget.

—David Ben Gurion, Israel's first prime minister, speaking of the Palestinians forced to live as refugees, 1969[1]

"PEACE. PEACE," YELLED HODA KHALIL. "WITH THEIR TONGUES the Israelis say they want peace, but their actions are different. Treachery is something in their blood. They talk peace, and then they do something different," she said, tears welling up in her large eyes.[2] Her fury rose and she talked again of the sister she never knew, gripping the back of her aging mother's chair in the hot sitting room of their home in the Egyptian village of Bahr el-Bakr. She cried for her sister, while her mother wept for her dead daughter, a six-year-old when five bombs were dropped from an Israeli aircraft onto the school at Bahr el-Bakr at 9:00 A.M. on April 8, 1970. Nineteen children died when the school roof fell in and crushed them. A few days earlier I had not heard of Bahr el-Bakr, the River of Cows as it is called in English. It is deep in the Nile delta, down long, straight roads lined by eucalyptus trees, which cross the canals that feed Egypt's breadbasket. Beyond the town of Zagazig, the road leads toward the northeast, toward the Suez Canal and Sinai. In this area, between the 1967 Arab–Israeli war that brought Israel deep into Egyptian territory with the seizure of the Sinai and the 1973 war that saw Egypt send thousands of troops into the captured desert in a surprise crossing of the canal that eventually led to Israel's withdrawal nine years later, a low-level war continued between the major conflicts. Throughout the period 1967–1973, Israeli fighter jets fought with what remained of Egypt's air force after much of it had been destroyed in 1967, and the skies above Bahr el-Bakr were one of the battlegrounds.

My journey to the town had taken much longer than the hours it took to drive there from my home in Cairo. Bahr el-Bakr was where a journey into what I had hoped would be the heart of at least one part of the Arab–Israeli conflict would reach not only an end but a conclusion. It had begun when I was sitting with a friend, an Egyptian lawyer, at a pizzeria in Cairo. We talked about Israel and the peace treaty it had signed with Egypt on March 26, 1979, twenty years before. In passing I asked him and his wife, an anthropologist, to dinner. The Israeli ambassador to Cairo would also be there. My friend's reaction was swift, and angry. He had been for dinner at my house numerous times, but this time no. He did not want to meet the ambassador, and would never do so. Aside from the political implications of somebody from a distinguished Egyptian family meeting with the Israeli ambassador, his reaction was personal, and I could feel his sense of insult; I felt apologetic, and we moved on to other subjects. The ambassador came for dinner, and I was left to consider whether I had any real idea of the true nature of the conflict that boils between Israel and its neighbors. I realized, despite my efforts to see through the bias in the Western media of which I was reluctantly a part, I had not even begun to scratch the surface. Over time, I came to realize that the conflict drives to the heart of what it is to be an Arab.

THE IRON WALL

Raouf Nasmi is an Arab hero, an Egyptian Christian who writes newspaper columns in Cairo under the name Omar Mahjoub. In 1967, while Egypt's ill-prepared army was being trounced as Israel seized the Sinai Desert, he assembled a team of doctors to help the wounded Arabs. His valiant gesture led him into the inner circle of Yasser Arafat's Fatah movement within the Palestinian Liberation Organization. He has remained on close terms with them ever since. On the wall of his office in the al-Arab library on Cairo's Kasr al-Aini street was a photograph of Khalil al-Wazir, better known as Abu Jihad. The PLO's head of operations in the West Bank had been assassinated by Israel in Tunis on April 16, 1988, and took pride of place on Raouf Nasmi's wall. Nasmi had been close to Abu Jihad, but eleven years later he was sanguine: "No Arab is speaking about cleansing the Israeli people. Israel is a state, which has given us Israelis, half of whom are not Zionists. Those who are not, will go on living with us. The others have a choice, of living with us or not," he told me. "What lies in our Arab conscience is the old history, which is now driving us and them back toward the need for coexistence. But I don't think Israelis trust anybody: not Muslims, not Christians, not even Jews. Mistrust is a characteristic."[3]

Nasmi is a Copt but, he said, "a Muslim by culture." How can such complexity become a part of the intricate pattern of relations

Palestinian leader Yasser Arafat (front center) accompanied by President Ben Ali of Tunisia (front right) and President Suleiman Demirel of Turkey (front left).

that one day might sow the seeds of an accommodation between Israel and its Arab neighbors? The conflict—the *intifada* or uprising—that had preceded the peace accord that was agreed to in Oslo in 1991 and was reignited following deliberate provocation by the then Israeli opposition leader and now Prime Minister Ariel Sharon in 2000, will only be fully addressed when the reality of the Middle East is a part of the peace deal. Arab Israelis, Palestinian Christians, and Oriental as opposed to European Ashkenazi Jews, are part of an equation reduced to the two elements: Jew and Arab. Russian Jews, Jewish fundamentalists, American Jewish settlers, and Muslim extremists are all parts of the complexity, but none are really part of the negotiating equation. "The basic principles of Jewish fundamentalism are the same as those found in other religions: restoration and survival of the 'pure' and pious religious community that presumably existed in the past," write Israel Shahak and Norton Mezvinsky, two Jewish authors, one Israeli the other American.[4] To create God's country on earth is not a far cry from the demands of Muslim fundamentalists. The problem is the land: For Israelis and Palestinians it is the same strip of land between the Mediterranean Sea and the Jordan River.

"The Palestinians have learned through agonies and failures that their only way to get redress for the historical injustice committed against them is not to eliminate Israel," Tahseen Bashir told me.[5] For much of the 1970s, Bashir had been the spokesman for Anwar al-Sadat, the Egyptian president who in 1979 had reached a peace agreement with Israel and in doing so had profoundly reshaped the political map of the region. Bashir's role had been to explain and justify to a skeptical Arab world the policy that resulted in Egypt's isolation from other Arab states and Sadat's assassination on October 6, 1981, by Muslim fundamentalists opposed to a deal with Israel. "Elimination is not doable. But to get along with Israel. This will give them an intermediate position. That's in many ways better then putting their stake against Israel. This is the working assumption. But even so, the most profoundly liberal of Zionists have not come to terms with what to do with the Palestinians. They are keen to come to peace with every Arab country, but not the Palestinians," Bashir told me.[6]

Acceptance of—or perhaps resignation to—the practical necessity of a peace deal has become entrenched within a section of the Arab world. As Bashir said: "Sadat wanted to take the yoke off Egypt" by coming to an agreement. The presence of Israel could not be ignored. There was a need—forced upon the Arabs by Israeli military superiority and the U.S. support it received—to realize that there was little choice but to accept Israel's existence. But still the issue of negotiated settlements remains more than just one of political-military facts on the ground. For Raouf Nasmi, the land rather than the cultural variety emerged as the source of conflict only when politics shattered a historical Muslim–Jewish coexistence, when Israeli claims to the entirety of Jerusalem succeeded in wresting from Muslim hands the third holiest site in Islam. Access to the land implies access to Islam's cultural heritage, with the one being dependent upon the other, and both dependent on Israel and its ally, the United States. They must recognize the full national rights of the Palestinians and allow them to become the Arab and Muslim guardians of those aspects of Islamic culture and religion that control over territory would imply: elements crystallized in the Palestine National Council's "Declaration of Independence," issued at the height of the Palestinian *intifada* in 1988, which opened:

> Palestine, the Land of the three monotheistic faiths, is where the Palestinian Arab people was born, on which it grew, developed and excelled. The Palestinian people was never separated from or diminished in its integral bonds with Palestine. Thus the Palestinian Arab people ensured for itself an everlasting union between itself, its land and its history.[7]

Throughout the troubled decade or more of negotiations that have taken place since Israel was forced to the negotiating table in Madrid on October 30, 1991, the same issue has remained: "The central problem is the official Israeli refusal to recognize or deal with the fact of Palestinian nationalism," the Palestinian-American writer Edward Said wrote in 1992.[8] Despite recognition of the Palestinian Liberation Organization (PLO) as the representative of the Palestinian people,[9] Israel's plans for the West Bank have betrayed its real attitudes toward Palestinian statehood and thereby have implied its attitude toward the idea of Palestinian nationhood, nationalism, and identity. The brutal frankness of Israeli thinking has never been in doubt, as Ben-Gurion made clear long ago:

> If I were an Arab leader, I would never sign an agreement with Israel. It is normal; we have taken their country. It is true God

promised it to us, but how could that interest them? Our God is not theirs. There has been Anti-Semitism, the Nazis, Hitler, Auschwitz, but was that their fault? They see but one thing: we have come and we have stolen their country. Why would they accept that?[10]

As the most brutal expression of this attitude—in my view, often more than even the armed response to unrest—Israeli settlement building, and the expansion of existing settlements, has continued throughout the years of negotiations. Every new illegal Israeli home has either driven another Palestinian from his land or confirmed in the minds of Palestinians that while on the one hand Israel may be talking, it is only prepared to do so as a smokescreen behind which its colonial land grab may persist. Within mainstream Israeli opinion there is no acceptance of the right of the Palestinians to have a self-governing state. This denial is not necessarily the result of a belief that peoples do not have the right to have states. It is the result of a belief that the Palestinians do not have a right to have a state on land to which Israel either lays claim or in which it retains an interest on the basis that such a Palestinian state may impinge on Israel itself. While extremist prime ministers such as Benjamin Netanyahu routinely provoked Palestinian ire by referring to the area occupied by Israel as Judea and Samaria rather than the West Bank, others simply saw, and still see, the loss of the territory as a security issue. The failure has been to create a dispensation whereby the cultural coexistence—which survived for thousands of years before Israel was created in 1948, though with the inevitable crises and violence along the way with which all history is marked—is not dependent upon the physical control of the land upon which that coexistence is taking place. Is political power over territory the necessary prerequisite for assuring the cultural freedom both communities demand?

"If we allowed a Palestinian state to be created, the only thing it would produce would be the total destruction of Israel," David Bar Illan, spokesman for former Israeli prime minister Benjamin Netanyahu, told me. "This really is giving the Sudetenland to Hitler. You can have peace with the Palestinians without giving them any part of Jerusalem. Anything outside the municipal boundaries of Jerusalem would be acceptable."[11] The evocation of Jewish suffering under the Nazis slipped off Bar Illan's tongue with an ease that reduced the horrors of the worst crime humanity has ever committed to the status of a political game. For most Arabs, Nazis mean very little, as they are a part of a European history and culture from which European and American Jews like Bar Illan were transplanted into the Middle East. The Nazi past is evoked for the benefit of European journalists, who can perhaps be made to swallow the idea that the Arab attitude toward Israelis somehow resembles that of the Germany of Adolf Hitler, which it does not.

"Under a certain situation there will always be the threat of annihilation,"[12] Pinchas Wallerstein, spokesman of the Israeli settler community in the West Bank, told me, continuing:

Very few Israelis like the peace agreement with Egypt. It's there, but it can change if the leadership changes. There's not a democratic government there. There exists a very deep fear by the Israeli population of the Arab population. But I definitely believe in a dialogue. Before the Intifada I had many many meetings with them.

The optimal situation would be one where there was no "permanent status." There would be *de facto* peace between the Israelis and the Palestinians. No one believed in the permanent status situation. Definitely, it won't work. The moment that it's clear to the Palestinians that the Jewish population is staying here for good, there will be a status quo of peace.[13]

We were sitting in the living room of one of the neat houses among the well-watered gardens of Kibbutz Ofra in the occupied West Bank, as he told me: "It's clear that most settlers aren't interested in withdrawal [from the Occupied Territories.]. . . We need one barrier against terror, and one barrier against attack from the east. There must be roads linking Jewish settlements and roads linking Palestinian settlements, and the roads must have no linkage."[14] The apartheid—the policy of separateness that formalized the black–white divide in South Africa from 1948 until majority rule in 1994—sought by Wallerstein and the settler movement in the late 1990s has now become even more brutal. Today it has manifested itself in an eight-meter-high wall constructed by Israel along the "border" it has declared with the areas of Palestinian land envisaged as outside direct Israeli administration. According to B'Tselem, an Israeli human rights group that closely follows the situation in the West Bank, the wall and the security zones on either side of it will amount to the grabbing of a further forty thousand acres of the West Bank, or 3 percent of the ever-shrinking land mass available to the Palestinians.[15]

The vision of the early Israelis is now coming true: "Between ourselves it must be clear that there is no room for both peoples together in this country. We shall not achieve our goal if the Arabs are in this small country. There is no other way than to transfer the Arabs from here to neighboring countries—all of them. Not one village, not one tribe should be left,"[16] wrote Joseph Weitz, head of the Jewish Agency's Colonization Department in 1940, eight years before the creation of Israel and long before any form of organized armed Palestinian resistance to Israeli encroachment had taken place. Weitz was following in an established tradition of Jewish nationalist thinkers, perhaps the most ardent of whom was Ze'ev Jabotinsky, whose writings in 1923 crystallized the strategy of confrontation with the Arabs of Palestine long before the first Jewish terrorist groups had fired the conflict's opening shots:

> We cannot promise any reward either to the Arabs of Palestine or to the Arabs outside Palestine. A voluntary agreement is unattainable. And so those who regard an accord with the Arabs as an indispensable condition of Zionism must admit to themselves today that this condition cannot be attained and hence that we must give up Zionism. We must either suspend our settlement efforts or continue them without paying attention to the mood of the natives. Settlements can thus develop under the protection of a force that is not dependent on the local population, behind an iron wall which they will be powerless to break down. . . .
>
>   I do not mean to assert that no agreement whatever is possible with the Arabs of the Land of Israel. But a voluntary agreement is not possible. As long as the Arabs preserve a glimmer of hope that they will succeed in getting rid of us, nothing in the world can cause them to relinquish this hope, precisely because they are not a rabble but a living people.[17]

The horrors that have determined so much of Jewish history lie at the heart of Israel's character, as the Israeli writer Benjamin Beit-Hallahmi states: "Anti-Semitism has created the bond of common Jewish fate. What all Jews had in common was the externally imposed definition of being regarded as Jews. . . . It is the gentiles who have kept the Jewish identity alive and have revived Jewish nationalism. Jews have been forced into adopting their nationalism because Europe has rejected them."[18] The determination of Israelis to visit on the Palestinians their revenge for European anti-Semitism is both the key source of Arab anger and a major reason for the inevitable failure of any agreements between Palestinians and Israelis that do not have at their core the assimilation of Israelis into Middle Eastern society. If European anti-Semitism produced Zionism and the Israeli nationalism that emerged from it, then a durable solution can only be sought in rediscovering cultural roots beyond Europe's shores. "Either the Arab societies accelerate their steps toward westernization and globalization, or the Israelis will decide that they should live in the area as Middle Eastern Hebrews," said Gamil Mattar, director of Cairo's Arab Centre for Development and Future Research.[19] He continued:

> But on neither the Arab side nor the Israeli side are they ready for the transformation. The process of transformation will bring tremendous problems of identity. Agreements with Israel can freeze the conflict. I don't think we can build upon agreements. You just freeze a situation that has been imposed. You don't have strong societies in the region that are sure of themselves. All of them: Arab and Israeli.[20]

Mattar's identification of the weaknesses of the conflicting societies in the region is vital. Israel emerged to challenge Arab identity at a time when that identity was seeking to emerge from European colonialism. Already by 1948—the year of Israel's creation—Arab states had seen the evolution of political Islam, the emergence of Arab nationalism, and the passing of the old order; all was as if nullified by the sudden appearance of a wholly new European colony, whose condition was a sign that the liberation from colonialism was forever going to be incomplete, as Israeli writers like Benjamin Beit-Hallahmi recognized in 1993:

> What has been done to the Palestinians is so fantastic and stunning that many simply cannot conceive of it as real. Invasion, defeat, humiliation and expropriation followed like thunder after lightning. The natives have been robbed, deprived of their identity

and history. They had their homeland pulled out from under them. They have the right to ask why all this has befallen them. The answer is that they should not have been a part of the story, and have no real relation to it. They were innocent bystanders in the wrong place at the wrong time. . . . The Palestinian majority became a minority because its members were passive, peaceful and disorganized, no match for Zionism. . . . The victors did not want to create real genocide, but they did want to erase the memory and the identity of their victims.[21]

It is a major irritation to many Israelis, and to their supporters in the United States, that their efforts to dim that "glimmer of hope" talked of by Ze'ev Jabotinsky in 1923 have been such a failure. More than eighty years after Jabotinsky had identified the parameters in which it was necessary to work to ensure that Zionism would be sustained as a force, Benjamin Netanyahu, prime minister in the late 1990s, continued with the aim "to reduce Palestinian expectations. With the settlement activity and the road building it becomes clear: You're going to find it impossible to draw state lines and have a viable solution," a senior European diplomat told me in Tel Aviv. "Netanyahu will gamble that the Arabs will sell the Palestinians down the river. So, Syria and Lebanon would do deals. Lebanon wants Syria off their back."[22] But again, it did not happen as Israel had apparently hoped. The Arabs remained firm, and Israeli disillusionment with the Netanyahu government turned to disgust. As the Oxford scholar Avi Shlaim wrote in 2000: "The assumption [by Netanyahu] that the Arabs would suddenly abandon their long struggle for the recovery of occupied land was not simply naïve but also provocative. It created a dangerous tide in the relations between Israel and the Arab world."[23]

As had been the case throughout the peace process launched after the Declaration of Principles—the Oslo accords, agreed to by the Palestinian Liberation Organization and Israel on August 19,

1993, and signed in Washington on September 13—Jewish settlement building in the West Bank continued. The creation of new settlements on occupied Arab land, as well as the expansion of existing settlements, was daily proof to the Palestinians that even under Yitzhak Rabin, the prime minister who had signed the Oslo accord and shaken the PLO leader Yassir Arafat's hand in Washington, the "spirit of Oslo" was less a benchmark than a hurdle to be leapt over at every opportunity. "The Oslo process actually worsened the situation in the occupied territories, and confounded Palestinian aspirations for a state of their own," wrote Avi Shlaim.[24] The Oslo agreement had not spelled out that settlement building should stop. But the aim of the agreement was to build confidence, and the settlement building, which accelerated under Rabin and escalated as deliberate policy under Netanyahu after his election in 1996 and then under Ehud Barak and Ariel Sharon, shattered whatever faith the Palestinians had developed in Israeli commitment to a peace process. These blatant signs that the colonization of the Occupied Territories was going to continue even while talks to end that colonization were taking place sowed a distrust among Arabs that lies at the heart of their attitudes toward Israel's sincerity and that now, in mid-2004, has turned the Occupied Territories and Israel into a bloodbath. Little seemed to have changed since Uri Lubrani, former prime minister David Ben-Gurion's special adviser on Arab affairs, had threatened in 1960: "We shall reduce the Arab population to a community of woodcutters and waiters."[25] In 1998, two years into the Netanyahu premiership, I sat with the Palestinian negotiator Sa'eb Erekat in his Jericho office. He told me: "We see the peace process slipping out of our fingers like sand, and we see that the people who said they would stand beside us are not."[26] He continued:

Netanyahu has destroyed everything that has allowed Palestinian moderation. Netanyahu's strategy is to use all this coming and going to show that the peace process is going on. Meanwhile he is changing the facts on the ground. There is a war being waged against us. There is ethnic cleansing. Every hour there is something that he is doing. Netanyahu is leading us to an inevitable confrontation. He wants to blame us. That's the endgame.

What do the Israelis want from our side? Do they want a real democracy next to them? Or do they want anyone who can deliver against terrorism? I think they want the latter. The Netanyahu government wants a Palestinian neighbor that they can blame. That's weak, that has no credibility. They can never reach a point where they can have a partnership.[27]

THE SPOILS OF DIVISION

In a broadcast on Radio Israel, the four-year-old Jewish state's foreign and defense minister, Moshe Dayan, announced on February 12, 1952: "It lies upon the people's shoulders to prepare for the war, but it lies upon the Israeli army to carry out the fight with the ultimate object of erecting the Israeli Empire."[28] Two years later, Dayan, in a speech to Israeli army officers, further elaborated his strategy for building the "iron wall" first envisioned by Jabotinsky:

> We could not guard every water pipeline from being blown up and every tree from being uprooted. We could not prevent every murder of a worker in an orchard or a family in their beds. But it was in our power to set a high price on our blood. A price too high for the Arab community, the Arab army, or the Arab governments to think it worth paying. . . . It was in our power to cause the Arab governments to renounce "the policy of strength" towards Israel by turning it into a demonstration of weakness.[29]

Half a century later, the brutality of the Israeli–Palestinian conflict leaves Dayan's assessment looking relatively resigned, even moderate. Four hundred meters below sea level in a hot café in the West Bank town of Jericho, a bottle of mineral water tells part of the story of what has changed. Jericho was handed over to Palestinian control, along with part of the Gaza Strip, at a ceremony in Cairo on May 13, 1994. Six weeks later, Yasser Arafat arrived in the town—the first time he had been to Palestine in twenty-seven years. The agreement, said one Israeli human rights activist, "means that Arafat is now annexed by the American-Israeli security system. In return he will get nothing except permission to be a local dictator."[30] When asked what she thought of the agreement that was supposedly the first actual step to handing over territory to the Palestinians, Hanan Ashrawi, a Palestinian delegate to the Madrid conference, recounted in her autobiography: "We are legalizing apartheid in this agreement and entering a diminished phase of nation building with sorrow and reluctance. The fact that our first sign of independence is the arrival of the police force encapsulates the irony."[31] The size of the administrative area within which the Palestinian Authority was to operate in and around Jericho had been reduced to one-sixth of what had been outlined on the maps originally pored over by Israeli and Palestinian negotiators. By the Cairo agreement, the Palestinian Authority essentially became a tool of Israel, which retained control over thirty-three public services and reduced Arafat's administration to municipal bureaucracy with a plethora of armed security services with which to assert his authority, rather than the embodiment of a new national government.

The water issue was symbolic of Israel's stranglehold; in the Jericho cafeteria, the label on the bottle of water stated that it came from Israel. But from where in Israel? Was it from a future Palestine, or perhaps the Israeli-occupied Syrian Golan Heights? Was it from the Israel defined by the United Nations in 1948 and reaffirmed in UN resolution 242 after the seizure of the West Bank and Gaza? When Dayan was admitting that water pipelines could not be guarded from attack, he was speaking of a time before Israel occupied the West Bank and seized the main water supply: the Jordan river and its associated tributaries and groundwater sources. Just as the Palestinian–Israeli conflict is fundamentally an issue about control over land, the associated issues of water, agriculture, and economy dominate the lives of those involved. For the Israeli settlers in the colonized West Bank and in a few heavily-guarded outposts in Gaza who retain the religious idea of a greater Israel or Dayan's "Israeli empire," the land is part of the heritage; for the Palestinians, the area is the fundamental pillar of statehood, and Jerusalem the heart of the Palestinians' role as guardians of Islam's third holiest site. But the land, its resources, and the livelihood it can provide are the real purpose of the fight. The issue of water is at the heart of the conflict now raging, simply because by 2009 there will not be enough to meet the needs of the Arab and Israeli populations now living in Israel, the West Bank, and the Gaza Strip.

During the 1993–1995 discussions that led to the signing of the Interim Agreement of September 28, 1995, "the worst battles [on infrastructure issues] were waged on water," Uri Savir, Israel's chief negotiator, wrote in his account of the discussions.[32] He continued:

> Amounts [of water] may seem objective, but there are as many views on this subject as there are experts—from the alchemists, who forecast a dry and perilous future for Israel, to the scientists, who put their faith in technology for solutions. The solution to this problem must be regional, and therefore the best source of water is peace.[33]

This view is widely shared. "The Israeli–Palestinian water agreement is really one of the victims of the faltering of the peace process," Sherif Elmusa, a water consultant who advised the Palestinian delegation during the 1995 Palestinian–Israeli negotiations on water rights, told me. "Palestinians are dependent on the Israeli water company, and this dependence won't disappear unless their quota is increased. Only the peace process can do this."[34]

The recognition of Palestinian rights to water that was under Israeli control was part of the September 28, 1995, Taba Interim Agreement, called Oslo II, but the details were left to the final status negotiations due to end by May 1999. They never took place. Israeli water commission figures show that 1.8 billion cubic meters of water a year is available from various sources between the Jordan River and the Mediterranean Sea—the area inhabited by Israelis and Palestinians. Israel uses 1.6 billion cubic meters a year and the Palestinian Authority areas 200,000 cubic meters. According to the Palestinian Centre for Human Rights, by March 2002, 88 percent of the water sourced in Israeli-occupied Palestinian areas was diverted by Israel for use either within Israel itself or by the Israeli settlements in the Occupied Territories.[35] "The crucial problem is not scarcity but distribution inequity. Israeli policies restricted Palestinian water consumption to around 110–125 million cubic meters (mcm) per year (mcm/y)," Alwyn Rouyer, a Middle East specialist at the university of Idaho, wrote in 2002.[36] One aspect of the illegality of Israeli actions during the post-1967 occupation was that it banned new drilling for water in the territories, a ban that was illegal, because under the Jordanian law applicable in the West Bank before the Israeli invasion, new drilling was permitted. It almost goes without saying that Palestinian applications for permits to drill new wells legally were hardly ever issued after the Israeli occupation. Meanwhile, Israeli consumption and use of water sourced in Palestinian areas mounted, most dramatically for the illegal settlements in the West Bank. According to the 1990 report of the Israeli state comptroller, Israeli state-owned wells in the West Bank yielded an annual average 750,000 mcm/year, compared with 13,000 mcm/year for Palestinian wells.[37] Israeli settlements in the West Bank had exceeded their annual quotas by 35 percent in the 1980s, which, according to Rouyer, contributed "to the drying-up or deterioration of the more shallow, nearby Arab wells."[38] The issue was a major source of friction during the 1993–1995 peace talks. Uri Savir relates how one Israeli negotiator, Noah Kinarti, had said a Palestinian needed less water than an Israeli, "implying that we were cleaner."[39] Savir, the head of the delegation, asked Kinarti to adopt a less aggressive posture in the discussions, to which Kinarti is said by Savir to have replied: "Let me do it my way. We'll reach an understanding in the end. Because without an understanding on water, there won't be an Interim Agreement."[40]

The Taba agreement of 1995 allotted a major role to the United States as the arbiter and overseer of the establishment of a more equitable system of water distribution and usage. In the end, what the agreement did was to encourage the drilling of a plethora of wells in the West Bank as a response to the huge, unmet demand. Rouyer's view is that:

> For a sustainable agreement to be reached, Israel must definitively accept the fact that Palestinians have a right to an equitable share of the region's water supply, and they should outline a plan of action aimed at achieving this goal. The [Palestinian Authority] must accept the fact that Israel depends on West Bank water and has a legal and historical right to a proportional share of that water. Moreover, a sustainable agreement will only be achieved when both parties are willing to go beyond legal and historical debates over often-minute divisions of the already scarce water supply.[41]

In his Tel Aviv office, Meir Ben-Meir, Israel's water commissioner, was blunt. "The very existence of Israel depends on this quantity, of 1.6bn cubic meters. . . . The Palestinians claim they have water rights that have been taken by Israel. But decreasing the 1.6bn cubic meters available to Israel would mean Israel would have to turn to desalination. Which it is not prepared to do," he said, though it was an option he said he favored.[42] The cost of desalinated water could be met by Israelis, whose incomes are higher than those of the Palestinians, while the latter would require major subsidies.

But aside from the mathematics, the injustice of the situation the Palestinians find themselves in is illustrated by the fact that the 1995 agreement recognized Palestinian water rights over areas that in fact would provide a more than adequate supply for the Palestinian population if they were handed over to the Palestinian Authority. The main area of contention has been the wells in the Palestinian-controlled town of Jenin, from which Israel extracts 1.4 million cubic meters of water from wells. Israel rejected Palestinian requests to be allowed to drill in Arab areas, on the grounds that it would interrupt supply to Israel's West Bank settlements. But in return Israel takes the water from Palestine, and the appalling cycle of injustice goes on. To meet growing need, Meir Ben-Meir estimates that Israel would by 2008 have to install desalination plants capable of providing 100 million cubic meters of water a year to meet combined Israeli and Palestinian water demand, on the basis that the combined Israeli and Palestinian populations would reach ten million by that year.

The shared interest in resources was clearly recognized in the negotiations of 1993–1995. But the process of recognizing these mutual concerns during negotiations intended to lead to the creation of two separate states allowed the parameters of dispute that eventually brought about the complete collapse of the negotiations at the instigation of the future Israeli prime minister, Ariel Sharon. The two-state solution is not a solution, because the resources are too scarce and will always be fought over if the two populations are kept apart and are forced to see the sharing of resources as a matter of losses and gains. Only the sharing of resources in a single country can meet the needs of the people living between the Mediterranean Sea and the River Jordan. The need to share water, and the recognition by the Oslo peace process that the issue of water was a weapon with which both sides would arm themselves to establish their credibility as negotiators, have been used simply as a tool in the ongoing conflict. A study by the Applied Research Institute of Jerusalem of Israel's use of water from both its legal territory and illegally occupied territories states that: "The obvious conclusion is that Israel is flagrantly violating international water law. Unfortunately for Israel's co-riparians of the Jordan basin, questions of rights, justice and equity are being ignored. Instead Israel is pursuing its own agenda, centered purely upon a perception of its own 'water security.'"[43]

Similar to the "tool" of water is the process of economic "closure," whereby Israel punishes all Palestinians for the actions of the suicide bombers, by transforming the Palestinian territories into little more than concentration camps when it closes the "border" with the West Bank and Gaza to prevent Palestinians employed in Israel from going to work. But the most vivid means by which the process of negotiation has been subject to the blackmail that is at the heart of Israel's readiness to use as tools of war the very tools that are supposed to be the ingredients of peace, is the theft of Palestinian land itself. In an interview in the *New York Times* in 1983 General Raphael Eitan, then the Israeli Defense Force's chief of staff, made clear that: "When we have settled the land, all the Arabs will be able to do about it will be to scurry around like drugged cockroaches in a bottle."[44] According to the Palestinian Centre for Human Rights,[45] 1.2 million Palestinians in Gaza subsist on 60 percent of the land in this sliver of territory, while most of the 42 percent of the Gaza Strip under Israeli military control is reserved for six thousand Israeli settlers, who constitute only 0.5 percent of the population. This also includes nonsettlement areas under Israeli military control, such as military bases, bypass roads, and some rural areas inhabited by Palestinians.

The bypass roads linking settlements to Israel disrupt the contiguity of Palestinian areas; in the West Bank alone there are 340.8 kilometers of bypass roads, which, with buffer zones, cover 51 square kilometers of land. Under the Fourth Geneva Convention, it is illegal for an occupying power to transfer parts of its own population into territory it occupies, nor is it permissible to introduce any permanent changes to an occupied territory that are not for the benefit of the occupied population. Thus, all Israeli settlements are illegal, as they are intended to be permanent and are reserved exclusively for the settlers at the exclusion of the indigenous population. By March 2002, there were 308 Israeli built-up areas in the Occupied Territories, which were home to 400,000 settlers, according to PCHR, excluding military sites. The Oslo agreement allowed the settlements to remain temporarily by deferring a decision on their future to the "final status negotiations." The agreement did not require Israel to withdraw from any settlements, and the post-accord period saw Israel expand its settlements at an unprecedented pace, increasing the number of settlers by 72 percent from September 1993 to March 2001, excluding expansion in east Jerusalem.

During the period between the two *intifadas*, when peace seemed possible, proof of Israeli's sincerity in being ready to cede territory was the greatest need of Palestinians and Arabs farther afield, if a negotiated end to the decades-long conflict were ever to be achieved. The settlement building that accelerated under Yitzhak Rabin and Shimon Peres was the means by which the "nonnegotiable" aspects of Israel's strategy were manifested. As Uri Savir, Israel's chief peace negotiator, wrote of the issues that were voiced regularly at meetings during the 1993–1995 period—specifically, the release of Palestinian political prisoners, the lifting of the economic "closure" of the occupied territories, and the demand for a total freeze on settlement building:

Each of these issues was of great importance to the Palestinian public, but they were not taken seriously enough by us because we regarded the conclusion of the Interim Agreement as a historic breakthrough and therefore often concentrated more on the negotiations than on the situation on the ground. So to a certain degree we scoffed at the Palestinians' complaints about such "banal" issues as the closure and the prisoners. In retrospect this was a mistake, for to have been more forthcoming on these issues would have created more goodwill, which would have helped other discussions, as well as our relationships in general.[46]

The May 29, 1996, Israeli election, which marked the end of the peace process with the arrival of Benjamin Netanyahu at the head of the Israeli government, brought with it a resurgence in the extremist positions that much of Israeli public opinion had sought to drown out during the Rabin years. On November 4, 1995, Yitzhak Rabin had been assassinated by a Jewish fanatic, and the doctrine of peace—dependent as it had been on the combination of personalities that circumstances had drawn together—unraveled. Netanyahu's extremism was widely seen in Israel as having stoked the fires that had encouraged Yigal Amir, Rabin's assassin, to take up his pistol.

But it is wrong to assume that support for Rabin within Israeli society was replicated among the mass of Palestinians. Rabin had overseen agreements with the increasingly corrupt and dictatorial Palestinian Authority of Yasser Arafat. When the foreign minister Shimon Peres succeeded Rabin as prime minister, the message that began to emerge was that Israel would pursue peace as part of a plan for a "New Middle East," which would have Israel at its center. "Most of Israel's neighbors were less than comfortable with this vision," Avi Shlaim writes, continuing:

Their principal fear was that Israel's military domination of the area might be replaced by economic domination. The Syrians saw the new rhetoric emanating from Jerusalem as no more than a cloak for Israel's perennial ambition to dominate the Levant. The Egyptians suspected that Israel wanted to take over their traditional role of political leadership in the Middle East. . . . Islamists throughout the Middle East were troubled by the prospect of Israeli-brokered Westernization in their countries. Even Arab intellectuals remained distinctly ill at ease with the vision of the New Middle East.[47]

Six days after taking over as premier, Peres rejected a deal—the Stockholm Accord—negotiated without his knowledge, which would have given the Palestinians a state on 96 percent of the West Bank. The accord was effectively the follow-up to the Oslo accord, in which Peres had played a key role. However, unlike Rabin—who had given the go-ahead for the Stockholm discussions—Peres was less accepting of the idea of a contiguous and independent Palestinian state. Peres had reservations and envisaged Palestinian control only over enclaves in the West Bank—akin, though he did not say so, to the *bantustans* to which South Africa's black majority had been confined by apartheid—while Israel would retain the Jordan River as its border. Peres was thus beset by doubts over his commitment to the relatively fast-track peace process launched by Rabin. He then made the catastrophic mistake of approving the assassination of Yahya Ayyash, a bomber known as "The Engineer," who was associated with the Hamas Islamic Resistance Movement, and whose activities had killed 50 Israelis and wounded 340 others. Ayyash's assassination by Israel's Shabak security service on January 5, 1996, unleashed a wave of Hamas reprisal bombings that killed sixty Israelis between February 25 and March 3. Peres's grip was

Shimon Peres, former Israeli prime minister and foreign minister.

shaken, and he sought to take the initiative to prove that he could be tough on terror. Peace talks with Syria, which backed Palestinian groups, were postponed; the Palestinian territories were closed; and all of Israel's military resources were put into confronting Hamas and Islamic Jihad. All of this played straight into the hands of Netanyahu, who could and did bathe enthusiastically in the tide of bloodshed that secured him election victory on May 29—as the guardian of the security he successfully portrayed Rabin and Peres as having thrown away.

COLLATERAL DAMAGE

Idriss, a Hebron butcher, unzipped a pocket in his leather wallet and showed me his front teeth. His street in the ancient city was lined by shops with neatly painted green metal shutters. Most were closed, or appeared to be so, though a glimmer of light from inside the partially closed doors could occasionally be seen if you got close.

The street was at the center of "historic" Hebron. Its cobbles had been cleaned, the buildings renovated, its shops opened by business-people selling the kind of goods that would be most attractive to tourists: traditional Palestinian ceramics, copper lamps, fabrics, and the like. The street was part of the "peace." On January 15, 1997, the Hebron Protocol had become Benjamin Netanyahu's attempt to show that he—and his right-wing Likud Party—could come to deals with the Palestinians, while also keeping his promise of "peace with security" made to the Israeli public. The Rabin government had been seeking a deal that would hand back parts of Hebron to Palestinian control in September 1995, but it delayed the with-drawal. Rabin had recognized that Israel's presence in an over-whelmingly Palestinian town for the sake of a small Jewish settlement was untenable. His view was hardened when Baruch Goldstein, a Jewish fanatic, slaughtered twenty-nine Muslims and injured three hundred more at a mosque in the town on February 25, 1994. It eventually fell to Netanyahu to take the initiative. In his characteristically ambiguous way, he argued in the Knesset, the Israeli parliament, that the division of the town into Palestinian and Jewish zones (a division of 80:20 in terms of the percentage of land) meant: "We are not leaving Hebron. We are redeploying from He-bron. In Hebron we touch the basis of our national consciousness, the bedrock of our existence."[48] He argued that the constant pres-ence of Israeli troops in the town to guard 450 Jewish settlers would give Israel the security guarantees it sought, while also allowing Palestinians to run their own lives.

Eighteen months after the Hebron deal Idriss the butcher was sitting outside his shop in the "historic" Palestinian zone of the town. He and his family and friends had been celebrating the Mus-lim festival *eid el-fitr* when Israeli troops had let off tear gas to break up the party. On paper, he lived in a Palestinian zone, but at each end of his street heavily armed Israeli troops peered out from behind sandbagged strongpoints, eyeing the enemy through binoculars. During the furor at the festival, he had been hit in the mouth with a rifle butt, and five of his teeth had been knocked out. He had kept them as evidence of the violence: Who was he going to show them to? He had no answer. No court was going to ask him to open his wallet and show his teeth. So he kept them, and in the meantime had had five new false teeth made and inserted to fill in the gaps. The absence of recourse to the law now dominated. But his complaint was directed far more strongly against the Palestinian Authority than the Israeli forces: "The leaders—our leaders—are not of the people. There will be war between the Palestinians," he told me. "The leaders are here to take money. Only that. Where has all the money gone? Millions of dollars, in one day it all just disappears. They are not of here. It will only get better when the leaders come from here, not from among those who have returned. But I fear there will be a war among the Palestinians."[49]

The Palestinian Authority leadership, seen by people like Idriss as outsiders who had returned from exile to run the lives of Palestinians who had remained in the Occupied Territories throughout the violent *intifada* of the late 1980s, had failed to match popular expectations. An explosive combination of factors lies behind this. Hebron, at the point when Netanyahu was receiving letters of adulation from the U.S. administration for having "redeployed" Israeli forces and thus given the impression of a commitment to meeting Palestinian aspirations,[50] was a microcosm. As Avi Shlaim pointed out, the Hebron Protocol gave 20 percent of the town to 0.5 percent of the population—the Jewish settlers—while the 160,000 Palestinians had the rest but "remained subject to numerous restrictions and limitations."[51]

Throughout the period of occupation, all economic activity in the territories was scrutinized by the Israeli Military Authority—a long and deliberately arduous process, which by both design and default limited economic growth in the West Bank and Gaza.[52] Permits and licenses took months to procure, new industrial equipment was forbidden from entering the territories, and Palestinians were forced to buy secondhand equipment from Israeli suppliers. Israeli taxation of Palestinian export products and imposition of import tariffs on consumer durable goods from neighboring Arab states also remain permissible within the agreements reached thus far.[53] By 2002, half of the taxes paid by Palestinians in the Occupied Territories "actually accrue[d] to the Israeli economy through these charges. This is in addition to the income and social security taxes paid by Palestinians working in Israel [but living in areas under Palestinian Authority control]."[54]

The end of the formal occupation of small areas of Palestinian territory in the wake of the Oslo agreement, and the complicated rearrangement of administrative and military authority into areas under either Israeli, Palestinian, or joint control, doubled the pressures on the Palestinian population by combining the repression of Israel and the shortcomings and incompetence of the fledgling Palestinian Authority. The result was to expose the Oslo accords as deeply flawed from the Palestinian point of view. "The Oslo Agreement changed the nature of the Arab–Israeli conflict in a fundamental way, but it did not and could not end it," wrote the Palestinian-American writer Said Aburish in his 1998 biography of Yasser Arafat.[55] He continued:

> It enhanced the positions of Israel and Arafat and the PLO, mostly in the eyes of the outside world and in terms of their ability to deal with each other, but the euphoria which accompanied the signing was short-lived. Arafat's concessions cast doubt on whether he would be able to carry his people with him; the most important issues had been relegated to the final status negotiations; and considerable ambiguity surrounded the articles of the Declaration of

Principles. What had been achieved was mutual recognition and a commitment to end the conflict through diplomatic means. Everything else depended on Israeli and PLO goodwill. . . . The participants in Oslo became [for the PLO leader Yasser Arafat] "my friends." He exhibited a sense of confidence, secure in the knowledge that the recognition put an end to the possibility that the PLO as it existed in Tunis [where it had been exiled in 1982] might be marginalized and replaced by local leadership [from among Palestinians in the West Bank or Gaza].[56]

The Oslo agreement was, however, the landmark deal to which at that time there appeared no alternative. In this obviously imperfect situation, there was a need to enhance the power of the dealmakers—however flawed they were as individuals, or self-seeking were their motives—to create a structure for negotiations. The task of selling the Oslo agreement to the Palestinian people fell to Arafat, and "initially, they accepted Arafat's word that peace and economic well-being were on the way. They looked forward to freedom and the emergence of a Palestinian state. But this enthusiasm was short-lived and their joy soon gave way to doubt," Aburish writes.[57] But these doubts were the result not only of skepticism about the credibility and intentions of the Palestinian leadership as it emerged but also Israel's ruthless weakening of that leadership. Aside from the appalling violence that has punctuated the conflict, the issue of land remained the core of the conflict. Successive Israeli leaders have used the atrocities of suicide bombers, over which none of the Palestinian Authority leadership has any direct control, as a stick to beat that leadership, strengthen support for Israel in the United States, and demand concessions from the Palestinian population. The cause of the suicide bombings—whether in the 1990s or more recently—rests almost solely with the anger felt by Palestinians at Israel's refusal to abide by agreements, withdraw from Palestinian land, and negotiate sincerely with Palestinian leaders. The brutality of Israel's occupation—whether it be in the form of bullets fired on civilians from helicopter gunships, the stealing of Arab land, the uprooting of olive groves, or the demolition of Palestinian homes—is an aspect of the crisis that, because it is marginally less dramatic than the aftermath of a bus bomb in an Israeli street, has been sidelined by a peace process whose course has been heavily influenced by how the two sides are represented in the media. It is vital to remember that at least three times more Palestinians than Israelis have been killed in the ongoing uprising provoked by Ariel Sharon in September 2000. Successive American presidents can—rightly—condemn the appalling suicide bombings, but it is also convenient for them that they are rarely asked to respond to Israel's violence, whether it be rocket attacks on crowded streets or the demolition of Palestinian family homes. Ultimately, both acts of violence add up to the same thing: For the dispossessed Palestinians, the loss of home, land, orchards, fields, and livelihood, coupled with loss of hope and dignity, has now been driven so hard into the Palestinian psyche by Israel's ruthless determination that life is a form of death. The despair and hatred that have swollen the ranks of the suicide bombers are the result. When the bombers pull the cord, however, they are condemned for their atrocities; when Israel rampages through their lives, the most that any U.S. president has ever said is that Israel's actions are "unhelpful."

Knowing that Israel will never be criticized in any meaningful way by its closest ally—the consequences of which are examined in the following chapter—Benjamin Netanyahu continued in the great Israeli tradition of appearing to negotiate on the one hand, while ruthlessly pursuing land theft on the other. In his first act of deliberate provocation, he ordered the opening of a tunnel linking Jerusalem's Wailing Wall with a tourist site nearby. The opening of the tunnel was a blatant violation of the understanding that the future of Jerusalem would be negotiated. It was also a calculated insult to Muslims, as it passed beneath the Dome of the Rock and thus impinged on the sanctity of Islam's third holiest site. Violence erupted, leaving eighty Palestinians and fifteen Israeli soldiers dead, and leaving some to conclude that after only four months in power, with the opening of the tunnel "Netanyahu blasted away the last faint hope of peaceful dialogue with the Palestinians."[58]

He had started as he meant to continue. His next provocation followed soon after. Photographs taken in 1997 of Jebel Abu Ghneim—the hill east of Jerusalem called Har Homa by Israelis—show a long hill clad with trees. Now there is a town on the hill, a huge Jewish settlement, the starkest piece of evidence that the peace process was for Israel an issue of security, not rights, with the controversial settlement intended as part of a "defensive" wall that would ultimately become the frontier between the illegally seized land of Arab east Jerusalem and the city's eastern suburbs and the western border of the West Bank. The plan to build 6,500 homes for 30,000 Israelis at Jebel Abu Ghneim was launched by the previous Labor government under Shimon Peres, at a time when Palestinians still clung—in vain—to the principle unsaid but enshrined in the spirit of Oslo that the "facts on the ground" should not be changed during the period between the signing of the Oslo accord in 1993 and the agreement on the final status of Jerusalem. On March 2, 1997, the Palestinian Authority's chief negotiator, Sa'eb Erekat, said that Arafat intended to ask President Clinton to "intervene personally to get Mr. Netanyahu to revoke his decision [to build the settlement]. We feel Clinton is the only one who can save the peace process from collapsing if bulldozers take to the land on Abu Ghneim."[59] He was probably correct in his belief, but Clinton did nothing. The bulldozers tore up the ground, and U.S. criticism did not rise above a murmur, despite the regional outcry. Moshe Fogel, the Israeli government's spokesman, said Israel did not intend to change its mind. "Israel's policy on Jerusalem may not be easy for them to swallow . . . but in the final analysis we're going to have to act on our convictions."[60]

The following day, David Bar-Illan, Netanyahu's spokesman, announced that to ensure that the Palestinians would abide by the Oslo accord, the Palestinian Authority had to close four of its offices in Jerusalem. "It is impossible for the peace process to continue, for the redeployment and other obligations which Israel has, to continue, without the closing of these offices," said Bar-Illan.[61] Palestinians must play by the rules; Israel must never be expected to. The Netanyahu government's strategy was becoming clear: Squeeze the Palestinians, encourage them to resort to violence, blame them for failing to be "partners in peace," and then abandon the entire peace process.

That this was Israel's strategy was not lost on the Arab states: "Building the settlement in east Jerusalem is tangible proof that Netanyahu is not thinking of the peace process, but of provoking the Arabs and the whole world," said Faruq al-Shara, Syria's foreign minister.[62] In an effort to fully exploit Yasser Arafat's shaky control over Palestinian affairs, Netanyahu on March 21 also sent his foreign policy adviser Dore Gold to Cairo to inform President Hosni Mubarak that Israel wanted to complete talks on the final status of Jerusalem within the coming six months rather than by May 1999 as specified in the 1993 Oslo agreement. Netanyahu clearly saw that Arafat wanted to deliver something to his people, and the offer of a deal over Jerusalem could perhaps be made to seem tempting, particularly as the furor over the illegal settlement building at Jebel Abu Ghneim was now in the equation. But the Egyptians, keen to retain their pivotal role in the talks by retaining links with Israel while also influencing Arafat, were merely dismayed: "The question of bringing forward the final status talks is not serious. It is to strengthen [Netanyahu's] own hand, and keep him in control of the territory as he gets involved in issues he can't solve. Meanwhile, Israel keeps hold of the land. It's against the logic of the [1995] Interim Agreement," a senior Egyptian official told me.[63]

However he dressed up issues in flowery rhetoric and talk of "the bedrock of our existence," Netanyahu's characteristic opportunism was all that lay behind his strategy. It has always been vital for Israel that the Palestinian leadership remain weak. Israel needs to be able to demand the impossible of the Palestinian leadership—that it stop the suicide bombers, for example—to be able to diminish its stature and extract concessions that only a weakened administration would be forced to make. Netanyahu saw that Arafat was weak and believed he could seize the chance to ensure that deals could be agreed to that hugely favored Israel. As Avi Shlaim wrote of Netanyahu's strategy: "The main elements of his strategy were to lower Palestinian expectations, to weaken Yasser Arafat and his Palestinian Authority, to suspend the further redeployments stipulated in the Oslo accords, and to use the security provisions in these accords in order to assert Israel's dominant position."[64] The often violent consequences of the Palestinian leadership signing deals that fell far short of Palestinian popular aspirations were not and have never been remotely significant to Israel's leaders, and have often been a gift to Israeli leaders in their constant search for ways to benefit from the often violent consequences of Palestinian anger. Until Ariel Sharon in 2002 forced the Palestinians to replace their negotiating team and sideline Arafat altogether, the fact that bad deals have brought with them the violence of which Israel is the primary victim had never led to a modification or reversal of the Israeli strategy of weakening the Palestinian leadership. Sharon forced Arafat aside with the aim of replacing him with somebody even weaker. Weak interlocutors, weak negotiating positions, poor preparation for discussions, and haphazard or chaotic decisionmaking are the characteristics of the Palestinian Authority that Israel has thrived upon, encouraged, and exploited in its hunt for

deals that weigh vastly in its favor. This is what lay behind Netanyahu's attempt to rush to the final status talks.

Part of Arafat's weakness lay in his failure to draw Palestinian society together into a formidable and cohesive political body. Its main
division was between those who had fought the *intifada* on the
ground in Palestine from 1987 and those nine or ten thousand Palestinians—"ten thousand goons and a goalie" as Palestinian writer Said
Aburish derisively calls them[65]—who had returned to the West Bank
and Gaza from exile when it became possible to do so. Arafat gathered the latter around himself, eventually isolating democrats like the
education minister Hanan Ashrawi, and cocooning himself in the
Gaza Mansion House. Israel used various means to manipulate a
man they knew was isolated from the people he sought to lead; in so
doing, they further weakened him—deliberately so—by making it
obvious to the Palestinian masses that their leader was dependent for
his credibility upon his acceptance by Israel. Arafat was always a symbol many Palestinians—whether they personally liked him or not—
would rally to when the need arose, but in the context of the peace
process he was the identifiable international figure who signed pieces
of paper. However, he has failed to bridge the gulf between statesman
and man of the people as dramatically as that between guerrilla
leader and politician, and he has stumbled in the gray area between
the lofty ideal of nationhood and the base reality of corruption, brutality, and disastrous compromises that he has overseen.

Palestinian disenchantment with Arafat intensified in response to
both the failure to advance the moves toward statehood in the face of
Israeli resistance and the excesses of the Palestinian Authority. On
November 29, 1999, Arafat's dictatorial style led him to order the arrest of two of a group of twenty prominent Palestinians who had
gone one step further than previous critics by identifying Arafat himself in their condemnation of the Authority's "corruption, injustice
and tyranny."[66] The twenty had earlier issued a manifesto entitled

"The Nation Calls Us," which blamed Arafat for having "opened the doors to the opportunists to spread their rottenness through the Palestinian street. . . . The land is being plundered, Jewish settlements are expanding, refugees are being conspired against and our prisoners are being held in Israeli jails behind a tissue of trickery and lies." The declaration continued:

> [The Oslo accords] had turned out to be a bartering of the homeland for the enrichment of the corrupted and corrupting in the PA. The economic situation gets worse and worse and all institutions are threatened with collapse. [The Palestinian population should] confront this tyranny [and] . . . sound the alarm against the Palestinian Authority's misrule in every town and village, every camp and corner of the land.[67]

The Authority's response was to denounce the signatories as "deviationists" who had "strayed from the national path in publishing a petition full of lies and unfounded accusations."[68] But this response was rejected out of hand across the Palestinian areas, where condemnation of the "mafia" running the Palestinian Authority was loud and clear. One of the manifesto's signatories, Abdul Jawad Salih, told students at Bir Zeit University on the West Bank: "We say to these corrupt people, stop where you are. This is a country that gave martyrs for a homeland, not for a mafia."[69] Some weeks earlier, Arafat had decided to delay publication until further notice of the Authority's comptroller general's report, which two years earlier had revealed that nearly one-third of the budget had been diverted.

The risk taken by Palestinians critical of Arafat was substantial, not only due to the brutality of the various security forces Arafat had at hand as tools of his own repression, but also because of the extent to which such criticisms played into the hands of Israel. The undermining of Arafat from within the Palestinian population was grist to Israel's mill; far from showing there was free speech in Palestine, it was simply exploited as proof that Arafat was a dictator who would never become a democrat with whom deals could be struck. The manifesto of the twenty emerged after Netanyahu had lost the 1999 election, but its sentiments were already being widely felt and voiced in Palestine while he was prime minister. The growing evidence of Palestinian Authority corruption and brutality during his term was integral to his campaign against Arafat, which was particularly galling to neighboring Arab states whose own records on corruption and brutality resembled those of the Palestinian Authority. Their response to Netanyahu's strategy was a combination of bewilderment and anger; Egypt, in particular, saw years of effort, genuine sacrifice, and numerous compromises of its own in pursuit of peace with Israel in danger of being squandered. On April 1, 1997, Arab League foreign ministers agreed to halt moves toward normalizing relations with Israel, in protest to the illegal settlement building at Jebel Abu Ghneim. Arab and Israeli representative offices—the precursor to the opening of embassies—were closed, and the long-standing though largely token economic boycott was reimposed.

Ever determined to sow division and portray the aggressor as victim, Netanyahu told Israel radio that these measures amounted to an attempt to overthrow the coalition government he led: "Certain elements in the Arab world have perhaps developed an illusion they can dictate to the people of Israel who their government will be. The Arab world is testing us. But it is completely clear that returning to the tactics of the economic boycott will not succeed. They did not succeed when Israel was small, economically and otherwise, and they will not succeed today when we are much stronger."[70] Egypt sought to defuse the crisis by inviting Netanyahu to talks in the southern Sinai resort of Sharm el-Sheikh. Netanyahu had by then gone further in trying to portray himself as the vulnerable victim of circumstance, by playing up the threat from members of his own coalition—in particular a seventeen-member bloc known as the Land of Israel Front—to withdraw from the government if construction of the illegal settlement at Jebel Abu Ghneim were suspended.[71] The night before the May 27 Sharm el-Sheikh meeting with the Israeli premier, Mubarak met with Arafat in Cairo. Mubarak was trying to find a way out of a situation whose solution he could not deliver. All he could do was keep the sides talking, which is why he was prepared to accept a visit by Netanyahu. But the result was that the illegal settlement building continued as if no discussions had taken place. "Har Homa is a constant, and Israel hasn't changed its commitment to Har Homa,"[72] Dore Gold, Netanyahu's spokesman, said on June 8, as part of the strategy of showing that efforts by Egypt—Israel's vital interlocutor in the Middle East—were also incorporated into its attitude of dismissive disdain toward all Arabs and their governments. But what was also becoming clear was that Netanyahu was backing himself into a corner with this approach. "If Netanyahu becomes reasonable, he will alienate his extreme right," a senior Egyptian official told me at the height of the crisis.[73] "Har Homa is a symbol or a test of the overall direction. Even if the Israelis freeze construction there, it will be extremely difficult to convince any Palestinians that the Israeli government is acting in good faith."[74]

Ariel Sharon's election as prime minister of Israel on February 6, 2001, was as much a sign of the crisis in Israeli political life as it was a mark of how little progress there had been in the process of peacemaking in the region. The anxiety his rise to the premiership sent through Palestinian and broader Arab circles stemmed not simply from the concern that another Likud government would pursue the games that Benjamin Netanyahu had played in place of negotiations. Sharon was a wholly different threat to peace, because of a reputation borne of his role in the massacre of Palestinians at the Sabra and Chatila refugee camps in Beirut on September 16–18, 1982. The slaughter of up to 3,500 Palestinians in the camps by the

Christian Phalangist militia was preceded by the encirclement of the camps by Israeli tanks working in concert with the Phalangists against their common enemy: the Palestinians. According to a case brought in a Belgian court against Sharon, who was Israel's defense minister at the time and had overseen the invasion of Lebanon and Israel's capture of West Beirut in the summer of 1982, the future prime minister approved the Phalangists' advance into the camps.[75] On September 11, Sharon had announced that "2,000 terrorists" had remained inside the Palestinian refugee camps around Beirut, and agreed at a meeting with Lebanese President-elect Bashir Gemayal in the Lebanese resort town of Bikfaya that the militia would enter the camps. The subsequent slaughter by the Lebanese caused an uproar, not least in Israel. A commission of inquiry was launched. Sharon's callousness was severely criticized, and he was forced to resign as defense minister, though he was kept on as minister without portfolio. The Kahan commission of inquiry said of the future prime minister:

> As a politician responsible for Israel's security affairs, and as a Minister who took an active part in directing the political and military moves in the war in Lebanon, it was the duty of the Defense Minister to take into account all the reasonable considerations for and against having the Phalangists enter the camps, and not to disregard entirely the serious consideration mitigating against such an action, namely that the Phalangists were liable to commit atrocities and that it was necessary to forestall this possibility as a humanitarian obligation and also to prevent the political damage it would entail. From the Defense Minister himself we know that this consideration did not concern him in the least, and that this matter, with all its ramifications, was neither discussed nor examined in the meetings and discussion held by the Defense Minister. In our view, the Minister of Defense made a grave mistake when

he ignored the danger of acts of revenge and bloodshed by the Phalangists against the population in the refugee camps.[76]

Twenty years later, Ariel Sharon has confirmed the worst fears of Palestinians and other Arabs. With the enthusiastic support of the administration of U.S. President George W. Bush, Sharon has turned the decade-long effort at peacemaking in the Middle East into an era that may soon be regarded as an interlude between wars. By making clear to Palestinians from the start of his premiership in 2001 that they should abandon hope of a state on anything like the lines envisaged in the Oslo accords, Sharon was laying the foundation for a conflict that now—in mid-2004—looks only a short way off. While still in opposition as Likud leader, Sharon made his intentions unequivocally clear on September 29, 2000, when he took a highly publicized walk through a Muslim holy site, the *Haram al-Sharif* in Jerusalem, as a gesture intended to stamp Israeli authority on the entire city. By signaling that Palestinians should give up any claims to the Arab area of the city that houses Islam's third holiest site, his action precipitated the *al-Aqsa Intifada,* the uprising that had killed around 2,828 Palestinians[77] and 958 Israelis[78] by April 2004. Sharon made it clear to the Israeli electorate that a vote for him in 2001 was a vote for conflict. His victory confirmed the popular will in Israel and emphasized that the country no longer saw negotiation and compromise as an acceptable way to achieve its security. His reelection on January 28, 2003, showed how deep-rooted this sentiment had become. Like Netanyahu before him, Sharon has sought to provoke Palestinians in order to justify a devastating Israeli response to Palestinian violence as a means of diminishing Palestinian expectations and driving them toward accepting whatever Israel is prepared to offer.

Sharon's strategy of isolating Yassir Arafat in the hope that it would lead to the appointment of more malleable interlocutors within the Palestinian Authority (PA) isolated not only the PA president but the entire Authority. The rise to prominence of Hamas, the Islamic Resistance Movement, in the Gaza Strip, has been the result. Arafat has failed to deliver statehood to his people and, today, sits in the rubble of his headquarters in Ramallah, under intense Israeli surveillance of his every move in the expectation that at some point the order will be sent by the Israeli prime minister to have him assassinated. The policy of assassination has encircled him, since the Israeli government declared that it would carry out the murder of Palestinians it alleges have masterminded terrorist attacks in Israel. As with the election of Sharon, the policy of state-sanctioned murder has revealed the severity of the crisis in Israeli political life. As the Oxford scholar Avi Shlaim wrote in June 2003: "As a soldier and politician, Sharon has always championed violent solutions. He has yet to learn you cannot have a winner and a loser in a peace process; that resolution of a conflict requires two winners. Nor does he understand Israel ought to end the occupation, not as a concession to the Palestinians, but as a favor to itself if it wishes to preserve its democratic and Jewish character. As Marx observed, a nation that oppresses another cannot itself remain free."[79]

Sharon's vision, rather than Palestinian violence, has brought the two sides to the crisis of today. The Bush administration's amoral position on the crisis—dressed up disingenuously as one dominated by its supposedly moral position on terrorism, against the background of its strong affinity with Israel—has greatly encouraged the violence, in part by feeding the anti-Americanism that has taken root globally as a result of the rise of the sentiments articulated by al-Qaeda. By the time Sharon made the decision to provoke the current uprising of Palestinians—the *al-Aqsa Intifada*, as it has become known—by taking his walk through the Haram al-Sharif in Jerusalem, Hamas had engaged in cease-fire talks nine times since 1994. Some of these offers were in response to PA pressure, some to pressure from the United States or the European Union, and most were dismissed by Israel as a tactic intended to give the organization a respite during which it planned more violence. The cease-fire that ended on August 21, 2003, in response to Israel's killing of the Hamas official Ismail Abu Shanab in Gaza following the Palestinian suicide bombing of an Israeli bus, marked the end of one phase and the beginning of another. It reached its appalling twin climax on March 22, 2004, when the Hamas leader Shiekh Ahmed Yassin was blown to pieces by a rocket fired from an Israeli helicopter as he was being pushed home in his wheelchair. His killing was then followed on April 17, 2004, by a rocket attack on his replacement as leader, Abdel Aziz al-Rantissi, which killed him and his bodyguards.

COLD PEACE

The killings of the Hamas leaders were condemned widely, though the United States further eroded its influence and credibility (as examined in Chapter 7) by abstaining from a vote at the UN condemning the murder of Yassin. John Negroponte, the then U.S. ambassador to the UN who has since been nominated U.S. ambassador to Iraq, stated:

> The United States is deeply troubled by the killing of Sheikh Yassin. Israel's action has escalated tensions in Gaza and the region, and could set back our effort to resume progress towards peace. . . . [Events] must be considered in their context and this Security Council does nothing to contribute to a peaceful settlement when it condemns one party's actions and turns a blind eye to everything else occurring in the region. . . . This resolution condemns the killing of Sheikh Yassin, the leader of HAMAS, a terrorist organization dedicated to the destruction of Israel. . . . This resolution also, as indi-

cated in the preambulatory language, refers only to the situation in
the Occupied Territories, ignoring the tragic events which are occur-
ring in Israel. The Council should be focused on ways to advance the
goal of the two states, Israel and Palestine, living side by side in peace
and security. The one-sided resolution before the Council does not
advance that goal. One-sided, unbalanced resolutions by the Security Council, such as the one before the Council today, would only
detract from the efforts of the Quartet and the international community to resume progress on the path towards peace.[80]

President Bush then further isolated the administration from the
Arab side by endorsing Sharon's plans to permanently retain some
West Bank settlements while withdrawing Israelis from the Gaza
Strip. "In light of new realities on the ground, including already existing major Israeli population centres, it is unrealistic to expect that
the outcome of final status negotiations will be a full and complete
return to the armistice lines of 1949,"[81] Bush said at a joint press
conference with Sharon at the White House on April 14, 2004. The
endorsement ended half a century of expectations that Israel would
retreat to the area it had been allotted at its creation. It made clear
that the United States and Israel no longer regard Palestinian involvement in the negotiating process as of fundamental importance,
by revealing a readiness to make fundamental decisions without
Palestinian involvement. The endorsement also revealed the readiness of the United States to accept that principle was no longer at
the heart of negotiations: After a decade during which illegal settlement building was accelerated to change the demography of the
West Bank, Israel was rewarded for destroying the trust necessary
for the negotiations to succeed and for creating the conditions for
the escalation of violence. Ahmed Qorei, the Palestinian prime minister, despaired. "Any words that may encourage settlements or
building the wall would mean a dangerous destruction of the peace

process and will leave nothing left to negotiate with the Israelis,"[82] he said on hearing of Bush's statement.

The injustice was thus cemented, in the mistaken belief that by accepting what is "realistic" the move toward peace could be accelerated. But a durable peace in the Middle East will not emerge in the near future unless justice emerges first. The silencing of the guns and the termination of the bombing campaigns that are the result, not the cause, of the violence—if such things could be achieved— would not bring peace unless there were an end to the illegal occupation of the West Bank, the return of Palestinian homes and property stolen by Israel, compensation for land and property that has been grabbed by the Israeli authorities, and the creation of a credible legal system within the sovereign Palestinian areas. Ariel Sharon's plan to withdraw the 7,500 Israeli settlers from Gaza was roundly rejected in a referendum by members of his ruling Likud party on May 5, 2004. But even if he manages to push through his plan, the withdrawal will do nothing to build trust among the Palestinians of the West Bank now that his aim of permanently retaining settlements there has been made known and given U.S. approval.

Trust will be the key feature of any future negotiations, and for now it has disintegrated. It took ten years for the people who fled the horrors of Bahr el-Bakr to gather the confidence to return. By then, Egypt and Israel had signed their piece of paper, a milestone had been reached, and Anwar el-Sadat had been assassinated as the price for signing an agreement against the wishes of the people over whom he ruled. The school has now been rebuilt and is named after "The Martyrs of Bahr el-Bakr." Some of the mud streets of the farming village have been named after the children who died. A simple brick monument, about as high as the eleven-year olds who were the oldest pupils to die, bears the names of the dead. Their school bags and bloodied clothes have been gathered in a small museum in the new school. "Of course we want to see peace. Enough of death. But peace can disappear over small things," said Nabilah Hassan, called in the village simply Mother of the Martyr Mamdouh, in memory of the son she lost in the bombing. "It has nothing to do with religion. It has to do with their behavior."[83]

In Bahr el-Bakr there is more anger and distrust than faith in the ability of Arabs and Israelis to turn agreements on paper into a new reality. Nine carefully worded articles, with a preamble, two annexes, and an exchange of letters, officially brought an end to Israel's conflict with Egypt on 26 March, 1979. The deal cited the conviction that in itself it was "an important step in the search for comprehensive peace in the area and for the attainment of the settlement of the Arab–Israeli conflict in all its aspects."[84] The peace treaty signed by Sadat and the former terrorist leader Menachem Begin, who had become Israeli prime minister at the head of a hawkish government on May 17, 1977, was the first test of whether deal making could address the Arab–Israeli crisis.

But are pieces of paper the solution?

An integral aspect of the 1979 treaty was the understanding reached at the Camp David talks that "the parties are determined to reach a just, comprehensive, and durable settlement of the Middle East conflict through the conclusion of peace treaties based on Security Council Resolutions 242 and 338 in all their parts."[85] The former resolution binds Israel to withdraw from Arab territories it occupied in the 1967 war. The latter binds Israel to abide by the first resolution. But Israel has not withdrawn, and the refusal of successive Israeli governments to accept that Arab unity on the issue of Palestine—despite major diversions and disagreements among the Arabs along the way—has generally been retained. Egypt may have had a peace with Israel, while most Arab countries do not, but this has not brought anything more than an end to hostilities and an opportunity for Egypt to pursue a dialogue with Israel even at times of major crisis.

The peace is cold, because Israel has failed to accept that however successfully it feels it has lured some Arabs into striking deals, it has not convinced any Arabs—neither countries, governments, nor peoples—that its purpose is to deepen ties with its neighbors on anything other than its own superior and advantageous terms. "For the dialogue to be a fruitful exchange between equals some serious soul-searching on the part of the Israelis is in order," Mohamed Sid Ahmed, the Egyptian political commentator, told me just after the fall of the Netanyahu government on May 17, 1999. He continued: "So far, their attitude towards the Arabs has been fundamentally racist—regarding Egyptians and, more generally, Arabs, as objects, not subjects, of history, as mere instruments to be discarded, neutralized, and, if necessary, eliminated, so that Israel can achieve its objectives. Unless there is a real shift in Israel's perception of the Arabs, an attempt at normalization is doomed to fail as long as [Israel] fails to demonstrate by deeds, not only words, that its presence in the area is more beneficial to the Arabs than its absence."[86]

The fall of Netanyahu could have brought with it a real possibility—fueled by the still recent memory of Yitzhak Rabin's efforts coupled with the apparent rejection by Israeli society of the Iron Wall that Netanyahu's fall seemed to imply—that trust could lead to genuine peace. For all Arabs, Egypt's experience is an important litmus test. Its near-quarter century of peace with Israel provides a valuable insight into what deals can bring and what they fail to achieve between peoples. "In Israel there are agonies and struggles akin to something like a reformation," Tahseen Bashir, Sadat's former spokesman, told me in the wake of Netanyahu's defeat. "In the Muslim world, you're talking about a community that hasn't gone through a reformation. Both of us are caught in a dilemma. And neither of us has come with a clear, consistent answer. Sadat hated Begin, and he left it to the future to weave the tissue of the future. In the meantime, a historical mosaic has been compromised. We need to create a new mosaic."[87] Israel's existential travails have their comparisons among its Arab neighbors. The Arab–Israeli conflict had been a rallying call for Arab nationalists and was thus associated with the political creed of Gamal Abdel Nasser. The fact that the conflict has long outlived Nasser is proof enough, however, that its root is much deeper than a single phase in the political evolution of nations. "Whatever the politicians decide, the question of normal relations depends on the people. This isn't a problem of Palestinians or Egyptians or Israelis. It's a cultural problem," said Raouf Nasmi, the Egyptian commentator with close ties to the Palestinian leadership. "If you look at the map of the world, the Israelis are part of the West. And they will be a part of the West until the majority of Israelis return back to their Oriental origins. If we are speaking of peace between peoples, there's no problem from the Arab side. The Arabs are not xenophobic. But the Israelis are, and especially the Ashkenazi [European Jews]. And [Israeli Prime Minister Ehud] Barak is always talking about [Israeli-Palestinian] separation, though in the long run they will dissolve among us."[88]

Such predictions seem futile, however, and are one reason why a durable peace is unlikely to be achieved in the near future. The negotiating structure built up since the fall of Netanyahu has been consistent with the foundations he laid, whatever the political hue of the governments in Jerusalem. The strategy of striking deals has been developed because it is the easiest way for Israel to assert itself in the region; it has been dependent upon the region's soldier-kings and potentates for its existence. Their combination of autocratic power and military weakness has left them with little choice but to go to the negotiating table. Israeli leaders may deride their few Arab interlocutors with criticisms of their lack of democracy, but they have been wholly dependent upon the absence of democracy in the region to strike the deals made thus far. Until the election of Ariel Sharon and the decision to provoke the Palestinians into war, the result had been numerous agreements that had for the most part either collapsed or brought results that fell far short of Palestinian expectations. Far from building trust, deal making as a method of achieving peace instead became an even more inflammatory battleground. The failure to abide by agreements—which Israel has routinely done since 1967, with the enthusiastic support of the United States—has crystallized the cultural division between Israel and the Arabs as no other element could do. The underlying element in every deal struck since 1991 has been that Israel will withdraw to its 1967 borders, and that the Palestinians will have a functioning state created through negotiations. But it is clear that this is not accepted in Israel, despite the negotiations at least nominally retaining this basic premise even while successive Israeli leaders have stated publicly that they do not accept it. Deals are pieces of paper that the weak Palestinians often fail to abide by because they cannot, and which the Israelis fail to abide by because they seize every opportunity not to do so. Deals thus solidify the gulf rather than bridge the gap. Is it then the case that peace will only come when Israelis "dissolve" into the Middle East—as Raouf Nasmi asserts? If so, how? And if not, why not?

"The origins of Arab anti-Semitism can be found in a real conflict, and are not a matter of cultural prejudice,"[89] wrote the Israeli writer Benjamin Beit-Hallahmi, suggesting that the acculturation of Israeli society into the Middle East is not impossible. Denied the opportunity to renege on agreements, Israel would be forced to either use its nuclear arsenal to assert its regional primacy or—more likely—accept that as a part of the Middle East it is in its interest to adapt. The only durable solution is not only for that adaptation to bring with it Israel's full incorporation into the region, but for the limited resources that are the flashpoints of animosity between Israelis and Palestinians to be fully shared. Palestinians have long shown that they are ready to accept Israel; Israelis need the Palestinians as their partners in the peaceful construction of a state and as their inroad toward acceptance by the Arab world. Moreover, by 2020 Jews will make up only 45 percent of the predicted fifteen million people (as opposed to comprising 55 percent of the current ten million) in the area between the Mediterranean and the Jordan,[90] a fact that in itself will become an increasingly important determinant of policy. Demographic change is most likely to intensify Israeli concerns about being swamped. But only with the full and equitably distributed benefits of statehood—as secure and prosperous for Jews as for Arabs—will the necessary partnership be created, in a manner that dilutes animosity, reduces distrust, and decouples the Israeli–Palestinian conflict from the broad and complex regional picture. Only with the abandonment of the two-state solution and the creation of a single, multi-faith, democratic nation between the Mediterranean Sea and the Jordan River can this be achieved. But this will not happen, because it is not in the strategic interests of the one country whose role in the conflict will ultimately determine the outcome—the United States.

7

A CROSSROADS ON ARAB STREET

AMERICAN POWER AND THE MIDDLE EAST

AMONG THE VILLAS AND MANSIONS THAT SURROUNDED THE palatial headquarters of V Corps, the mechanics of America's future presence in the Middle East could be seen at their most vivid. The hub of the military machine was the only palace in which the power worked, so the chandeliers sparkled in the marble-floored halls, which thudded with the sound of military boots. Just before leaving London to go to Baghdad, I recalled seeing a television item in which the employee of an armaments factory in the U.S. Midwest had been asked for his views on the military campaign in which he—the assembler of three-thousand-pound bombs—had played his role. "If I had known what these bombs were going to be used for, I would have had a different view of my job," he had said, confusingly. His bombs had cleared the way for V Corps to reach Baghdad.

A month before, I had been asked to recall for a newspaper article my experience of a decade earlier, when I had stood under a

moonlit sky and awaited the arrival of U.S. forces on the beach of
Mogadishu. Emerging from victory in the Cold War and Gulf war,
President George Bush the elder had dispatched a mission to the
Somali capital in December 1992. The aim was to end a famine and
consolidate the "New World Order." Instead, the mission crossed
the line—subsequently called the Mogadishu Line—into urban
warfare, and thrust U.S. forces into a traumatic retreat. Navy Seals,
followed by nineteen thousand Marines, spearheaded the "humani-
tarian intervention." But the Somali reaction was one of deep ambiguity about the foreign presence.

By May 2003, a similar ambiguity had taken root in much of
Iraq. Iraqis did not, as Vice President Dick Cheney and Deputy
Defense Secretary Paul Wolfowitz had predicted in a variety of in-
terviews in early 2003,[1] unequivocally welcome the invading U.S.
and U.K. forces with open arms. Ten years earlier the ambiguity of
Somalis turned from skepticism into hostility, as suspicion of the
well-intentioned but ineptly executed foreign presence intensified.
On the streets of Mogadishu, militias opposed to the *gul*—the foreigners—exploited popular uncertainty about the occupation, used
civilians as human shields, gunned down U.S. marine patrols, ambushed Pakistani UN forces, and brought down U.S. military heli-
copters. Fierce pride fueled antagonism toward the foreign troops,
and after a battle between militiamen and U.S. forces in the city on
October 3, 1993, the foreign troops began a humiliating retreat
and left Somalia to its fate.

Fresh back from a day hunting for the weapons of mass destruc-
tion that had been the pretext for bringing America and Britain to
Iraq, the team of weapons specialists to which I had been attached in
May 2003 relaxed on the terrace of their Baghdad villa by watching
Black Hawk Down, a dramatic movie about the Mogadishu debacle.
The nineteen U.S. Rangers killed in Mogadishu that night were part
of an inspirational myth for their successors in Iraq ten years later,

who watched under the inky Baghdad sky, eyes fixed on the small screen as the story of heroism and bravery was told. With unwavering pride, they watched in silent admiration, barely drawing breath, as the tale of military error, bad planning, inadequate preparation, and a total absence of local knowledge passed them by, in a blaze of gunfire and tense music. And when the credits were rolling across the screen, they were impressed, even slightly in awe, when I told them that I had been in Mogadishu that night; that I had waded in inch-deep blood at a hospital to which the hundreds of Somalis injured or killed by the U.S. forces—none of whom were shown in the movie—had been taken, had been the first to visit the battle scene early the following morning, and had watched the bodies of the dead U.S. forces being dragged through the sandy streets of the city. For just as the armaments factory employee seemed genuinely to have no real idea that the bombs he was making were going to be used to tear America's enemies to pieces, so the forces that had invaded Iraq and with whom I spent time there in mid-2003 were driven by a sense of mission that required that they also remain one step away from the reality of what they were involved in. Remaining detached requires the capacity to romanticize the brutality of the military occupation of Iraq, in which U.S. troops are being killed on a daily basis. This in turn requires a firm belief in the moral rectitude of the mission and the unwavering conviction not only that it is a responsible use of global military superiority, but also that the consequences of unleashing that military power can be reconciled with the ideological principles that underpin the mission.

Between the launch of the war against al-Qaeda in October 2001 and that against Iraq eighteen months later, the rise to prominence of ideologues capable only of speaking the language of conflict with the Arab world allowed the Bush administration to construct a matrix of excuses in place of a Middle East policy. In an article entitled "Forget the 'Arab Street,'" Reuel Marc Gerecht of the

alarming and sinister American Enterprise Institute think tank in
Washington—from which the administration of George W. Bush
has seconded some twenty advisers to work in various government
departments—wrote in April 2002:

> The administration that has done so much to reverse the image of
> American weakness in the Muslim Middle East—weakness that is
> the jet fuel behind the appeal of bin Ladenism in the Arab
> world—may well deal, quite unintentionally, a severe blow to
> America's *hayba*, the majesty and magnetism that inhere in unchal-
> lengeable power. Without this mystique, there is no guarantee of
> peace and security for us and our friends in the region.
>
> If this happens in the next few months, it will be a very good
> idea for Bush and company to march to Baghdad as quickly as
> possible. They'll need to do something stunning to reverse Amer-
> ica's fortunes and keep the suicide bombers from our gates.[2]

Today, America's "friends in the region" can be counted on only
one finger: Israel. With every other country in the Arab world still
awaiting the long-term consequences of the invasion of Iraq, even
relatively long-term allies like Egypt, Jordan, and Kuwait are aware
that the inconsistencies in their relations with the United States cannot be obscured forever. The unraveling will emerge from the contradictions inherent in the exercise of American power in the region.
While the United States sought partners in the region—in pursuit
of oil, peace between the Palestinians and Israelis, trade development, and the longer-term goals of fostering religious harmony in a
region whose resonance is global—it was possible for the military,
diplomatic, and economic power it invested to bolster its Arab interlocutors to act as a counterweight to the deep popular resistance
to American goals. Now, the United States has only one partner in
the region, as the "peace process" in which it was able to engage the

region as a catalyst has collapsed, and the rapport it had developed with selected Arab leaderships is increasingly vulnerable to the deep popular antagonism felt toward U.S. influence and the U.S.–Israeli alliance.

In the article cited above, reference to the "unchallengeable power" of the United States is a sign of how isolated the United States has become, not only in its behavior but in its thinking. The awful success of the September 11, 2001, terrorist attacks in New York and Washington was in part the success of American power being challenged. America's weakness and failure were exposed for all to see. The Bush administration's response was to construct a wholly self-serving security policy, requiring all the countries of the world to wrap themselves in the straitjacket of U.S. interests. Many regimes—not least in the Arab world—saw some advantage to themselves in doing so, attacking dissident groups and silencing dissent under cover of the "war on terror," free from the accusation that they were engaged in human rights abuses by the fact of their once biggest critic—the United States—having become the most enthusiastic supporter of their robust actions. But just as the U.S. alliance with the soldier-kings and potentates of the region has long been fraught with dangerous contradictions, the new alliance can only be temporary, as interests diverge and the social currents of the Arab world divorce the United States from what is really taking place beneath the surface. No Arab leaders can or will deliver the region, in the way that current U.S. policymakers have made it clear they hope to see. Instead, the United States will turn to its only natural ally and seek to build it up into an impregnable fortress, surrounded by the "Iron Wall."

Official America's empathy with Israel is built on the same assumptions that are the barrier to a durable peace between Israelis and Palestinians. In an influential paper published with the aim of directing the course of the Netanyahu government when it came to power in 1996, a group of U.S. conservatives—several of whom have subsequently held senior positions in the administration of George W. Bush—advised the incoming Likud premier to make a "clean break" with the Rabin and Peres peace process.[3] The paper stressed the need for Israel to dump economic policies based on U.S. foreign aid, shed any semblance of the socialist ideals that had been an important part of the Jewish state's founding ethos, and establish a "new vision for the U.S.-Israeli partnership based on self-reliance, maturity and mutuality."[4] But most important, it portrayed Israel unequivocally as the bastion of "Western values" in the Middle East, stating: "Israel's quest for peace *emerges* from, and does not *replace*, the pursuit of its ideals. The Jewish people's hunger for human rights . . . informs the concept of peace and reflects *continuity with values with Western and Jewish tradition.*"[5] The writers of the paper advised the Netanyahu government to intensify pressure on the Palestinians by demanding that the Palestinian Authority "be held to the same minimal standards of accountability as other recipients of U.S. foreign aid."[6] Thus, Israel was being advised that the Palestinians' apparent obligations to the *United States* were a weapon Israel *itself* should seek to use in its relations with the Palestinians. The paper continued:

> Israel has no obligations under the Oslo agreements if the PLO does not fulfill its obligations. If the PLO cannot comply with these minimal standards, then it can be neither a hope for the future nor a proper interlocutor for the present. To prepare for this, Israel may want to cultivate alternatives to Arafat's base of power. Jordan has ideas on this.[7]

The paper thus added to the already deeply rooted view within the incoming Netanyahu administration that demanding the Palestinian Authority assert an authority it was known not to have—at least in terms of its ability to create watertight security for Israel—

would be a useful tactic in undermining its credibility. This was a strategy Netanyahu used consistently throughout his premiership. Moreover, the fact that Israel itself had hitherto refused to abide by an understanding not to continue settlement building in the Occupied Territories during the period of the peace process—the issue that has always been the major proof that Israel does not abide by agreements and is thus the cause of the Palestinian distrust that lies behind the violence against Israel—was not mentioned in the paper. By stressing Israel's role within the security strategy of the West, the paper firmly reestablished the concept of the Iron Wall first conceived by Jabotinsky in the 1920s. "Israel can under these conditions better cooperate with the U.S. to counter real threats to the region and the West's security,"[8] the paper stated, adding: "When Israel is on a sound economic footing, and is free, powerful, and healthy internally, it will no longer simply manage the Arab-Israeli conflict; it will transcend it."[9]

The primary aim of U.S. conservatives is not to create the conditions for Arab–Israeli peace but to build a pro-U.S. island in the Middle East. All countries seek allies around the world. The United States is not exceptional in wanting a genuine ally in the Middle East, as opposed to relations with Arab states like Saudi Arabia that are based purely on the need for oil and the expansion of the market for U.S. and U.K. arms manufacturers. As one European diplomat, reflecting on the refusal of the United States to pressure the Israeli government to end its attacks on the peace process, told me during the Netanyahu premiership in mid-1998: "The French can work with Lebanon and Syria. The British can work with Jordan and the Palestinians. The U.S. can get the Israelis to jump. But it's a failure of political will. If they put the pressure on, there are any number of things that they can do. But it's inconceivable that they are going to."[10] But in seeking to build up Israel so that it may "transcend" the Arab–Israeli conflict, U.S. conservatives have created in their minds ambitions that have replaced the interests of the region with those of the United States. The United States may even be seen to be exploiting the Israeli presence in the region. Writing before the Oslo process became known, the Israeli writer Benjamin Beit-Hallahmi was a rare voice when he doubted the validity of the main foundation of both Zionist claims and the U.S. policy that stems from these claims:

> Can Israel's problems be tied to "Jewish fate?" No. They are not merely a continuation of past experience. Existence in West Asia as settler colonialists is unlike anything else in Jewish history. It is radically different from "Jewish fate" in Eastern Europe or the U.S. Claims about "Jewish fate" ignore the real difference between Jewish and Israeli history. Unlike the situation of Jews persecuted for being Jews, Israelis are at war with the Arab world because they have committed the sin of colonialism, not because of their Jewish identity.[11]

The ambitions harbored by U.S. conservatives and the interests of Israel itself are not easy bedfellows, do not guarantee Israel's long-term future, and ignore altogether the fact that the U.S. tendency to see the entire Middle East through the prism of the Palestinian–Israeli conflict has created a warped and superficial attitude toward the Arab world, its complexity, and its diversity. As Benjamin Beit-Hallahmi wrote:

> The incredible attachment of some American Jews to Israel, the way they worship Israelis, or their fantasy of Israel, is proof of their insecurity in their own society, their alienation, their feeling of incompleteness. There is a terrible weakness in this psychological dependence on Israel. . . . U.S. Jews are stagehands or extras in the dramas of Israel, where the real action is. . . . Most of them would

never dream of practicing what they preach [by going to live in Israel]. They leave that to others, but they enjoy offering the most tortuous defenses for the Zionist faith.[12]

He continues with a suggestion: "The argument that Israel is the only safe refuge for Jews has been dispelled by the establishment of the U.S. as everybody's refuge. . . . New York City may be the real answer to the nineteenth century 'Jewish Question' posed by [Theodor] Herzl, as both Diaspora Jews and young Israelis flock to its boroughs."[13]

But such pragmatism is alien to the "men of destiny" who feed the political hunger of Washington, which in turn stokes the extremism—itself the result of personal insecurity and anxiety among those living in Israel—that builds walls rather than bridges between the adversaries. The fellows of the American Enterprise Institute—to whom President George W. Bush has paid regular homage—today provide clear signs of the myopia now stalking official thinking. The new lease on life given to the American Right by the September 11 terrorist attacks has given them carte blanche to accuse any opponent of Israeli strategy of being a terrorist. "Terrorism continues to work for Arafat, even with the first American administration that has largely defined itself by a war against Middle Eastern terrorism," wrote the strident Reuel Marc Gerecht.[14] Referring to the various attempts to negotiate an end to the Israeli–Palestinian conflict, he continued:

The "peace process" is over, and some form of Israeli occupation of these lands is inevitable, yet few foreign-policy professionals are prepared to admit that American and Israeli policy for years has been founded on an illusion. . . . On the streets of Israel, the West Bank and Gaza, people are more honest and straightforward. "Oslo," "Mitchell," and "Tenet"—the terms of the "peace process" desiderata that make the Palestinian terror war against Israel sound like battling spouses hunting for some new marriage-counseling technique—have absolutely no meaning.[15]

Gerecht does not specify with whom he spoke on the "streets of Israel, the West Bank and Gaza," and from whom these insights were gleaned. The absence of views from the "Arab street"—a term used widely to denote Arab public opinion—about which he is so derisive, suggests that in fact his views have been generated from within the maze of cubbyhole offices and unmarked doors that make up the think tank for which he works.

The relevance of Arab public opinion is meanwhile a major challenge facing American "foreign policy professionals" seeking to influence administration strategy on the Middle East. State control of the media in much of the Arab world—either through ownership or less direct influence—is cited as a reason for arguing that ordinary Arabs would be less opposed to Israel if they had the "freedom" to think for themselves and enjoyed Western-style democracy and press freedom. In fact the opposite is probably true; the Arab press generally reflects the Arab view of Israel, whether it be the views of governments or "the street." In Egypt, for example, popular anti-Israeli opinion is probably far more strident than that expressed in state-owned media that occasionally fall little short of being anti-Semitic. If there were democracy in the Arab world, it is likely that Islamists would become the major power bloc in key countries, making the prospect of Israel's acceptance in the region even less likely. On the other side, it is an important part of the Israeli and pro-Israel propaganda machine to identify all Arabs—governments and peoples—as roughly similar, and in particular to daub them all as either actual or potential terrorists. In its June 9, 2003, "Middle East Report," the American Israel Public Affairs Committee—known by its acronym AIPAC—which leads Israel's lobbying efforts in the United States, reported the following: "Arab countries have demonstrated an un-willingness to truly combat the suicide bombings and other attacks against Israeli citizens."[16] In view of the fact that the demise of Saddam Hussein in Iraq two months earlier was supposed to have removed the vital conduit for Palestinian terrorist backing, the ap-parently ongoing support from other "Arab countries" is baffling; Israel has yet to provide any evidence that Palestinian suicide bombers are continuing—if they ever did—to receive assistance from other Arab countries. Moreover, the sweeping generalization failed to identify whether, in the absence of Saddam Hussein, it was now Jordan, Egypt, Morocco, Qatar, Oman, or others—countries that had sought to improve their ties with Israel when Israel had ap-peared ready to make peace—that were now providing assistance to terrorists bent on destroying Israel. The paper did not say, leaving the impression that all Arabs are the same. Two weeks later AIPAC issued an analysis of European attitudes toward Palestinian terror-ism, which it headlined: "The EU has been reluctant to cut off funding for Palestinian terrorist groups."[17] Ignoring the vigorous ac-tion taken by European Union (EU) states against terrorist groups long before and in the wake of the September 11 attacks, the analy-sis sought to act on the Bush administration's behalf, highlighting apparent differences between the British position—which stated that the political wing of the Hamas Islamic Resistance Movement should not receive EU funding because of its ties to Hamas's military wing—and that of the EU itself, which drew a distinction between the two sides. The report sought to suggest that the EU was some-how pro-terror. But its analysis was also flawed by the simple fact that in neighboring Lebanon, the British government provides financial assistance for social projects overseen by the political wing of Hizbollah—the Iranian and Syrian-backed group—whose mili-tary wing is also in conflict with Israel over the latter's continued oc-cupation of an area of southern Lebanon called Shebaa farms.[18]

The role of AIPAC as a lobbyist has focused on demonizing the Arabs. It presents a version of history intended to minimize understanding within the United States of the motivation behind Arab actions and responses to Israeli actions. Its chronological account of Arab–Israeli relations[19] is intended to show Israel as the party ready for peace and the Palestinians as embarked on inexplicable acts of violence. It is blunt in its assessment that "peace is not possible without firm American backing for Israel. Israel's potential peace partners must know that the bond between the U.S. and Israel is unbreakable, even if there are occasional disagreements. . . . Israel must negotiate from a position of strength backed up by U.S. aid."[20] The view is reciprocal; at a March 2003 AIPAC conference, Condoleeza Rice, the U.S. national security adviser, stated:

> AIPAC is an important advocate for strong friendship between the United States and Israel and is, thus, a great asset to our country because we share so much with Israel, but most importantly we share values. You can have lots of friends, but friends who share your values are the ones who are most steadfast and most important, and I want to thank you for your support of our good friend, Israel.[21]

But even with the friendship and advice of the pro-Israel conservatives who are the fabric of the Bush administration, Israel is in no more of a position now to "transcend" the peace process—as Richard Perle and others envisioned in the mid-1990s—than it was in 1996 when Benjamin Netanyahu came to power. It must negotiate if it ever wants to see peace. But to succeed where other negotiations have failed, it is the United States that must first establish whether it is peace in the interests of America or the Middle East that it is seeking. In the same speech to AIPAC, Rice drew clear linkages between the fate of Israel and the war in Iraq, which by then had been advancing for ten days, telling her audience:

We will help Iraqis build institutions that are democratic that protect the rights of all Iraqi citizens. . . . A free Iraq can, after all, add
momentum to reform throughout the Middle East. . . . We should
join hands with those in the Middle East who want to build a different future for the Middle East. . . . We see signs that this new
thinking also extends to a new generation of Palestinian leaders
and it is one of the reasons that President Bush is very hopeful that
success in Iraq can set a new stage for Middle Eastern peace.[22]

In fact the Bush administration's focus on the Israeli–Palestinian
issue as a part of the post–Iraq war framework—which suffered from
the same chaos and ineptitude as all aspects of the postwar planning
for Iraq itself—emerged largely at the insistence of U.K. Prime Minister Tony Blair. Blair's government did not regard the overthrow of
Saddam Hussein as having created a Middle East "peace dividend"
similar to that which prevailed at the end of the Cold War and out of
which the Madrid conference on the Palestinian–Israeli confict
emerged. Instead, officials in London knew that to retain credibility
in the eyes of regional governments, from their new interlocutors like
Syria, Libya, and Iran to established allies in Egypt and Jordan, they
had to seek ways of diluting deep popular distrust of the West in the
region, by accelerating improvements in the lot of the Palestinians.

The problem for the Bush administration in creating the link as
it did—between Iraq, Palestine, Israel, and international terrorism—was that these were connections it needed to conjure up to
justify launching the war that overthrew Saddam Hussein. But as
has emerged since, the links were spurious: Saddam's role as a backer
of terrorism was not of such importance that his overthrow has
removed a major impediment to Israeli–Palestinian peace, as his
financial gifts to the families of Palestinian suicide bombers are far
from proven to have inspired more attacks on Israelis, and nor did
he have links to al-Qaeda. Saddam was a limited threat within the

region, and no real threat to the United States at all. The true extent of his threat to Israel is also likely to remain potential, though it is probable that he would have turned the potential into reality if he had had the means. But he did not.

The United States thus has far less capital to draw upon from its "victory" in Iraq than its prewar positions suggested. The reason for this is simple: The war was not really about Iraq at all, but about Saudi Arabia. When the U.S. Congress on July 25, 2003, issued its 858-page report on the intelligence failures that had permitted the nineteen hijackers to launch the September 11, 2001, attacks, twenty-eight pages mostly referring to Saudi Arabia were deleted from the public version and have remained secret.[23] Clearly there is a great deal the U.S. government wishes to hide about the extent to which its relations with the kingdom have collapsed. The fact that fifteen of the hijackers were Saudis was a thunderbolt striking U.S. attitudes toward Saudi Arabia. While Saddam Hussein was an irritation in the region, the imposition of no-fly zones over parts of Iraq, the strict embargoes imposed on the regime in the wake of the 1991 Gulf war, and deep distrust of Saddam and his henchmen felt by Arabs across the region had reduced the threat to one of potentialities rather than realities. In the wake of the September 11 attacks, however, Saudi Arabia emerged as a much greater threat—the extent of financial support for al-Qaeda emanating from within the kingdom, and the deep-rooted loathing there of the United States, having become clear. The September 11 attacks transformed Saudi financial power, oil reserves, and facilities for key U.S. military installations in the region from features of a U.S.–Saudi alliance into potential weapons of war. The subsequent U.S. strategy has been nothing but rational from the perspective of U.S. national interests: reducing its reliance upon Saudi Arabia by greatly diminishing its military presence there, relocating its facilities, and—most important—seizing Iraq and its oil resources to reduce reliance on Saudi reserves. As the Palestinian writer Said Aburish wrote bluntly in 1998, when discussing U.S. support for Saudi Arabia and its impact on the Middle East:

> Until the need for oil, the Cold War and the desire to manipulate the outcome of the Arab–Israeli conflict forced it into the open as the dominant power in the Middle East, republican non-colonial America was acceptable to the Arabs. Even in the late 1930s the Arabs believed in America's neutrality on the problem of Palestine. . . . But America discarded its ideology, followed oil interests, turned a blind commitment to anti-communism into a wish to involve all people in this issue and manifested a desire to please Zionism and win elections at home at the expense of the Arabs. America has, during the past four decades, followed its replacement of the old, tired colonial powers by adopting policies similar to theirs. In the process America became colonialist and made the Middle East unsafe for democracy.[24]

Because the real motive for war in Iraq was not what was presented, the foundations for a *new* dispensation in the Middle East are in reality barely laid, while expectations that—as Condoleeza Rice claimed—"a free Iraq can . . . add momentum to reform throughout the Middle East" are deeply ambiguous. There is no doubt that current and future U.S. engagement in the Middle East will shape events there. The combination of substantial military, financial, and diplomatic power will inevitably have an impact. The question is whether the commitment of resources can actually introduce change that is durable, or—as in the case of Somalia a decade ago—be all sound and fury until the failure becomes too expensive and the effort is abandoned. Such is the stake the Bush administration—and the United States as a world power—now has in the Middle East, that the destiny of the United States is inextricably linked to what emerges in both Iraq and in the land between the Mediterranean Sea and the Jordan River. The weakness of U.S. engagement in the region is that it is now led more by a focus on U.S. and Israeli security than on the aspirations of the Arab populations, as former U.S. ambassador to Israel Martin Indyk accurately characterized in an otherwise strangely argued proposal in May 2003 for the creation of a U.S.-controlled trusteeship in Palestine: "Without some form of international intervention, Israelis and Palestinians will continue to die and their circumstances will continue to deteriorate, fueling vast discontent and anger at the United States in the Muslim world and placing Israel's future well-being in jeopardy."[25]

RED LINES

For most Arab states, the U.S. agenda is not based on responding to regional needs but on determining those needs, as President Bush made clear on June 24, 2002, when he firmly placed all aspects of the Palestinian response to Israel's aggression into the category of "terror," which now strikes such a powerful chord with the American public. In demanding that Palestinians replace Yasser Arafat, Bush sought to blackmail the Palestinians into ending their resistance to Israeli aggression, and made only a feeble request that Israel halt the settlement building that lies behind so much of the anger among Palestinians. Bush effectively demanded the capitulation of the Palestinians to U.S. and Israeli demands if they ever wanted to secure their own state, portraying the Palestinians as the cause of the violence that had raged since September 28, 2000, when Ariel Sharon found a way to promote antagonism by visiting the Muslim holy site *Haram al-Sharif,* making clear that it would never become part of a Palestinian state. "The Palestinian Authority has rejected your offered hand and trafficked terrorists,"[26] Bush said of Israel in June

2002, then taking further the Israeli strategy of blaming the Palestinian Authority for the weaknesses it undoubtedly has, but which are as much the result of Israel's deliberate weakening of it as they are the result of its own corruption, ineptitude, and brutality. "Ultimately, Israelis and Palestinians must address the core issues that divide them if there is to be real peace, resolving all claims and ending the conflict between them," Bush continued, specifically "that the Israeli occupation that began in 1967 will be ended through a settlement negotiated between the two parties, based on UN Resolutions 242 and 338, with Israeli withdrawal to secure and recognized borders."[27]

Such language may have appeared forthright, breaking various taboos rejected by Israel. But the speech offered nothing original in terms of bargaining strategy and merely served to recognize that the only way to bring peace was through negotiation. This is, of course, what had been happening throughout the preceding decade. What was new was the extent to which U.S. national security interests were implicitly recognized as being at the heart of the administration's thinking. For Bush the benchmark was terror: "This moment is both an opportunity and a test for all parties in the Middle East; an opportunity to lay the foundations for future peace, a test to show who's serious about peace and who is not."[28] Less than a year later, Condoleeza Rice would try to combine the logic of U.S. preoccupations with domestic national security and the administration's support for Israel with the need to build a vision of a democratized post–Iraq war Middle East, by claiming there were also certain "principles" at play, where in fact practice was far more significant: "Some say that this is a vision that is too ambitious for the Middle East. Some say that the United States of America is too exuberant in its support of democracy. Some say that there is a kind of naïveté to a belief in these principles."[29]

But it is not so much the attachment to democratic principles— of which the Bush administration has tended to project itself as the world's sole guardian, however offensive this has proved to Europeans whose democracies are far older and less subject to the financial power of candidates than the U.S. system—as the past failure to put them into practice that has dominated the formulation of the Bush administration's policy. Much of what Rice and Bush have said about how to resolve the Israeli–Palestinian issue has been said before; the main distinction has been in exploiting the post–September 11 atmosphere as a means of levering Yasser Arafat out of the way, to engineer the installation of a Palestinian leadership that will be less "obstructive" and will therefore make even more concessions to Israel than Arafat was prepared to do. But instead of creating new conditions for peace, such a strategy can only create the conditions in which bad deals may be signed under duress, inevitably creating the conditions for further conflict, as has been seen in the rise of Hamas.

The reasons for the failure of previous agreements must be forensically examined and frankly recognized, if the most recent proposal—the "road map" presented by the "Quartet" of the United States, the European Union, the United Nations, and Russia on April 30, 2003—is to be rescued from collapse. Bush, in his June 24, 2002, speech, said: "A Palestinian state will never be created by terror. It will be built through reform. And reform must be more than cosmetic change or a veiled attempt to preserve the status quo. True reform will require entirely new political and economic institutions based on democracy, market economics, and action against terrorism."[30] Bush clearly held the incumbent Palestinian Authority responsible for the failure to build a state, and in so doing exposed how deeply partisan the United States is, and how deeply attached it remains to the game plan first put in place by the Netanyahu government in 1996.

In an effort to flesh out his charade of seeking "peace with security," Netanyahu was forced to go through the motions of negotiations when he met Arafat at Wye Plantation in Maryland in October 1998. The agreement, signed on October 23, was intended to address two key issues: Israeli anxiety over security and the need of the Palestinians to secure enough territory on which to create a viable state. The agreement provided for Israel to withdraw from 13 percent of the West Bank and bound the two sides to negotiate further withdrawals at final status talks scheduled to be held by May 4, 1999. In return, the Palestinian Authority would combat terrorist organizations, prevent illegal weapons distribution, and amend articles in the Palestinian National Charter that Netanyahu viewed as threatening aggression toward Israel. The accord was in effect part of the piecemeal series of interim agreements begun after Oslo, intended to build up to the final status negotiations, which would deal with Jerusalem, water arrangements, and the return of Palestinian refugees. After the signing ceremony, King Hussein of Jordan, who died from cancer soon afterward, told the signatories: "It's time that, together, we occupy a place beyond ourselves, our peoples, that is worthy of them under the sun, the descendants of the children of Abraham. . . . I think that we have passed a crossroad."[31]

Even if fully implemented, the Wye accord would have meant that Israel retained control of 82 percent of the West Bank, while 400,000 Israeli settlers would have maintained their presence on 180 illegal settlements in the Occupied Territories. It was not surprising that the agreement was widely criticized: Palestinians said the land from which Israeli troops would withdraw was regarded as grossly inadequate, and would anyway remain subject to Israeli security control; meanwhile, action against terrorist groups would necessitate the Palestinian Authority arresting Hamas and Islamic Jihad supporters, many of whom were involved in providing much-needed social services to the Palestinian population and not in terrorist actions. On the Israeli side, half of Netanyahu's cabinet opposed Wye. These pressures meant it was doomed to fail. The Palestinians did amend the charter and rounded up scores of militants, while Israeli forces did withdraw from part of the West Bank. However, Israeli settlement building continued apace, so the withdrawal from one area was nullified by its illegal expansion in another. In December 1998, as his government was beginning its head-long plunge toward electoral defeat, Netanyahu canceled all Israeli troop withdrawals after accusing the Palestinian Authority of failing to register or confiscate illegal weapons or outlaw the "support structure" of terrorist organizations, despite the U.S. administration's recognition that it had taken action against terrorist activity.

Five months later, in the grand hall of Alexandria's beachside presidential palace, the ebb and flow of peace was as regular as the waves that rolled up against the sea wall. Netanyahu had fallen from power on May 17, 1999, replaced by the former army chief of staff and Israel's most decorated soldier, Ehud Barak, who secured 56 percent of the votes. "The new government of Israel has clear guidelines. We are not going to build new settlements and we are not going to dismantle ones,"[32] Barak told the gathering of skeptical reporters—myself among them—in Alexandria, while President Mubarak of Egypt stood beside him listening intently to see if the man who had ousted Netanyahu would deliver on the promises his predecessor never saw as his responsibility to keep. In fact, new homes for twenty-two thousand settlers were built in the Occupied Territories during the Barak premiership. "The whole issue of settlements should be settled in the final settlement agreement. The real intention in our government is to move forward in the peace process, making clear that if peace could be achieved in the Middle East we will achieve it. I am determined to go in the footsteps of my commander, mentor and great leader, Yitzhak Rabin," Barak asserted, stating that he would implement the Wye accord signed and then canceled by Netanyahu, on the basis that "Israel abides by international agreements."[33] However, he remained vague about how he would pursue this commitment, and did not commit the new government to halting the expansion of existing settlements. More-

Ehud Barak, Israeli prime minister 1999–2001.

over, he made clear that there were "red lines" that Israel would not cross, the key one being that Israel would not withdraw to its 1967 border, that "Greater Jerusalem, the eternal capital of Israel, will remain united and complete under the sovereignty of Israel,"[34] and that Jewish settlements would remain in "Judea, Samaria and Gaza."[35] Thus, Barak made clear that UN resolutions would be ignored, and that the foundation of the dialogue with the Palestinians was doomed to fail from the start, as the right to build a real state in the West Bank and Gaza was clearly not going to be the result.

Avi Shlaim, the Oxford scholar who is at his most scathing when writing of Netanyahu, described the 1999 election as "a political earthquake. But it was more than an earthquake. It was the sunrise after the three dark and terrible years during which Israel had been led by the unreconstructed proponents of the iron wall."[36] But the optimism that prevailed with the demise of Netanyahu and the arrival of Barak was derived from wishful thinking. Barak's "red lines" meant that even while he sought a negotiated solution, he was not going to deliver what was envisaged in the Oslo Declaration of Principles that had been agreed to by his "mentor and great leader." So what was he trying to achieve? His efforts focused on overcoming the intense pan-Arab distrust of Israel that had become the hallmark of the Netanyahu premiership and on creating an atmosphere more conducive to negotiation. At heart, he sought to give the impression that he was simply different from his predecessor, "not fixated on the idea of Israel being surrounded by predators. . . . But at the same time there could be little doubt that Barak intended to govern as he campaigned—as the political heir to Rabin the soldier-statesman, not [Shimon] Peres, the poet-philosopher,"[37] Shlaim writes.

The interplay between building trust and signing agreements is a major element in the cynical political conflict that has determined the course of the negotiating process and has served to undermine it. In his speech after the signing of the soon-to-collapse Wye accord, King Hussein went on to say:

> I think such a step as is concluded today will inevitably trigger those who want to destroy life, destroy hope, create fear in the hearts and minds of people, trigger in them their worst instincts. They will be skeptical on the surface, but if they can, they will cause damage, wherever they are and wherever they belong.[38]

Opponents of the peace process throughout the 1990s have clearly sought to undermine it by using violence, as in the case of the Palestinian suicide bombers or Israeli extremists such as Rabin's assassin, Yigal Amir, or the murderer of Palestinian worshippers, Baruch Goldstein, at the Hebron mosque. The horrifying violence has shaken—as it is intended to do—both sides, as actions and reprisals spiral and confidence is lost. The readiness or not to keep an eye on the bigger picture—as King Hussein was advocating—has varied according to the agendas of successive political players in the awful drama. Netanyahu demanded rigid Palestinian Authority adherence to every letter of every agreement—while ignoring Israel's own obligations—largely to slow the process. As Ariel Sharon has since done, Netanyahu made demands intended to discredit the Palestinian leadership and thus bolster Israel's negotiating position, fully aware that a weak Palestinian Authority could not negotiate any deal that would be accepted by Palestinians and that a strong Palestinian Authority would only accept a deal that brought with it the creation of a state whose substance Israel would regard as a threat. In a crisp assessment of both sides' strategies for the interim period between Oslo and the planned final status negotiations, Robert Malley, President Clinton's special assistant for Arab–Israeli affairs, and Hussein Agha of Oxford University wrote in 2002:

> Lacking a clear and distinct vision of where they were heading, both sides treated the interim period not as a time to prepare for an ultimate agreement but as a mere warm-up to the final negotiations; not as a chance to build trust, but as an opportunity to optimize their bargaining positions. As a result, each side was determined to hold on to its assets until the endgame. Palestinians were loath to confiscate weapons or clamp down on radical groups; Israelis were reluctant to return territory or halt settlement construction. Grudging behavior by one side fueled grudging behavior by the other, leading to a vicious cycle of skirted obligations, clear-cut violations, and mutual recriminations.
>
> By multiplying the number of obligations each side agreed to, the successive interim accords increased the potential for missteps and missed deadlines. Each interim agreement became the focal point for the next dispute and a microcosm for the overall conflict. . . . Yet another interim agreement could not cure ills that are inherent in the culture of interim agreements. . . . As all these factors suggest, the current confrontation is not an argument in favor of acting small, but rather a call to start thinking big.[39]

When, after just over a year in power, Ehud Barak sat down with Yasser Arafat and President Clinton at Camp David in Maryland on July 11, 2000, for what the Israeli leader described as "the moment of truth,"[40] he did so at a moment when the need to break down the Iron Wall was still a potent element in the thinking on both sides. He then sought to use this relatively productive atmosphere to push through an agreement of which Netanyahu himself would have been proud: Jerusalem would remain Israeli, the "1967 borders would be amended,"[41] the "overwhelming majority of the settlers in Judea, Samaria and the Gaza Strip will be in settlement blocs under Israeli sovereignty,"[42] and there would be no Palestinian army in the West Bank. "We are arriving at a decisive crossroads in the future relationship between us,"[43] Barak said, accurately. Fifteen days later, President Clinton emerged from the marathon negotiating sessions to announce: "I have concluded with regret that they will not be able to reach an agreement at this time."[44]

The ground rules for the Camp David talks were tough: "Nothing is agreed until everything is agreed," was what the negotiators had decided in advance. The talks had been preceded by a campaign by hawks in Israel and the United States intended to sow fear in the minds of Israelis that Barak was about to compromise Israel's security. Dore Gold, the former Netanyahu confidante and Israeli ambassador to the United Nations, now a senior adviser to Ariel Sharon, wrote an article, widely circulated by the Project for the New American Century think tank, which has since formulated many of the ideas at the heart of the Bush administration's Middle East policy. In the article the military threat from neighboring Arab states was elucidated as if the year was 1948 and the Arab states were about to attack. Referring to the Allon Plan for Israeli security, which was based on control of specific areas of high ground in the Jordan Valley, Gold wrote: "Indications are that this cornerstone of Israeli policy and diplomacy is about to go down the drain, as the

current US administration attempts to organize a three-way summit. . . . Israel is about to concede the strategic barrier of the Jordan
Valley in order to close a deal with the PLO."[45] Gold's argument was
that Israeli concessions over land would require greater Israeli reliance on U.S. military technology to maintain its military capability ahead of any threat from outside. Like Richard Perle and the
others who had written the 1996 paper advocating reduced Israeli
reliance on the United States, Gold rejected the idea of a deal that
implied the United States "taking an active part in shaping Israel's
future."[46] The process of peacemaking during the Clinton years is
seen by some as having had as its central premise U.S. power—pax
Americana—rather than a durable peace between the parties. As
Stephen Zunes of San Francisco University, a former executive director of the Institute for a New Middle East Policy, wrote during
the Netanyahu premiership:

> Most observers believe true peace requires a comprehensive settle-
> ment to the Arab–Israeli conflict, a dramatic reduction in military
> expenditure, and support for democratization and human rights.
> US policy in the 1990s worked contrary to these goals—that is,
> with American economic and strategic interests in the region tak-
> ing precedent—which means that a comprehensive peace which
> allows the region to form its own terms was impossible.[47]

Zunes portrays more than two decades of U.S. involvement in
the peace process, which began with the Carter-Sadat-Begin Frameworks for Peace signed at Camp David on September 17, 1978, as
having "successfully derailed ongoing efforts to organize an all-
parties conference, by working out a separate peace between Egypt
and Israel, and not effectively including the PLO. . . . [Moreover,
by] including promises of strategic cooperation and more than
$5bn of military aid annually to the two countries, the [1978]

Camp David Accords were more of a tripartite military pact than a true peace agreement."[48] Zunes identifies the Clinton administration as being "the first in US history to see the West Bank and Gaza as disputed territories, insinuating that the Israelis and Palestinians had equal claim to the land, rather than the view of the UN and others in the international community which continued to recognize East Jerusalem and other lands gained during the Israeli advances in 1967 as territory under foreign military occupation."[49] As a result, wrote Zunes, more than a year before the failure of the July 2000 Camp David talks:

> It was inevitable that a Clinton Administration-directed peace process would not lead to a settlement meeting legitimate Palestinian demands for self-determination. Rather, the goal seemed to be the establishment of economic and political structures that would severely limit the [Palestinian Authority] *vis-à-vis* Israel and thus lead to virtual continuation of Israeli control.[50]

The failure at Camp David was the clearest evidence that the foundation of discussion had to change fundamentally if negotiation was to bring a solution to the conflict. Among many elements revealed by the discussions was the significance of Palestinian—and particularly Yasser Arafat's—isolation. The process of weakening the Palestinians had been as concerted under Barak as under Netanyahu. Barak had done it by intensifying expectations of the Camp David meeting to fever pitch, while at the same time retaining his "red lines" and therefore knowing that he was not going to be offering the Palestinian leader the concessions he knew to be the only ones Arafat could successfully take back to the Palestinian people. Robert Malley, Clinton's adviser on Arab–Israeli affairs, who was present at Camp David throughout the talks, would later write that Arafat had "told us on numerous occasions that he had not wanted to go to Camp David. He thought that Israeli and Palestinian negotiators had not sufficiently narrowed the gaps separating their positions before the summit, and once there, made clear in his comments that he felt both isolated from the Arab world and alienated by the close Israeli-American partnership."[51] Barak had called the meeting "a moment of truth" and would continue after the failure to reach agreement to portray it as such; the truth was that "Arafat was afraid to make the historic decision necessary at this time in order to bring about an end to the conflict,"[52] the Israeli Prime Minister claimed.

This was far from the truth, however, and it was a major blow to the longer-term negotiating process that Barak and Clinton insisted on holding Arafat solely responsible for the collapse of the talks, by blaming him for his failure to accept Israeli proposals that he—and they—knew he could not sell to the Palestinians. The trust that some had thought had replaced the suspicion prevailing throughout the Netanyahu years disintegrated, as Israel and the United States in concert took to blaming the Palestinians for apparently being "not ripe for peace."[53] Barak's proposals to Arafat were clear: Israel would annex 9 percent of the West Bank and would in exchange give the Palestinians an area one-ninth the size of the annexed area; the new Palestinian state would thereby cover 91 percent of the West Bank, as well as Gaza, but would depend upon popular Palestinian acceptance of this unequal land exchange. In Jerusalem, a Palestinian government would have sovereignty over Arab neighborhoods in the east of the city and the Muslim and Christian quarters of the Old City, but Israel would retain sovereignty over the *Haram al-Sharif*— the third holiest site in Islam, known as the Temple Mount by Jews. On the vital issue of the return of the 3.5 million Palestinian refugees, nothing was decided, and Arafat feared the worst.

From the Palestinian perspective, the inadequacy of the Israeli proposals was as pronounced as the readiness of the Palestinians to make concessions. Dominating the vitriolic exchanges that took place after the talks collapsed has been the accusation that Arafat simply kept saying "no." Barak himself would say two years later that Arafat "did not negotiate in good faith, indeed, he did not negotiate at all."[54] But like Clinton, Barak was keen to go down in history as a man who had sought to make history, and he wanted history to be kind to him. This necessitated casting aside the detail of what he had offered Arafat, all along stressing the undoubted truth that nobody had theretofore offered the Palestinians a better deal. But it was a deal that was not good enough. As the official Palestinian assessment of what was offered makes clear, "Israel's Camp David proposal presented a 're-packaging' of military occupation, not an end to military occupation."[55] On the key issue of Jerusalem—the issue specified by Barak as the cause of the talks collapsing—the Palestinian position was that the Israeli proposals "would create Palestinian ghettos in the heart of Jerusalem,"[56] which "would remain separated not only from each other but also from the rest of the Palestinian state."[57] Regarding the rest of that state, the Palestinian position was that Israel's assertion that the Camp David proposals would return to the Palestinians most of the territory seized in 1967 was false. Since the signing of the Oslo accords, the Palestinians have recognized Israeli sovereignty over 78 percent of historic Palestine. But the 9–1 ratio of the proposed land swap in the Occupied Territories, and Israeli requests for long-term leases on a further 10 percent of the land there, would prevent the creation of a viable and independent state, and were "so unfair as to seriously undermine belief in Israel's commitment to a fair territorial compromise," the Palestinian statement read.[58] The Palestinians did agree to a 1–1 land swap in adjacent areas, but this was not offered.

Meanwhile, the Palestinian state envisaged by Barak was to have been divided into five noncontiguous areas, four in the West Bank split from each other by access roads leading to Israeli settlements, and the fifth covering the area of the Gaza Strip. The movement of people and economic activity between them would be under Israeli control, and "such a Palestinian state would have had less sovereignty and viability than the Bantustans created by the South African apartheid regime," the PLO argued.[59] Finally, on the question of the return of Palestinian refugees—and their descendants— forced out of the area when Israel was created, the Palestinian view was that the issue was never seriously discussed at Camp David because Barak "declared that Israel bore no responsibility for the refugee problem or its solution." But the Palestinian view remained clear that any settlement must include an agreement on the rights of the refugees, which would include addressing Israeli concerns that any right of return would be negotiated, and that Palestinian refugees might claim land and property seized from them by Israel in 1948. Instead, the issue was sidestepped.

MYTHS AND MAPS

On February 6, 2001, Barak's government fell. The *al-Aqsa intifada* had erupted five months before, encouraged by the visit on September 29, 2000, of the Likud leader Ariel Sharon and one thousand Israeli police and troops to the *Haram al-Sharif,* as a gesture laying Israeli claim to the Jerusalem site. Sharon was rewarded for his extremism by being appointed prime minister when Barak gave up. As the *intifada* raged, Arafat placed the blame for the outbreak of violence firmly on Sharon's shoulders, and told Arab leaders on October 21, 2000:

> The bloody events that resulted from the Israeli aggression against our Palestinian people have shown that the dangers of the absence of a just and lasting peace are not limited to a specific geographical

area; instead these dangers spread and threaten international security and stability.

Allow me, dear brothers, to say more than this, and address the United States, not just because it is a peace process sponsor, but also because it is the world power with distinctive responsibilities on the universal level and because it is directly interested in all areas of conflict in our world. The Middle East peace process has suffered from the absence of the balance needed to offer real chances for the progress of this process and the reaching of effective results in it. . . . I would like to draw attention to an issue where political dimensions mix with morals, where the concept of impartial sponsorship of the peace process does not go in line with the excessively harsh stands against the Palestinian people. These stands are embodied in many of the US Congress's decisions, which adopt a stand hostile to the Palestinian people and their rights.[60]

Clinton's failure at Camp David was just that: a failure of U.S. diplomacy. There can be no expectation of success in U.S.-led diplomacy in the Israeli–Palestinian conflict while the U.S. plays both arbiter and one-sided ally. Seeming desperate to secure his place in history before leaving office at the end of January 2001, Clinton drew up a new plan for Middle East peace in the weeks before his presidential term ended. The so-called Clinton Plan of December 23, 2000, was forensically torn to pieces by Palestinian negotiators, who concluded that the proposals—called the "parameters" by both sides—"fail to satisfy the conditions required for a permanent peace."[61] A week later, on January 7, 2001, Clinton responded in a speech to the Israel Policy Forum in New York, revealing the extent to which he himself doubted the Palestinian commitment to a peaceful settlement, and emphasizing the role of Arabs whom he saw as bent on using the Palestinian issue as a vehicle for a "whole different agenda."[62] Taking further the view that

Arafat's rejection of the Camp David proposals was the result of obstinacy rather than pragmatism, Clinton lashed out at the Palestinian leader, saying: "All the people that are saying to the Palestinian people: 'Stay on the path of *no*', are people that have a vested interest in the failure of the peace process that has nothing to do with how those kids in Gaza and the West Bank are going to grow up and live and raise their own children."[63]

But even as he was making these statements, it was becoming clearer that it was Clinton's own failure—and that of the United States as a world power capable of wielding influence in a manner that drew upon what it knew of the world rather than what it would like to see serving its own interests—that was at the heart of the problem. The reasons for the failure at Camp David have subsequently been subject to the most outrageous manipulation by those involved, adding vast amounts of fuel to an already raging fire; by blaming Arafat, both Clinton and Barak further undermined the Palestinian leader and lent huge credibility to the incoming government of Ariel Sharon in its subsequently near successful campaign to force Arafat out of the picture altogether. There is something vengeful about the way Clinton and Barak—both of whom have applauded each other's roles in the discussions—have misrepresented Arafat's approach during the talks as a way of concealing the true extent to which U.S. bias toward Israel has failed both Palestinians and Israelis by failing to play a genuine role as arbiter. What Arafat actually offered at Camp David was entirely consistent with long-held Palestinian positions—positions that have their foundations in UN resolutions, are to be found in the text of the Oslo Declaration of Principles signed by Barak's mentor Yitzhak Rabin, and are generally accepted by Palestinians as the basis of their nationhood and of Israel's right to exist as their neighbor. Robert Malley, the Clinton adviser present throughout the discussions, who has presented the only straightforward assessment of why Camp David failed, has made it clear that Arafat made substantial concessions regarding Israeli sovereignty over areas of East Jerusalem and Jewish settlements in the West Bank, as well as the negotiated return of Palestinian refugees. "No other Arab party that has negotiated with Israel—not Anwar al-Sadat's Egypt, not King Hussein's Jordan, let alone Hafez al-Assad's Syria—ever came close to even considering such compromises," Malley wrote in 2001.[64] A year later, in response to a long interview given by Ehud Barak to the *New York Review of Books*, Malley and Hussein Agha of Oxford University wrote scathingly of the way in which Barak and subsequently Ariel Sharon had gratuitously exploited the failure at Camp David as the basis for an entire policy of confrontation with the Palestinians, even though the premise—that the failure had been Arafat's fault alone, and that he orchestrated the violence that followed—was wholly inaccurate. "The failure at Camp David and the start of the second Palestinian intifada are directly linked in accounts by Barak and others to argue that Arafat's response to the unprecedented offers was to scuttle negotiations and seek to achieve his goals through terror," they wrote in 2002.[65] Specifically, they strongly rejected Barak's view that the right of return for Palestinian refugees amounted to a Palestinian plan to swamp Israel with Arabs and destroy the Jewish state:

> Barak's assessment that the talks failed because Yasser Arafat cannot make peace with Israel and that his answer to Israeli's unprecedented offer was to resort to violence has become central to the argument that Israeli is in a fight for survival against those who deny its right to exist. So much of what is said and done today derives from and is justified by that crude appraisal. . . . The one-sided account that was set in motion in the wake of Camp David has had devastating effects—on Israeli public opinion as well as on US foreign policy.[66]

The presidency of George W. Bush has seen the myths of the Israeli–Palestinian conflict take on far more importance than the realities. Barak's portrayal of the Palestinians as intent upon "the destruction of Israel as a Jewish state"[67] and as being "the products of a culture in which to tell a lie . . . creates no dissonance"[68] had permitted the Bush administration to isolate Arafat long before the September 11, 2001, terrorist attacks in New York and Washington allowed them to emerge with a foreign policy after nine months of wayward sniping at global issues. Arafat was characterized as having unleashed the *intifada* as a strategy that was somehow an alternative to negotiations. In fact he did not. On April 30, 2001, a five-man team led by former U.S. senator George Mitchell presented their conclusion as to why the violence started and what should be done to stop it. The Mitchell report flew in the face of Barak's later claim that Arafat had planned the violence, stating: "We have no basis on which to conclude that there was a deliberate plan by the Palestinian Authority to initiate a campaign of violence at the first opportunity."[69] But the process of manipulating public opinion—particularly in the United States—had already started to produce a picture of Arafat as the negotiator who does not accept the right of Israel to exist and is planning its demise. As one analyst in the *Washington Post* wrote in July 2002: "This view has become prevailing wisdom in the Bush administration and among most Israelis, and combined with the September 11 attacks, has been fatal for peace talks and nearly fatal for Arafat. Even if suicide attacks stopped, it would be awkward at best for Israel to go back to the bargaining table."[70]

The result was a focus on trying to revive security cooperation between the Palestinian Authority and Israel, rather than any substantive effort to address the underlying issues; in March 2002, George Tenet, the CIA director, presented a "security work plan,"[71] followed by the "Zinni Paper,"[72] which called on both sides to end attacks, collect weapons, and cooperate against "terrorist threats." President Bush then clarified the administration's approach in his June 24, 2002, speech. His conclusions—demanding the replacement of Arafat[73]— were delivered as if much of the Mitchell report had never been written, the truth about what actually happened at Camp David had never been aired, and the reality of being a Palestinian subject to the brutality of Israeli aggression had never dawned on him. The speech laid blame for the failure to achieve peace squarely on the structure of the Palestinian administration, and thus on Arafat, the embattled Palestinian leader who had watched Israeli tanks blast all but a few rooms of his Ramallah headquarters to dust while he was inside. Israel was blameless, according to Bush, and Palestinian suffering was something that the president said he understood as being the result of their having "been treated as pawns in the Middle East conflict. Your interests have been held hostage to a comprehensive peace agreement that never seems to come," he said. Clearly, in Bush's view all the Arab states that had ever involved themselves in Palestinian affairs were to blame for the Palestinian predicament, while the one country whose ambitions had forced Palestinians off their land had played no part in creating the suffering that had brought with it anger and violence.

Bush's warped perspective and unlimited bias against the Palestinians mean that the U.S. role in the search for peace between Israelis and Palestinians will hinder rather than help. With this in mind, the "road map" agreed to in October 2002, the sidelining of Arafat, and the installation of Mahmoud Abbas as a short-lived Israeli- and U.S.-approved Palestinian prime minister are elements riddled with familiar shortcomings. Launched as Israel is constructing a four-meter-high wall that will become a non-negotiated border between Israel and the West Bank that Israel will declare at a time of its choosing, the "road map's" three-year program—culminating theoretically in 2005 with the creation of a Palestinian state—focuses on Bush's idea that Palestinian "reform" is the key to bringing an end to the violence. The determination of the Bush administration to identify the Palestinian character as being the main fault line—rather than as being the consequence of the crisis—is a major weakness in the process. Pressuring the brief Abbas administration to tailor its functions to Israeli requirements will edge the underlying reality of the Palestinians' plight further outside the negotiating process. As Hasan Abunimah, a former Jordanian ambassador to the United Nations, and Ali Abunimah, founder of the Palestinian Web site Electronicintifada.com, wrote in the *Financial Times* in July 2003:

> Despite the declaration of a unilateral Palestinian ceasefire with Israel, and the frequent meetings between Israeli and Palestinian leaders, the "road map" for peace is in serious trouble. This is because the Bush administration, the plan's chief sponsor, has allowed Israel to reinterpret it so that it is gutted of the elements that offered hope of progress.
>
> . . . As the Bush administration does nothing to check Israel—and simultaneously piles pressure on the deeply unpopular Mr. Abbas, whose appointment as Palestinian prime minister it engineered—it is only a matter of time before the situation explodes in a new and sustained round of violence.
>
> Perhaps the only hope of saving the process lies with strong intervention by the European Union, which nominally co-authored the road map. Hitherto, the EU has acquiesced in US leadership, even when it has disagreed with US positions. And the US has been willing to ignore Europe on those rare occasions when it has asserted itself, as the Iraq crisis demonstrated. But, ironically, US difficulties in Iraq may give Europe the leverage to demand real action towards Palestinian freedom and Middle East peace as a prerequisite for help in extricating the Americans from their own unravelling occupation of Iraq.[74]

Despite the United States's ability to remain active, convene meetings, and appear involved, its efforts have failed at most stages, if considered in their own terms. All U.S. administrations have sought to portray their initiatives as historic, when in fact they have ended up being part of a painfully slow and incremental process of building ties between the opposing sides—ties that may perhaps one day merge as common interests leading to the creation of the single state that is the only real hope for stability. Clinton in particular stressed the historic—taking his lead from Ehud Barak—but in the end accepted that reality would always raise its head. The emphasis on the historic act has also been a key part of the highly destructive public relations element in the process of U.S.-led negotiations, in which lobbyists secure more importance than players, impressions become more important than facts, and platitudes take the place of credible ideas, as the post–Camp David analyses offered by Robert Malley have shown. Ultimately, however, the only real moments of history have been instigated by the players themselves, or by minor countries capable of subtle diplomacy: Anwar al-Sadat's visit to Israel and address to the Knesset on November 20, 1977; the Norwegian-led Oslo accords; King Hussein of Jordan's personal apology to the families of Israeli schoolchildren shot by a Jordanian soldier. These are the real moments of history. The U.S. role has been dominated by words rather than deeds and by a search for a U.S. place in history that distinguishes it from all other nations on the basis of its intellectual weight rather than merely its financial and military resources. But the United States has often been responsible for undermining its capacity to achieve this status. On the one hand, it has sought the role of "sponsor" and arbiter, but on the other it has provided the loan guarantees for illegal settlement building—$9 billion more of which were agreed to with Israel on August 20, 2003—and does nothing to discourage American Jews from going to live illegally in the Occupied Territories; it provides the military equipment Israeli routinely unleashes on Palestinians; and it never votes against Israel at the United Nations. It was against this background that Fouad Ajami, professor of Middle Eastern studies at Johns Hopkins University, wrote in the wake of the September 11, 2001, terrorist attacks:

> In the best of worlds, Pax Americana is doomed to a measure of solitude in the Middle East. This time around [as the United States sought allies against al-Qaeda], the American predicament is particularly acute. Deep down, the Arab regimes feel that the threat of political Islam to their own turfs has been checked, and that no good can come out of an explicit public alliance with an American campaign in their midst. Foreign powers come and go, and there is very little protection they can provide against the wrath of an angry crowd. It is a peculiarity of the Arab-Islamic political culture that a ruler's authoritarianism is more permissible than his identification with Western powers—think of the fates of Sadat and the Pahlavis of Iran.
>
> Ride with the foreigners at your own risk, the region's history has taught. . . . So in thwarted, resentful societies there was satisfaction on September 11 that the American bull run and the triumphalism that had awed the world had been battered, that there was soot and ruin in New York's streets. We know better now. Pax Americana is there to stay in the oil lands and in Israeli-Palestinian matters. No large-scale retreat from those zones of American primacy can be contemplated. American hegemony is sure to hold—and so, too, the resistance to it, the uneasy mix in those lands of the need for the foreigner's order, and the urge to lash out against it, to use it and rail against it all the same.[75]

In the Middle East, the United States is a lonely superpower now trying to reorganize a region of the world in which its interests are substantial. Martin Indyk, former U.S. ambassador to Israel, insists that "Only the United States can credibly sponsor such an initiative [as international trusteeship of Palestine], because only it enjoys the essential trust of both parties."[76] His characterization of the U.S. position is highly optimistic. There is no region of the world in which the U.S. reputation is so clearly seen—in particular on the "Arab street"—as that of an aggressor; beyond its unshakable alliance with Israel, its allies are the despots targeted by the Islamists. Having played no constructive role in the Israeli–Palestinian conflict prior to the September 11 terrorist attacks, the Bush administration simplistically used "terror" as the label to define the good and the bad in the conflict, and sought to portray the crisis as one with which it was ready to engage only if the Palestinians capitulated.

The Palestinian Authority has had no choice but to accept a U.S. role, despite Washington's bias against it, for the simple reason that no other body has presented itself as a viable alternative as mediator. However, U.S. credibility should not be seen as invincible. Foreign policy failure has been the hallmark of the Bush administration since its election. Compensating for that failure is what lies behind the launch of the "Global War on Terror" or GWOT, as well as the creation of the entirely spurious "Axis of Evil" and the plan to lead the political transformation of the entire Middle East. But circumstance rather than vision has lain behind the Bush project since September 11, 2001, the administration's image being that of a militaristic roller coaster that is out of control rather than a political force equipped with credible and durable plans for global betterment. As the November 2004 election approaches, the *fragile myths* underpinning the administration's credibility have started to emerge. The testimony of former White House counterterrorism chief Richard A. Clarke to the commission investigating the September 11 terrorist attacks amounted to an allegation that the Bush administration had been complacent about the threat from al-

Qaeda. Clarke told the commission: "The Bush Administration saw terrorism policy as important but not urgent, prior to 9-11. The difficulty in obtaining the first Cabinet level (Principals) policy meeting on terrorism and the limited Principals' involvement sent unfortunate signals to the bureaucracy about the Administration's attitude towards the al-Qaida threat."[77] Clarke has since vilified the administration in his book, *Against All Enemies*.[78] The extent of the administration's apparent complacency was revealed in the declassified President's Daily Brief—the secret intelligence assessment presented to the president each day by the CIA—of August 6, 2001. The brief stated: "FBI information since [1998] indicates patterns of suspicious activity in this country consistent with preparations for hijackings or other types of attacks, including recent surveillance of federal buildings in New York."[79]

Regarding the August 6 brief, Condoleeza Rice, Bush's national security adviser, told the Commission: "There was nothing in this memo that suggested that an attack was coming on New York or Washington, D.C. There was nothing in this memo as to time, place, how or where. This was not a threat report to the president or a threat report to me."[80] The difficulty of infiltrating al-Qaeda means it would be unreasonable to argue that the administration could have known about the details of the September 11 attacks in advance. But what is clear is that little had been done to maximize efforts to respond to what *was* known and had been revealed in the August 6 brief. The extent to which U.S. homeland security measures have been transformed in the wake of the September 11 attacks has revealed the extent to which such reform was required and has exposed the administration as having in reality been less preoccupied with the security of Americans than it might have been. Globally, the impact of the GWOT has been to tailor U.S. foreign policy to the domestic security needs undertaken to compensate for this past failure. No other nation is threatened by al-Qaeda in the way the United States is, but the GWOT has created the impression that the destinies of all nations are tied to that of the United States, which they are not. The United States has diminished its ability to act as an arbiter on issues that require an impartial player. Its major failure has been on the Israeli–Palestinian issue, where the Bush administration has contributed to the crisis by fueling anger at its failure to play the role of intermediary it inherited but to which it is clearly no longer entitled.

The consequences of diplomatic failures to which the United States has been integral have brought a growing need to widen the scope of discussions and bring more players into the equation in more than the symbolic roles the United States allots to the "Quartet." The initial isolationism that the Bush administration has been forced to dilute in pursuit of its own security interests has been a key element in this shift. Part of Osama bin Laden's success has been to clarify Western, and particularly U.S., interests in the Arab world in a manner that has starkly exposed his own primacy as a political force. The "war against terror" has brought the most vehement Middle Eastern enemies of Islamism into the open as potential allies of the United States, among them Libya and Syria. Both, from the Islamists' perspective, are regimes that are vulnerable to criticism as human rights abusers. President Bush's "you're either with us or you're with the terrorists" choice was foisted on Arab regimes, who for a very short time hoped for leverage over U.S. policy in return for their commitment. But even America's long-term allies—Egypt, Jordan, and Morocco—have secured no additional leverage, particularly on the vital issue that concerns them all: the Israeli–Palestinian conflict. Most Arab governments had anyway already neutralized the substantial Islamist threat—in Syria as long ago as 1982, in Egypt in 1997, in Libya in 1999—which is the very reason why the Islamists left the region and decided to hit the mainland United States instead. Thus, the United States garnered support for *its* war, giving little or nothing to its allies in the region—in which sensitivities to Western behavior are most high—other than threats if they did not jump aboard. The regimes have now been left empty-handed, a fact from which their domestic political opponents will draw invaluable political capital.

This scenario is a familiar one to the Arab world, the history of Arab relations with Europe and the United States being littered with similar episodes of Western opportunism. It is the core reason why bin Laden and others like him will cement division with the West, on the basis that it is duplicitous and cannot be trusted. If the United States were evenhanded in its treatment of the Israeli–Palestinian conflict and went further, for example, than calling the killing by Israeli aerial bombardment of fourteen Palestinians—among them nine children—in Gaza in July 2002 merely "heavy-handed," if the war in Iraq had been portrayed as being in Arab as well as U.S., U.K., and Israeli interests, then the waves from the Middle Eastern epicenter of the al-Qaeda network would have less global resonance and bin Laden's task would be more difficult. Instead, distrust of U.S. motives has escalated, with the fault lines appearing both *within* the West and beyond, intensifying debate within the United States over whether the superpower knows what to do with its power: "Just because the United States is strong enough to act heedlessly does not mean that it should do so. Why not?" asked Stephen Brooks and William Wohlforth, academics at Dartmouth College, in a daunting analysis of U.S. military might. "Because it can afford to reap the greater gains that will eventually come from magnanimity. . . . After all, it is influence, not power, that is ultimately most valuable."[81]

EPILOGUE

The Palestinian–Israeli conflict is one of numerous issues influencing Arab political life. It is far from being the only issue. Its importance in the eyes of the world is in part a reflection of the imbalance of power that is the dominant feature of the region's relationship with the rest of the world, and with the West in particular. The fact of the conflict being a defining issue in this relationship is a cause of the tension and enmity that dominate that relationship and the image of the Arab world in the eyes of others. It is the West that has made this so. In the United States in particular, Arabs, and Arab states, peoples, religions, communities, and societies, are widely judged through the prism of the Arab–Israeli conflict and the consequences it has for U.S. national security concerns. It is as if the ebbs, flows, and horrors at Israeli bus stops and on the streets of Gaza or Ramallah are the only valid benchmarks of the entire region. The Arab world is not taken seriously in and of itself but is judged by the extent to which it adapts or not to Western interests, expressed either directly or by the litmus test of Israel.

The West's disdain for Arab and Islamic culture is not lost on the victims of this attitude. The most vocal opponents of Western influence in the Arab world, the extreme Islamists, are no longer seeking dialogue with the West. They remain adamant that dialogue is intended solely to engineer the capitulation of the Arabs to Western interests under the guise of "modernization." The architects of current U.S. policy in the Middle East would argue that Islamists have never sought dialogue with the West. This is not true, as the close relationship between the Islamists who evolved into al-Qaeda and the U.S. government that backed them during the 1980s in the fight against the Soviet occupation of Afghanistan showed. The confrontation that evolved into the September 11 terrorist attacks in New York and Washington is the extreme response to both self-loathing among Arabs who now despair of the Arab failure to extricate the region from the grip of Western power and the failure to build a modern identity for the region that is the result of internal evolution rather than external pressure.

Western power is the source of the enmity, tension, and misunderstanding that now dominate the Arab region's perceptions of itself and its place in the world. But the sentiments behind this conflict are far more complex than merely a critical attitude toward Western lifestyles. Arab history is strongly influenced by the sense of a once dynamic, innovative, and politically and religiously pluralist past having been lost, and possibly having been thrown away by irresponsible Arab leaders who sold out to the Europeans. It is also strongly influenced—though most strongly among Islamists—by the view that this past can be regained, and the perception is that it is Western power that is preventing the region from doing so. To truly begin to develop, the Arab world must first extricate itself from this debilitating habit of judging its worth and credibility through a process of comparison with the West. But central to the frustration that has now found voice in extremism is the realization that the avenues to such self-confidence are elusive. In his collection of essays, *What Went Wrong? The Clash between Islam and Modernity in the Middle East,*[1] the Harvard scholar Bernard Lewis writes:

If they can abandon grievance and victimhood, settle their differences, and join their talents, energies, and resources in a common
creative endeavor, then they can once again make the Middle
East, in modern times, as it was in antiquity and in the Middle
Ages, a major center of civilization. For the time being, the choice
is their own.[2]

This is a startling conclusion from one so well-versed in the
trail of events in the region, written before choice was largely taken
out of Arab hands by the decision of the second Bush administration to deliver the region an ultimatum to either meet U.S. demands for reform or face the fate of Iraq. In this calamitous
environment, the idea of "choice" is fundamental. Do the Arabs
have a choice? If so, is it in their hands, and if so, in which Arab
hands does that choice lie? When the Israeli government of Ariel
Sharon refused to work with Yasser Arafat, and the United States
did the same, this gave the Palestinians a choice: They must abandon either their democratically elected leader and the symbolic
focus of their long struggle for justice, or abandon dialogue with
their opponent. The choice was hardly theirs to make. Now, having
crossed the Rubicon and invaded Iraq, the United States and its
ally, the United Kingdom, are faced with the fact that as conquerors of a sovereign state, the choices they would like to see the
country have are those that they as conquerors are prepared to put
to the few people prepared to deal with them. What is clear now, in
May 2004, is that the Iraqis and other Arabs who are setting the
agenda in Iraq, have little intention of negotiating with the invaders. It barely matters what choice the U.S. regime in Iraq puts
to Iraqis; the fact that it has been offered by an "infidel" force allied
with Israel means that U.S. plans will be routinely opposed and
never fully implemented. The lesson will perhaps be learned sooner
or later, that whatever offer an invader makes will be rejected, not

because the offer is necessarily unattractive, but because of who made it.

It is a mark of how deep the crisis facing the Arab world now is that the foreign powers whose meddling in the region has done so much to stoke the fires of extremism throughout the past century are now becoming more rather than less influential, even as the Arab world's rejection of Western influence grows. In the conclusion of his classic tome *The Scramble for Africa*, Thomas Pakenham observed the following shift in the attitudes of European colonialists between the two world wars:

> [An] irreversible change had occurred in the world's attitude to colonies in the twenty-seven years since the end of the First World War. Gone was the empire-building alliance of God and Mammon that had helped to launch the Scramble. Now the imperialists were on the defensive. Both the men of God and the men of business had begun to see that formal empire was counter-productive. Colonies were becoming unfashionable.[3]

Now the alliance is back, in the form of a U.S. strategy intended to reshape the Middle East entirely, by abandoning diplomacy and enforcing hegemony through the military force that is leading and forging U.S. foreign policy. There being no audible note of approval from within the region for the plan Washington appears to have for the region, it is a plan that will necessitate increasing force, probably lead to increasingly violent resistance, and eventually result in the recognition that hegemony is as "counterproductive" as colonialism. The only way to form enduring relations with other nations, peoples, and cultures is to learn about them and the language they speak, understand them, seek out areas of common interest, and then establish mutually beneficial ties. Such cooperation was possible in the aftermath of the September 11 terrorist attacks, but the opportunity has since been squandered. The invasion of Iraq by a force whose ignorance of all these things is a major cause of the friction that exists between the occupying force and the Iraqi population, and has created the conditions in Iraq for a catastrophe that will have major reverberations in Saudi Arabia, Iran, and the Gulf states. As former U.S. Secretary of State Madeleine Albright wrote in September 2003, in an impressive critique of administration policy:

> [Was] invading Iraq the right way to start building democratic momentum in the Arab world? The answer will depend on how divided Iraq remains, and how dicey the security situation becomes. US soldiers will have a hard time democratizing Iraq if they are forced to remain behind walls and inside tanks. And US officials will lack credibility preaching the virtues of freedom if they feel compelled to censor broadcasts, search houses, ban political parties, and repeatedly reject Iraqi demands for more complete self rule.[4]

The Bush administration's scandalous failure to plan in detail and in advance what it was going to do in Iraq once Saddam Hussein's regime had been overthrown was the clearest sign that U.S. hegemony is a military phenomenon and will remain so even after the planned handover of administrative power to Iraqis on June 30, 2004. The neoconservative agenda spearheading administration actions does not offer even the vaguest idea of how a political agenda borne out of quite understandable U.S. national security interests can be exported to an area of the world where the United States has only one natural ally and is regarded with deep suspicion by the people.

American exasperation with the rejection by the mass of the Arab world of its power, influence, and sense of moral rectitude is the sore now irritating the U.S. body politic. Confrontation on the battlefield of Iraq is the clash that both sides have been moving toward since Osama bin Laden first lay down his challenge in 1996.

Just as the September 11 terrorist attacks forced the Bush administration out of the foreign policy shell from within which it had been content to snipe insults at the rest of the world in the first nine months of its term, so the decision to "preemptively" invade Iraq is a turning point in Arab history that reverses the trend that preceded it. Arab political life was born out of the imperial incubator. Across the spectrum, from the Muslim Brotherhood to the secular nationalists, the political edifice of the modern Arab world was built on foundations cut and shaped by the imperial experience. Among other former colonies, in sub-Saharan Africa for example, the continued interference of the former colonial powers and the United States in their affairs throughout the Cold War determined the course of political life. For Arab states, the forceful identification of Arab interests, their greater economic power, and the proximity of the Arab world to Europe meant that they could not be manipulated quite so extensively. However, the assertion of an identity that would mark the break with the colonial past, which could then be built up as proof that all that was good in the world was not necessarily European or American, has proved far more tortuous for the Arab world than for any other region that suffered under the colonial yoke.

The reason for this is straightforward: The Arab world is trapped. While Bernard Lewis can argue that the region should shed its sense of victimhood, he omits to mention that the reason for this self-perception among the Arabs of the Middle East is that there *are* a vast number of victims. Around 3.5 million Palestinian refugees remain the victims of the European fascism from which emerged the momentum that led to the creation of Israel; of the European colonialism that facilitated the theft of an entire country from the Palestinians; and of the U.S.-equipped, financed, and supported attacks on Palestinians by Israel. The refugees will never be allowed to return to their stolen homes in Palestine, and the process of their incorporation into the states in which they are stateless will be long, violent, and destabilizing for the entire region. The trap in which the Arab world now finds itself is one constructed during the multiple processes of responding feebly but with much venom to issues beyond its control—in particular, the creation of Israel—while seeking to build a political life that reflects both Arab modernity and Arab history. The leaders of the Arab world have allowed their people to fall into this trap by failing to create a balance within their own societies that would allow their fragile grip on power to be channeled into a credible process of nation building, and out of which popular legitimacy could perhaps grow. Now, faced with the presence of an occupying force at the heart of the Arab world, their credibility as leaders of an unforgiving population in search of dignity can only be further undermined. With a new era of foreign interference in the Middle East apparently in the making, the potential for Arabs to build their own nations is now in danger of being taken out of their hands altogether, with the injustices wrought by Western influence likely to become the foundations of the new regime. The current climate of tension and distrust can only hinder the Arab world from being drawn out of the crisis in which it finds itself. It is into this already raging and hate-filled inferno that a whole new generation of fighters are stepping, intent upon launching the ultimate and certainly futile *jihad* with the aim of expelling the infidel from the land of Islam.

NOTES

Prologue

1. Halim Barakat, *The Arab World: Society, Culture and State* (Berkeley, Los Angeles, London: University of California Press, 1993), 42.
2. Ibid., 9.
3. Albert Hourani, *A History of the Arab Peoples* (London: Faber & Faber, 1991), 454.

Chapter 1

1. Gamal Abdel Nasser, prime minister (1954–1956) and later president of Egypt (1956–1970), quoted in David Hirst and Irene Beeson, *Sadat* (London: Faber & Faber, 1981), 40.
2. Interview with the author, February 15, 1998.
3. Ibid.
4. Interview with the author, Cairo, January 16, 1999.
5. Mohammed Saeed al-Sahaf, press conference, Baghdad, January 13, 1999.
6. Dispatch, Saudi Arabian News Agency, Riyadh, January 14, 1999.
7. Interview with the author, Baghdad, March 16, 1998.
8. Interview with the author, Cairo, April 5, 2001.
9. Youssef Boutros-Ghali (minister of economy and foreign trade, Egypt), interview with the author, Cairo, March 29, 1998.

10. Eberhard Keinle, *A Grand Delusion: Democracy and Economic Reform in Egypt* (London and New York: I. B.Tauris, 2000), 195.

11. Interview with the author, Cairo, March 30, 1998.

12. Interview with the author, Cairo, May 7, 1998.

13. Interview with the author, Cairo, April 20, 1999.

14. Ibid.

15. Interview with the author, Cairo, June 21, 1999.

16. Interview with the author, Cairo, April 8, 1999.

17. Interview with the author, Rabat, September 17, 1995.

18. Interview with the author, Sale, December 15, 1995.

19. Interview with the author, Rabat, January 9, 1996.

20. Interview with the author, Rabuny, Algeria, May 28, 1996.

21. Interview with the author, Rabuny, Algeria, May 28, 1996.

22. Ahmed Marzouki, interview by author, Rabat, November 11, 1995. For Ahmed Marzouki's account of Tazmamart see: Ahmed Marzouki, *Tazmamart: Cellule 10* (Paris: Editions Paris-Mediterranee, 2000).

23. Interview with the author, Rabat, November 11, 1995.

24. Interview with the author, Rabat, December 4, 1999.

25. For the full story of the Oufkir family, see Stephen Smith, *Oufkir, Un Destin Marocain* (Paris: Calmann-Levy, 1999); and Malika Oufkir with Michele Fitoussi, *Stolen Lives: Twenty Years in a Desert Jail*, trans. Ros Schwartz (New York: Talk Miramax Books, 2001).

26. G. Douin, *La Mission de Baron de Boislecomte* (Cairo: n.p., 1927), quoted in Albert Hourani, *Arabic Thought in the Liberal Age, 1798–1939* (Cambridge: Cambridge University Press, 1983), 261.

27. C. Ernest Dawn, "The Origins of Arab Nationalism," in *The Origins of Arab Nationalism*, ed. Rashid Khalidi, Lisa Anderson, Muhammad Muslih, and Riva Simon (New York: Columbia University Press, 1991), 11.

28. Ibid., 23.

29. Hourani, *Arabic Thought*, 260.

30. Interview with the author, Kuwait City, July 3, 1999.

31. Interview with the author, Kuwait City, July 7, 1999.

32. Interview with the author, Kuwait City, July 2, 1999.

33. Interview with the author, Kuwait City, July 1999.

34. Interview with the author, Kuwait City, July 3, 1999.

35. Interview with the author, Kuwait City, July 4, 1999.

36. Bernard Lewis, *What Went Wrong? The Clash between Islam and Modernity in the Middle East* (London: Weidenfeld & Nicolson, 2002), 70.

37. Ibid., 73.

38. Moncef Marzouki, human rights activist, interview with the author, Tunis, October 20, 1999. From 1989 to 1994 Dr. Marzouki served as president of the Tunisian League for Human Rights, and later as spokesperson for the National Council on Liberties in Tunisia. In 1994, after declaring himself the opposition candidate to Ben Ali, he was imprisoned for four months. In 1994 the Tunisian government shut down the Center for Community Medicine, a clinic he had founded that provided medical care to residents in the slums of Sousse, a city a hundred kilometers south of Tunis. In July 2000 Marzouki received a letter from the Ministry of Health, dismissing him permanently from his position as professor of public health at the University of Sousse, because of statements he had made during a visit to the United States. In October 2000 he was charged with the crime of "spreading false information intended to disturb the public order," in response to a paper he had written criticizing Tunisia's human rights practices, which was circulated privately at a meeting of human rights defenders in Morocco earlier that year. In December 2000 he was convicted and sentenced to one year in prison. In September 2001, responding to an international campaign on his behalf, the Tunisian government formally suspended the sentence. In December 2001, he left Tunisia and now teaches at the Faculty of Medicine of the University of Paris.

39. Interview with the author, Tunis, October 20, 1999. Along with Moncef Marzouki, Ben Jaafar had founded the Tunisian National Council for Liberty (CNLT), as well as the Democratic Forum party, which the authorities refused to register.

Chapter 2

1. Interview with the author, Cairo, May 28, 1998.

2. Interview with the author, Alexandria, June 4, 1998.

3. Albert Hourani, *Arabic Thought in the Liberal Age, 1798–1939* (Cambridge: Cambridge University Press, 1983), 349–50.

4. Bernard Lewis, *What Went Wrong? The Clash between Islam and Modernity in the Middle East* (London: Weidenfeld & Nicolson, May 2002), 159–60.

5. *Al-Ahram Weekly,* Cairo, May 18, 1998.

6. Interview with the author, Cairo, May 28, 1998.

7. Interview with the author, Cairo, May 28, 1998.

8. Interview with the author, Algiers, September 16, 1999.

9. Interview with the author, Algiers, September 19, 1999.

10. Ibid.

11. Ibid.

12. Ibid.

13. For my own account of the war during the mid-1990s, see Mark Huband, *Warriors of the Prophet: The Struggle for Islam* (Boulder, Colo.: Westview Press, 1998), chapter 3.

14. Habib Souaidia, *La sale guerre: Le temoignage d'un officier des forces speciales de l'armee algerienne, 1992–2000* (Paris: Gallimard, 2001), 246.

15. Interview with the author, Algiers, September 18, 1999.

16. Ibid.

17. Interview with the author, Algiers, September 19, 1999.

18. Interview with the author, Algiers, September 21, 1999.

19. Ibid.

20. Interview with the author, Algiers, May 29, 2000.

21. Interview with the author, Algiers, September 15, 1999.

22. Interview with the author, Algiers, May 26, 2000.

23. Interview with the author, Khartoum, June 3, 1997. Parts of this chapter are based on Mark Huband, *Warriors of the Prophet: The Struggle for Islam* (Boulder, Colo.: Westview Press, 1998), chapter 7.

24. Interview with the author, Khartoum, December 15, 1993.

25. Interview with the author, Khartoum, December 14, 1993.

26. Interview with the author, Khartoum, December 13, 1993.

27. Ibid.

28. Sadiq al-Mahdi, leader of the Umma Party, interview with the author, Khartoum, December 16, 1993.

29. The rejection of force is raised in the Koran in several different contexts: "Whoso doeth that through aggression and injustice, We shall cast him into the fire, and that is ever easy for Allah," Surah 4, Verse 30; "Fight in the way of Allah against those who fight against you, but begin not hostilities. Lo! Allah loveth not aggressors," Surah 2, Verse 190; "I do not worship that which you worship, and neither do you worship that which I worship. And I will not worship that which you have ever worshipped, and neither will you [ever] worship that which I worship. Unto you, your moral law, and unto me, mine," Surah 109, Verses 1–6.

30. This figure and other information on the domestic policy of the NIF at this time was provided by Mohamed Ahamed Abdelgadir al-Arabab, a former

provincial state minister who fled the country in March 1995. Interview with the author, Asmara, Eritrea, May 5, 1995.

31. Hassan el-Tourabi, "The Islamic State," in *Voices of Resurgent Islam,* ed. John L. Esposito (New York: Oxford University Press, 1983), 245–46.

32. *Tawhid* means the unity of God and human life, which deems all public life religious and the purpose of public life being to pursue the service of God as laid down in the religious law, the *sharia.*

33. El-Tourabi, "Islamic State," 247.

34. For a detailed account of Islamic rule in Sudan see Mark Huband, *Warriors of the Prophet: The Struggle for Islam* (Boulder, Colo.: Westview Press, 1998), chapter 7.

35. Interview with the author, Khartoum, May 31, 1997.

36. Interview with the author, Khartoum, November 3, 2001.

37. Interview with the author, Khartoum, May 31, 1997.

38. Interview with the author, Khartoum, November 3, 2001.

39. Ibid.

40. "Sudanese President Isolates Rival," *Financial Times,* May 8, 2000.

41. Ibid.

42. Interview with the author, Khartoum, November 6, 2001.

43. Ibid.

44. Interview with the author, Cairo, October 27, 1998.

45. Ibid.

46. Parts of this chapter appeared in "An Army in the Shadows," *Financial Times,* July 20, 2002.

47. Gilles Kepel, *Jihad: The Trail of Political Islam* (London and New York: I. B.Tauris, 2002), 371.

48. Ibid., 373.

49. See Mark Huband, *Warriors of the Prophet,* 73–93.

50. Bernard Lewis, *What Went Wrong? The Clash between Islam and Modernity in the Middle East* (London: Weidenfeld & Nicolson, May 2002), 151–52.

51. Ibid., 23.

52. Kepel, *Jihad,* 219–20.

53. Ibid., 207.

54. Ibid., 320.

55. Ibid., 256.

56. M. J. Akbar, *The Shade of Swords: Jihad and the Conflict between Islam and Christianity* (London and New York: Routledge, 2002).

57. Ibid., 191.

58. Ibid., 195.

Chapter 3

1. M. J. Akbar, *The Shade of Swords: Jihad and the Conflict between Islam and Christianity* (London and New York: Routledge, 2002), 76.

2. Ibid.

3. Interview with the author, Khartoum, November 7, 2001.

4. Ibid.

5. Interview with the author, Khartoum, November 8, 2001.

6. Interview with the author, Khartoum, November 7, 2001.

7. For a detailed account of this intelligence sharing, see Mark Huband, *The Skull beneath the Skin: Africa after the Cold War* (Boulder, Colo.: Westview Press, 2001), 272–75.

8. Interview with the author, Khartoum, November 7, 2001.

9. Bernard Lewis, *What Went Wrong? The Clash between Islam and Modernity in the Middle East* (London: Weidenfeld & Nicolson, 2002), 158.

10. Ibid., 159–60.

11. Parts of this chapter are adapted from Mark Huband, John Willman, et al., "Inside al-Qaeda," *Financial Times*, November, 28–30, 2001, 10–11.

12. Jamal Ahmed al-Fadl, court testimony, New York, Southern District Court, March 20, 2001–May 31, 2001.

13. Interview with the author, Khartoum, November 5, 2001.

14. I am grateful to my colleague Mark Turner for these details.

15. (London: Global Witness, April 2003).

16. Telephone interview with the author, April 16, 2003.

17. Telephone interview with the author, April 16, 2003.

18. L'Houssaine Khertchou, court testimony, New York, Southern District Court, March 20, 2001–May 31, 2001.

19. Interview with the author, Khartoum, November 7, 2001.

20. Part of this chapter appeared in Mark Huband, Farhan Bokhari, Charles Clover, Roel Landingen, and Victoria Burnett, "The CEO of al-Qaeda," *Financial Times*, February 15–16, 2003, 1–2.

21. I am grateful to my colleague Charles Clover for these details.

22. Ibid.

23. Ibid.

24. Mark Huband, *Warriors of the Prophet: The Struggle for Islam* (Boulder, Colo.: Westview Press, 1998), chapter 1.

25. According to the college Web site.

26. I am grateful to my colleague Victoria Burnett for these details.

27. Simon Reeve, *The New Jackals* (Boston: Northeastern University Press, 1999).
28. Abdel Hakim Murad, report of interrogation by Philippines police, transcript in author collection.
29. Interview with the author, Manila, November 22, 2002.
30. Telephone interview with the author, November 14, 2002.
31. Part of this chapter appeared in Huband, *Warriors of the Prophet*, chapter 1.
32. Interview with the author, Kabul, December 4, 1996.
33. Ibid.
34. Interview with the author, Kabul, December 4, 1996.
35. Interview with the author, Kabul, December 6, 1996.
36. Ibid.
37. Ibid.
38. Osama bin Laden, "Declaration of Jihad against the Americans Occupying the Two Holy Places," Khurasan, Afghanistan, August 23, 1996.
39. "Fatwa Urging Jihad against Americans," signed by "Sheikh Usamah Bin-Mohammed Bin-Laden; Ayman al-Zawahiri, leader of the Jihad Group in Egypt; Abu-Yasir Rifa'i Ahmad Taha, a leader of the Islamic Group; Sheikh Mir Hamzah, secretary of the Jamiat-ul-Ulema-e-Pakistan; and Fazlul Rahman, leader of the Jihad Movement in Bangladesh," published in *al-Quds al-'Arabi*, London, February 23, 1998, 1.
40. Interview with the author, Istanbul, November 22, 2003.
41. Interview with the author, Casablanca, March 29, 2004.
42. President Hosni Mubarak, address to Egyptian forces, Suez, March 31, 2003.

Chapter 4

1. First Lieutenant Tim McLaughlin, 3rd Battalion 4th Marines, quoted in "Victory in the 21-Day War," *The Times*, April 10, 2003.
2. Bernard Lewis, *What Went Wrong? The Clash between Islam and Modernity in the Middle East* (London: Weidenfeld & Nicolson, 2002), 160.
3. Ibid., 153.
4. Interview with the author, Washington, D.C., November 13, 2002.
5. Edward W. Said, "Apocalypse Now," in *Acts of Aggression: Policing Rogue States* (New York: Seven Stories Press, 1999), 8.
6. Ibid.
7. Ibid., 7.

8. Ibid., 8–9.

9. Interview with the author, Baghdad, March 14, 1998.

10. Interview with the author, Cairo, March 15, 1998.

11. Ambassador David Newton, U.S. State Department, press conference, Cairo, February 17, 1998.

12. Interview with the author, Cairo, March 15, 1998.

13. United Nations Special Commission on Iraq, charged with finding and destroying Iraq's weapons of mass destruction.

14. Noam Chomsky, *World Orders Old and New* (London: Pluto Press, 1996), 10.

15. Noam Chomsky, "Rogue States," in *Acts of Aggression*, 15.

16. Hosni Mubarak, official statement, Cairo, December 17, 1998.

17. OIC statement, December 17, 1998.

18. Interview with the author, Baghdad, March 16, 1998.

19. Ibid.

20. Hosni Mubarak, interview with *Al Ahram*, Cairo, January 1, 1999.

21. Interview by the author, Cairo, January 16, 1999.

22. President George W. Bush, televised speech, Washington, D.C., March 18, 2003.

23. "Pentagon Abandons Goal of Thwarting U.S. Rivals," *Washington Post*, May 24, 1992.

24. Paul Wolfowitz, House National Security Committee Hearings on Iraq, September 16, 1998.

25. "Images of Past Wars May Not Fit Present Foe," *Washington Post*, September 16, 2001.

26. John Bolton, U.S. Undersecretary for Arms Control and International Security, speech to the Heritage Foundation, Washington, D.C., May 6, 2002.

27. Interview with the author, Washington, D.C., March 27, 2003.

28. Interview with the author, Washington D.C., March 28, 2003.

29. Ibid.

30. Interview with the author, Washington, D.C., March 27, 2003.

31. President George W. Bush, State of the Union address, Washington, D.C., January 6, 2002.

32. Interview with the authr, Washington, D.C., February 28, 2002.

33. Project for the New American Century, "Statement of Principles," June 3, 1997, available at www.newamericancentury.org/statementofprinciples.htm.

34. Richard Perle, comments to the American Enterprise Institute, February 13, 2003.

35. Ibid.

36. William Kristol, "From Truth to Deception," *The Washington Post*, October 12, 2002.

37. PNAC, "Second Statement on Post-War Iraq," March 28, 2003, available at www.newamericancentury.org/iraqstatement–032803.htm.

38. Edward Said, "The Academy of Lagado," *London Review of Books,* April 17, 2003, 39.

39. Osama bin Laden, taped statement, al-Jazeera, November 12, 2002.

40. Osama bin Laden, taped statement, February 10, 2003.

41. Mark Huband, "Terrorism Comes in from the Edge of the World," *Financial Times,* September 5, 2002.

42. General Wesley Clark, on *Meet the Press,* June 15, 2003.

43. Ibid.

44. State of the Union address, Washington, D.C., January 28, 2003.

45. Mark Huband, "Taliban Promised to Reveal Iraq Link to Terror," *Financial Times,* March 6, 2003.

46. Alhaj Abdul Salam Zaeef to Mansour Ijaz, October 7, 2002. Copy in author collection.

47. Colin Powell, U.S. Secretary of State, presentation to the UN Security Council, February 5, 2003.

48. Ibid.

49. George Tenet, director of central intelligence, to Senator Bob Graham, chairman, Senate Intelligence Committee, October 7, 2002. See http://www.fas.org/irp/news/2002/10/dci100702.html.

50. Telephone interview with the author, January 29, 2003.

51. Interview with the author, Paris, October 4, 2003.

52. Interview with the author, London, April 18, 2003.

53. "Iraq's Weapons of Mass Destruction: The Assessment of the British Government," Joint Intelligence Committee, London, September 26, 2002.

54. Mohamed ElBaradei, director general, International Atomic Energy Agency, statement to the UN Security Council, New York, March 7, 2003.

55. Ibid.

56. Interview with the author, March 9, 2003.

57. Jonathon Powell to Alastair Campbell and David Manning, September 17, 2002, ref. CAB/11/0069.

58. Dr. David Kelly to Dr. Bryan Wells, June 30, 2003, ref. MOD/1/0019–21.

59. Interview with the author, Baghdad, May 15, 2003.

60. Interview with the author, al-Qaim, Iraq, May 17, 2003.

61. Maj. Ron Hann, U.S. Army, interview by author, Baghdad, May 15, 2003.

62. Interview with the author, Baghdad, May 16, 2003.

63. Interview with the author, al-Qaim, Iraq, May 17, 2003.

Chapter 5

1. "Iraq's Weapons of Mass Destruction: The Assessment of the British Government," Prime Minister's office, September 26, 2002.
2. Interview with the author, Abu Ghraib, Iraq, May 16, 2003.
3. Interview with the author, el-Kosheh, Egypt, October 8, 1998.
4. Interview with the author, el-Kosheh, Egypt, October 8, 1998.
5. Interview with the author, el-Kosheh, Egypt, October 8, 1998.
6. Ibid.
7. Interview with the author, el-Kosheh, Egypt, October 8, 1998.
8. Interview with the author, el-Kosheh, October 8, 1998.
9. Interview with the author, Cairo, October 4, 1998.
10. Interview with the author, Cairo, December 2, 1998.
11. Interview with the author, Cairo, January 25, 2000.
12. Interview with the author, Cairo, January 25, 2000.
13. Interview with the author, Cairo, April 5, 2001.
14. Interview with the author, Cairo, April 5, 2001.
15. Pew Research Center for People and Press, "Views of a Changing World 2003," June 3, 2003, available at http://people-press.org/reports/display.php3?ReportID=185.
16. Available at http://www.nytimes.com/library/opinion/friedman/080100frie.html.
17. Interview with the author, el-Harrach, Algeria, May 26, 2000.
18. Interview with the author, el-Harrach, May 26, 2000.
19. Ibid.
20. Ibid.
21. Interview with the author, Algiers, May 27, 2000.
22. Interview with the author, el-Harrach, May 26, 2000.
23. Interview with the author, Rabat, December 4, 1999.
24. Interview with the author, Rabat, December 4, 1999.
25. Interview with the author, Rabat, December 5, 1999.
26. Interview with the author, Laayoune, May 16, 2000.
27. Interview with the author, Laayoune, May 16, 2000.
28. Interview with the author, Laayoune, November 7, 1999.
29. Interview with the author, Laayoune, November 8, 1999.
30. Interview with the author, Sale, July 9, 1996.
31. Part of this chapter is updated from Mark Huband *Warriors of the Prophet: The Struggle for Islam* (Boulder, Colo.: Westview Press, 1998), chapter 5.
32. Pronounced *Sarlay*, the town is the twin of the Moroccan capital Rabat, from which it is separated by the Bouregreg River.

33. Interview with the author, Sale, July 9, 1996.

34. Interview with the author, Rabat, December 8, 1995.

35. Ibid.

36. Ibid.

37. *Makhzen*, an Arabic word with various pronunciations in the Arab world, means literally "those to whom taxes are paid." In Morocco the word is used as a general term identifying the ruling elite, at the center of which is the monarch, who holds absolute power despite the presence of opposition parties, a parliament, and a prime minister.

38. Interview with the author, Sale, July 9, 1996.

39. Interview with the author, Casablanca, December 7, 1995.

40. Morocco has several secular opposition parties, which have representation in parliament.

41. Interview with the author, Casablanca, December 7, 1995.

42. Interview with the author, Sale, July 9, 1996.

43. Interview with the author, Rabat, December 10, 1995.

44. Movement for Rebirth and Renewal.

45. Interview with the author, Rabat, December 10, 1995.

46. Mahdi Elmandjra, "Futures of the Islamic World," paper presented to the symposium on the Future of the Islamic World, Algiers, May 1990.

47. Interview with the author, Sale, February 3, 2000.

48. Sheikh Abdesalam Yassine, "An Open Letter," released by al-Adl Wal-Ihsane, Sale, Morocco, January 7, 2000.

49. Interview with the author, Sale, February 3, 2000.

50. Interview with the author, Sale, May 17, 2000.

51. Interview with the author, Temara, May 19, 2000.

52. Interview with the author, Casablanca, May 20, 2000.

53. Interview with the author, Casablanca, December 1, 1999.

54. Aisha d'Afailal, interview by author, Tetouan, March 3, 2000.

Chapter 6

1. *Sunday Times* (London), June 14, 1969.

2. Interview with the author, Bahr el-Bakr, Egypt, July 7, 1999.

3. Interview with the author, Cairo, June 20, 1999.

4. Israel Shahak and Norton Mezvinsky, *Jewish Fundamentalism in Israel* (London and Sterlin, Va.: Pluto Press, 1999), vii.

5. Interview with the author, Cairo, June 20, 1999.

6. Ibid.

7. Palestine National Council, "Declaration of Independence," November 15, 1988.

8. Edward W. Said, *The Question of Palestine* (New York: Vintage Books, 1992), 242.

9. Yitzhak Rabin, Israel's prime minister, to Yassir Arafat, September 9, 1993.

10. Cited in Nahum Goldmann, *Le Paradox Juif: Conversation en français avec Leon Abramowicz* (Paris: Stock, 1978), 121–22.

11. Interview with the author, Jerusalem, July 6, 1998.

12. Interview with the author, Kibbutz Ofra, Occupied West Bank, July 9, 1998.

13. Ibid.

14. Ibid.

15. B'Tselem report, cited in David B. Green, "A Wall of Ambivalence," *Prospect* (London) (August 2003): 45.

16. Joseph Weitz, "A Solution to the Refugee Problem," cited in Uri Davis and Norton Mezvinsky, *Documents from Israel, 1967–1973* (Los Angeles: Evergreen Book Distribution, 1975), 21.

17. Ze'ev Jabotinsky, "Writings: On the Road to Statehood," cited in Avi Shlaim, *The Iron Wall: Israel and the Arab World* (London: Penguin Books, 2000), 13.

18. Benjamin Beit-Hallahmi, *Original Sins: Reflections on the History of Zionism and Israel* (New York: Olive Branch Press, 1993), 45–46.

19. Interview with the author, Cairo, June 22, 1999.

20. Ibid.

21. Beit-Hallahmi, *Original Sins*, 88–89.

22. Interview with the author, Tel Aviv, July 8, 1998.

23. Shlaim, *Iron Wall*, 575.

24. Ibid., 530.

25. Uri Lubrani, cited in Sabri Jiryas, *The Arabs in Israel* (New York: Monthly Review Press, 1976), 41.

26. Interview with the author, Jericho, July 11, 1998.

27. Ibid.

28. Moshe Dayan, Radio Israel, February 12, 1952.

29. Moshe Dayan, "Military Operations in Peacetime" (Hebrew), *Ma'arachot* (May 1959), cited in Shlaim, *Iron Wall*, 204.

30. Cited in Dan O'Neill and Don Wagner, *Peace or Armageddon: The Unfolding Drama of the Middle East Peace Accord* (New York: Marshall Pickering, 1993), 56.

31. Hannan Ashrawi, *This Side of Peace: A Personal Account* (New York and London: Simon & Schuster, 1995), 293.

32. Uri Savir, *The Process: 1,100 Days That Changed the Middle East* (New York: Vintage, 1998), 213.

33. Ibid., 214–15.

34. Telephone interview with the author, July 22, 1998.

35. www.pchrgaza.org.

36. Alwyn R. Rouyer, "Between Desert Countries: The Political Economy of Water under the Israeli Occupation of the Palestinian Territories and Beyond," in *Structural Flaws in the Middle East Peace Process*, ed. J. W. Wright Jr., 115 (Basingstoke, U.K.: Palgrave, 2002).

37. Cited in ibid., 119.

38. Ibid.

39. Savir, *The Process*, 213.

40. Ibid.

41. Rouyer, "Between Desert Countries," 129.

42. Interview with the author, July 8, 1998.

43. Jad Isaac, "Core Issues of the Israeli-Palestinian Water Dispute," *ARIJ* (Bethlehem) (1996), at www.arij.org.

44. General Raphael Eitan, quoted in *New York Times*, April 14, 1983, available at www.pchrgaza.org/facts.htm.

45. See www.pchr.org.

46. Savir, *The Process*, 172–73.

47. Shlaim, *Iron Wall*, 552–53.

48. www.knesset.gov.il.

49. Interview with the author, Hebron, July 9, 1998.

50. See "US Secretary of State Warren Christopher: Letter to Israeli Prime Minister Benjamin Netanyahu, January 15, 1997," in *The Israeli-Arab Reader: A Documentary History of the Middle East Conflict*, 6th ed. (London and New York: Penguin Books, 2001), 523–24.

51. Shlaim, *Iron Wall*, 580.

52. For detailed accounts of the economic implications of the Israeli occupation, see, for example, Fadle Naqib, "The Limiting Structure of Palestinian Limited Self-Rule: Recent Historical Perspective," in *Structural Flaws in the Middle East Peace Process: Historical Contexts*, ed. J. W. Wright Jr., 14–25.

53. Ibid., 16–17.

54. Ibid.

55. Said K. Aburish, *Arafat: From Defender to Dictator* (London: Bloomsbury, 1998), 262.

56. Ibid.

57. Ibid., 264.

58. Shlaim, *Iron Wall*, 577.

59. Avi Machlis and Mark Huband, "Arafat Plea to Clinton over Jewish Settlement," *Financial Times*, March 3, 1997.

60. Ibid.

61. Judy Dempsey and Mark Huband, "Palestinians Reassess Israeli Peace Pledges," *Financial Times*, March 6, 1997.
62. Mark Huband, "Arab States May Hold Peace Summit," *Financial Times*, March 21, 1997.
63. Ibid.
64. Shlaim, *Iron Wall*, 575.
65. Aburish, *Arafat*, chapter 9.
66. David Hirst, "Arafat Hits Out at Dissidents," *The Guardian*, November 30, 1999.
67. Ibid.
68. Ibid.
69. Ibid.
70. Mark Huband and Avi Machlis, "Arab States Put Closer Links with Israel on Hold," *Financial Times*, April 1, 1997.
71. Mark Huband and Judy Dempsey, "Israel Refuses to Give Way on Homes," *Financial Times*, May 27, 1997.
72. Mark Huband, "Mideast Officials Resume Contacts," *Financial Times*, June 9, 1997.
73. Senior Egyptian official, interview with the author, Cairo, June 12, 1997.
74. Ibid.
75. http://www.mallat.com/articles/complaintenglish.htm.
76. http://www.israel.org/mfa/go.asp?MFAH0ign0.
77. Figures from Palestinian Red Crescent Society, available at http://palestinercs.org/intifadasummary.htm.
78. Figures from Israeli Ministry of Foreign Affairs, available at http://www.mfa.gov.il/MFA/Terrorism-%20Obstacle%20to%20Peace/Palestinian%20terror%20since%202000/Victims%20of%20Palestinian%20Violence%20and%20Terrorism%20sinc.
79. http://www.guardian.co.uk/print/0,3858,4686473-103552,00.html.
80. http://www.un.int/usa/04print_043.htm.
81. "Bush Endorses Sharon Plan for Unilateral Withdrawal from Gaza Strip," *AFX Newswire*, Washington, April 14, 2004.
82. Ibid.
83. Interview with the author, Bahr el-Bakr, Egypt, July 7, 1999.
84. Egypt and Israel Peace Treaty, March 26, 1979.
85. "Camp David Summit Meeting: Frameworks for Peace," September 17, 1978, cited in *Israel-Arab Reader*, 223.
86. Interview with the author, Cairo, June 18, 1999.
87. Interview with the author, Cairo, June 20, 1999.
88. Interview with the author, Cairo, June 20, 1999.

89. Beit-Hallahmi, *Original Sins,* 173.
90. Green, "Wall of Ambivalence."

Chapter 7

1. "My belief is we will, in fact, be greeted as liberators," Cheney said on March 16, 2003. "I imagine they will be welcomed," Wolfowitz said in an interview on April 3, adding later: "I think there's every reason to think that huge numbers of the Iraqi population are going to welcome these people . . . provided we don't overstay our welcome." See http://www.theage.com.au/handheld/articles/2003/08/10/1060454077509.htm.
2. Reuel Marc Gerecht, "Forget the 'Arab Street,'" *Weekly Standard,* April 1, 2002, also available at www.aei.org/include/news/newsID15645/mews_detail.asp.
3. Richard Perle, James Colbert, Charles Fairbanks Jr., Douglas Feith, Robert Loewenberg, Jonathon Torop, David Wurmser, and Meyrav Wurmser, *A Clean Break: A New Strategy for Securing the Realm* (Washington, D.C., and Jerusalem: The Institute for Advanced Strategic Studies, 1996), also available at www.israeleconomy.org/strat1.htm.
4. Ibid., 5.
5. Ibid., 2 (emphasis in original).
6. Ibid., 4.
7. Ibid.
8. Ibid., 5.
9. Ibid., 6.
10. Interview with the author, Tel Aviv, July 8, 1998.
11. Benjamin Beit-Hallahmi, *Original Sins: Reflections on the History of Zionism and Israel* (New York: Olive Branch Press, 1993), 215.
12. Ibid., 197.
13. Ibid., 183–84.
14. Gerecht, "Forget the 'Arab Street.'"
15. Ibid.
16. Available at www.aipac.org/documents/realner060903.html.
17. Available at www.aipac.org/documents/dividener062303.html.
18. *Daily Star* (Beirut), July 24, 2003, 4.
19. Available at http://www.aipac.org/timeline2.
20. "The US and Israel: Partners in Peace," available at www.aipac.org.
21. Condoleeza Rice, speech to AIPAC, March 31, 2003.
22. Ibid.

23. Available at http://www.fas.org/irp/congress/2002_rpt/911rept.pdf.

24. Said K. Aburish, *A Brutal Friendship: The West and the Arab Elite* (London: Indigo, 1998), 30–31.

25. Martin Indyk, "A Trusteeship for Palestine," *Foreign Affairs* (May/June 2003): 54.

26. President George W. Bush, public statement, White House, June 24, 2002, available at http://www.bitterlemons.org/docs/bush.html.

27. Ibid.

28. Ibid.

29. Condoleeza Rice, speech to AIPAC.

30. Bush, public statement, June 24, 2002.

31. King Hussein of Jordan, Wye River, October 23, 1998.

32. Ehud Barak, press conference, Alexandria, Egypt, July 9, 1999.

33. Ibid.

34. Israeli government, "Basic Guidelines," July 1999.

35. Ibid. Judea and Samaria are the Israeli names for the occupied West Bank.

36. Avi Shlaim, *The Iron Wall: Israel and the Arab World* (London: Penguin Books, 2000), 609.

37. Ibid.

38. Hussein of Jordan, Wye River.

39. Robert Malley and Hussein Agha, "The Last Negotiation: How to End the Middle East Peace Process," *Foreign Affairs* (May/June 2002).

40. Ehud Barak, comments before leaving for the Camp David talks, July 10, 2000.

41. Ibid.

42. Ibid.

43. Ibid.

44. President Clinton, statement after the Camp David Talks, July 25, 2000.

45. Dore Gold, "What Happened to Secure Borders for Israel? The US, Israel, and the Strategic Jordan Valley," June 23, 2000, available at http://www.newamericancentury.org/iraqjun2200.htm.

46. Ibid.

47. Stephen Zunes, "Between the Arms Race and Political Lobbyists: How Pax Americana Threatens Middle East Peace," in *Structural Flaws in the Middle East Peace Process*, ed. J. W. Wright Jr. (Basingstoke, U.K.: Palgrave, 2002), 25.

48. Ibid., 26.

49. Ibid., 27.

50. Ibid., 28.

51. Robert Malley, "Fictions about the Failure at Camp David," *New York Times*, July 8, 2001, sec. 4, 11.

52. Ehud Barak, statement after the Camp David talks, July 25, 2000.

53. Ibid.

54. Ehud Barak, interview with Benny Morris, *New York Review of Books* 49, no. 10 (June 13, 2002), available at www.nybooks.com/articles/15501.

55. Palestine Liberation Organization, Negotiation Affairs Department, "Camp David Peace Proposal of July 2000: Frequently Asked Questions," available at http://www.nad-plo.org/eye/news38.html.

56. Ibid.

57. Ibid.

58. Ibid.

59. Ibid.

60. Yasser Arafat, speech to Arab summit, Cairo, October 21, 2000.

61. Palestinian negotiating team, "Remarks and Questions Regarding the Clinton Plan, January 2, 2001," cited in Walter Laqueur and Barry Rubin, eds., *The Israeli-Arab Reader: A Documentary History of the Middle East Conflict*, 6th ed. (New York and London: Penguin Books, 2001), 567.

62. President William J. Clinton, speech to Israel Policy Forum, New York, January 7, 2001, in Laqueur and Rubin, *Israeli-Arab Reader*, 573.

63. Ibid.

64. Malley, "Fictions about the Failure at Camp David."

65. Hussein Agha and Robert Malley, "Camp David and After: An Exchange (2. A Reply to Ehud Barak)," *New York Review of Books* 49, no. 10 (June 13, 2002).

66. Ibid.

67. Ibid.

68. Ibid.

69. George J. Mitchell et al., "Sharm el-Shiekh Fact-Finding Committee Report," April 30, 2001, available at www.bitterlemons.org/docs/mitchell.html.

70. Steven Mufson, "Camp David: Whose Story Is It Anyway?" *Washington Post*, July 28, 2002, B01.

71. George Tenet, "Palestinian-Israeli Security Work Plan," March 27, 2002, available at www.bitterlemons.org/docs/tenet.html.

72. General Zinni, "Second US 'Joint Goals' Proposal," March 26, 2002, available at www.bitterlemons.org/docs/zinni.html.

73. See note 26.

74. Hasan Abunimah and Ali Abunimah, "The Holes in Israel's Road Map," *Financial Times*, July 21, 2003.

75. Fouad Ajami, "The Sentry's Solitude," *Foreign Affairs* (November/December 2001): 14.

76. Indyk, "Trusteeship for Palestine."

77. Richard A Clarke, testimony to the National Commission on Terrorist Attacks upon the United States, March 24, 2004, available at http://www.9-11commission.gov/hearings/hearing8/clarke_statement.pdf.

78. Richard A. Clarke, *Against All Enemies: Inside America's War on Terror* (New York: Free Press, 2004).
79. "Bin Laden Determined to Strike in US," President's Daily Brief, August 6, 2001. Available at http://www.gwu.edu/~nsarchiv/NSAEBB/NSAEBB116/pdb8-6-2001.pdf.
80. Condoleeza Rice, testimony to the National Commission on Terrorist Attacks upon the United States, April 8, 2004, available at http://www.gwu.edu/~nsarchiv/NSAEBB/NSAEBB116/testimony.htm.
81. Stephen G. Brooks and William C. Wohlforth, "American Primacy in Perspective," *Foreign Affairs* (July/August 2002): 201–26.

Epilogue

1. Bernard Lewis, *What Went Wrong? The Clash between Islam and Modernity in the Middle East* (London: Weidenfeld & Nicolson, 2002).
2. Ibid., 160.
3. Thomas Pakenham, *The Scramble for Africa* (London: Abacus, 1992), 673.
4. "Bridges, Bombs, or Bluster?" *Foreign Affairs* 82, no. 5 (September/October 2003): 98–117.

BIBLIOGRAPHY

Books

Aburish, Said K. *Arafat: From Defender to Dictator.* London: Bloomsbury, 1998.

_____. *A Brutal Friendship: The West and the Arab Elite.* London: Indigo, 1998.

Akbar, M. J. *The Shade of Swords: Jihad and the Conflict between Islam and Christianity.* London and New York: Routledge, 2002.

Ashrawi, Hannan. *This Side of Peace: A Personal Account.* New York and London: Simon & Schuster, 1995.

Barakat, Halim. *The Arab World: Society, Culture and State.* Berkeley, Los Angeles, and London: University of California Press, 1993.

Beit-Hallahmi, Benjamin. *Original Sins: Reflections on the History of Zionism and Israel.* New York: Olive Branch Press, 1993.

Chomsky, Noam. *World Orders Old and New.* London: Pluto Press, 1996.

Esposito, John L. *Voices of Resurgent Islam.* New York: Oxford University Press, 1983.

Global Witness. *For a Few Dollars More: How al-Qaeda Moved into the Diamond Trade.* London: Global Witness, April 2003.

Hirst, David, and Irene Beeson. *Sadat.* London: Faber & Faber, 1981.

Hourani, Albert. *Arabic Thought in the Liberal Age, 1798–1939.* Cambridge: Cambridge University Press, 1983.

_____. *A History of the Arab Peoples.* London: Faber & Faber, 1991.

Huband, Mark. *Egypt: Regional Leader and Global Player, a Market for the 21st Century.* London: Euromoney Books, 2001.

_____. *The Skull beneath the Skin: Africa after the Cold War.* (Boulder, Colo.: Westview Press, 2001.

_____. *Warriors of the Prophet: The Struggle for Islam.* Boulder, Colo.: Westview Press, 1998.

Keinle, Eberhard. *A Grand Delusion: Democracy and Economic Reform in Egypt.* London and New York: I. B.Tauris, 2000.

Kepel, Gilles. *Jihad: The Trail of Political Islam.* London and New York: I. B.Tauris, 2002.

Khalidi, Rashid, et al. *The Origins of Arab Nationalism.* New York: Columbia University Press, 1991.

Lewis, Bernard. *What Went Wrong? The Clash between Islam and Modernity in the Middle East.* London: Weidenfeld & Nicolson, 2002.

Marzouki, Ahmed. *Tazmamart: Cellule 10.* Paris: Editions Paris-Mediterranee, 2000.

O'Neill, Dan, and Don Wagner. *Peace or Armageddon: The Unfolding Drama of the Middle East Peace Accord.* New York: Marshall Pickering, 1993.

Oufkir, Malika, with Michele Fitoussi. *Stolen Lives: Twenty Years in a Desert Jail.* Translated by Ros Schwartz. New York: Talk Miramax Books, 2001.

Pakenham, Thomas. *The Scramble for Africa.* London: Abacus, 1992.

Reeve, Simon. *The New Jackals.* Boston: Northeastern University Press, 1999.

Rubin, Barnet, and Walter Lacquer. *The Israeli-Arab Reader: A Documentary History of the Middle East Conflict.* 6th ed. London and New York: Penguin Books, 2001.

Said, Edward W. *The Question of Palestine.* New York: Vintage Books, 1992.

Savir, Uri. *The Process: 1,100 Days That Changed the Middle East.* New York: Vintage, 1998.

Shahak, Israel, and Norton Mezvinsky. *Jewish Fundamentalism in Israel.* London and Sterlin, Va.: Pluto Press, 1999.

Shlaim, Avi. *The Iron Wall: Israel and the Arab World.* London: Penguin Books, 2000.

Smith, Stephen. *Oufkir, Un Destin Marocain.* Paris: Calmann-Levy, 1999.

Souaidia, Habib. *La sale guerre: Le temoignage d'un officier des forces speciales de l'armee algerienne, 1992–2000.* Paris: Gallimard, 2001.

Wright, J. W., Jr. *Structural Flaws in the Middle East Peace Process*. Basingstoke, U.K.: Palgrave, 2002.

Major Articles

Abunimah, Hasan, and Ali Abunimah. "The Holes in Israel's Road Map." *Financial Times*, July 21, 2003.

Agha, Hussein, and Robert Malley. "Camp David and After: An Exchange (2. A Reply to Ehud Barak)." *New York Review of Books* 49, no. 10 (June 13, 2002): 22–26.

Ajami, Fouad. "The Sentry's Solitude." *Foreign Affairs* 80, no. 6 (November/December 2001): 14.

Albright, Madeleine K. "Bridges, Bombs, or Bluster?" *Foreign Affairs* 82, no. 5 (September/October 2003): 2–19.

Barak, Ehud. Interview by Benny Morris. *New York Review of Books* 49, no. 10 (June 13, 2002).

———. Statement after the Camp David talks, July 25, 2000.

Brooks, Stephen G., and William C. Wohlforth. "American Primacy in Perspective." *Foreign Affairs* 81, no. 4 (July/August 2002): 201–26.

Bush, George W. Speech, June 24, 2002. Available at www.bitterlemons.org/docs/bush.html.

Chomsky, Noam. "Rogue States." In *Acts of Aggression: Policing Rogue States*, edited by Noam Chomsky. New York: Seven Stories Press, 1999.

Christopher, Warren. "US Secretary of State Warren Christopher: Letter to Israeli Prime Minister Benjamin Netanyahu, January 15, 1997." In *The Israeli-Arab Reader: A Documentary History of the Middle East Conflict*, 6th ed., edited Walter Laqueur and Barry Rubin, 523–24. London and New York: Penguin Books, 2001.

Dempsey, Judy, and Mark Huband. "Palestinians Reassess Israeli Peace Pledges." *Financial Times*, March 6, 1997.

Egypt and Israel Peace Treaty, March 26, 1979.

Eitan, General Raphael. "Israel Frees More Prisoners, but Arabs Are Not Mollified." *New York Times*, March 4, 1983, A10.

Elmandjra, Mahdi. "Futures of the Islamic World," Paper presented to the symposium on the Future of the Islamic World, Algiers, May 1990.

"Fatwa Urging Jihad against Americans." Signed by Sheikh Usamah Bin-Mohammed Bin-Laden, Ayman al-Zawahiri, leader of the Jihad Group in Egypt; Abu-Yasir Rifa'I Ahmad Taha, a leader of the Islamic Group; Sheikh Mir Hamzah, secretary of the Jamiat-ul-Ulema-e-Pakistan; and Fazlul Rahman, leader of the Jihad Movement in Bangladesh. Published in *al-Quds al-'Arabi* (London), February 23, 1998.

Friedman, Thomas. Letter to Mubarak. Available at www.nytimes.com/library/opinion/friedman/080100frie.html.

Gerecht, Reuel Marc. "Forget the 'Arab Street.'" *Weekly Standard,* April 1, 2002. Also available at www.aei.org/include/news/newsID15645/mews_detail.asp.

Gold, Dore. "What Happened to Secure Borders for Israel? The US, Israel, and the Strategic Jordan Valley." Available at www.newamericancentury.org/iraqjun2200.htm.

Green, David B. "A Wall of Ambivalence." *Prospect* (London) (August 2003): 45.

Higgins, Andrew, and Alan Cullison. "Failed Chechnya Mission by Egyptian Jihad Head Sowed Seeds of Sept. 11." *Wall Street Journal,* July 2, 2002, A1.

Hirst, David. "Arafat Hits Out at Dissidents." *The Guardian,* November 30, 1999.

Huband, Mark. "Arab States May Hold Peace Summit." *Financial Times,* March 21, 1997.

———. "Mideast Officials Resume Contacts." *Financial Times,* June 9, 1997.

Huband, Mark, and Judy Dempsey. "Egypt Lifts Hope for Middle East Peace." *Financial Times,* June 13, 1997.

———. "Israel Refuses to Give Way on Homes." *Financial Times,* May 27, 1997.

Huband, Mark, and Avi Machlis. "Arab States Put Closer Links with Israel on Hold." *Financial Times,* April 1, 1997.

Indyk, Martin. "A Trusteeship for Palestine." *Foreign Affairs* 82, no. 3 (May/June 2003): 54.

"Iraq's Weapons of Mass Destruction: The Assessment of the British Government." Joint Intelligence Committee, London, September 26, 2002.

Isaac, Jad. "Core Issues of the Israeli-Palestinian Water Dispute." *ARIJ* (Bethlehem) (1996). Available at www.arij.org.

Kristol, William. "From Truth to Deception." *The Washington Post,* October 12, 2002, A31.

Machlis, Avi, and Mark Huband. "Arafat Plea to Clinton over Jewish Settlement." *Financial Times,* March 3, 1997.

Malley, Robert. "Fictions about the Failure at Camp David." *New York Times*, July 8, 2001, sec. 4, 11.

Malley, Robert, and Hussein Agha. "The Last Negotiation: How to End the Middle East Peace Process." *Foreign Affairs* 81, no. 3 (May/June 2002).

Mitchell, George J., et al. "Sharm el-Shiekh Fact-Finding Committee Report." April 30, 2001. Available at www.bitterlemons.org/docs/mitchell.html.

Mufson, Steven. "Camp David: Whose Story Is It Anyway?" *The Washington Post*, July 28, 2002, B.01.

Palestine Liberation Organization, Negotiation Affairs Department, "Camp David Peace Proposal of July 2000: Frequently Asked Questions." Available at http://www.nad-plo.org/eye/news38.html.

Palestine National Council. "Declaration of Independence." November 15, 1988.

Palestinian Negotiating Team. "Remarks and Questions Regarding the Clinton Plan, January 2, 2001." Cited in *The Israeli-Arab Reader: A Documentary History of the Middle East Conflict*, 6th ed., edited by Walter Laqueur and Barry Rubin, 567. New York and London: Penguin Books, 2001.

Perle, Richard, James Colbert, Charles Fairbanks Jr., Douglas Feith, Robert Loewenberg, Jonathon Torop, David Wurmser, and Meyrav Wurmser. *A Clean Break: A New Strategy for Securing the Realm.* Washington and Jerusalem: The Institute for Advanced Strategic Studies, 1996. Also available at www.israeleconomy.org/strat1.htm.

"Rapport d'enquete sur les enjeux politiques, economiques et sociaux de la production et du traffic des drogues au Maroc." *Observatoire Geopolitiques des Drogues* (Paris) (February 1994).

Rouyer, Alwyn R. "Between Desert Countries: The Political Economy of Water under the Israeli Occupation of the Palestinian Territories and Beyond." In *Structural Flaws in the Middle East Peace Process*, edited by J. W. Wright Jr., 115. Basingstoke, U.K.: Palgrave, 2002.

Said, Edward W. "Apocalypse Now." In *Acts of Aggression: Policing Rogue States*, edited by Noam Chomsky, 8. New York: Seven Stories Press, 1999.

———. "The Academic Lagado." *London Review of Books*, April 17, 2003, 39.

"Statement of Principles." Project for the New American Century, June 3, 1997. Available at www.newamericancentury.org/statementofprinciples.htm.

Tenet, George. "Palestinian-Israeli Security Work Plan," March 27, 2002. Available at www.bitterlemons.org/docs/tenet.html.

Tenet, George, Director of Central Intelligence. Letter to Senator Bob Graham, chairman, Senate Intelligence Committee, October 7, 2002. Available at www.fas.org/irp/news/2002/10/dci100702.html.

"Views of a Changing World 2003." Pew Research Center for People and Press, June 3, 2003. Available at people-press.org/reports/display.php3? ReportID=185.

Weitz, Joseph. "A Solution to the Refugee Problem." Cited in *Documents from Israel, 1967–1973*, edited by Uri Davis and Norton Mezvinsky, 21. Los Angeles: Evergreen Book Distribution, 1975.

Willman, John. "Chance Find That Averted Airport Bombing." *Financial Times*, November 28, 2001, 16.

Wright, Lawrence. "The Man Behind Bin Laden: How an Egyptian Doctor Became a Master of Terror." *New Yorker*, September 16, 2002.

www.aipac.org/documents/dividener062303.html.

www.aipac.org/documents/realner060903.html.

www.aipac.org/timeline2.

www.fas.org/irp/congress/2002_rpt/911rept.pdf.

Zinni, General Anthony. "Second US 'Joint Goals' Proposal." March 27, 2003. Available at www.bitterlemons.org/docs/zinni.html.

Zunes, Stephen. "Between the Arms Race and Political Lobbyists: How Pax Americana Threatens Middle East Peace." In *Structural Flaws in the Middle East Peace Process*, edited by J. W. Wright Jr., 25. Basingstoke, U.K.: Palgrave, 2002.

INDEX